Back in from the Anger

Back in from the Anger

Roger Lucey

JACANA

First published by Jacana Media (Pty) Ltd in 2012

10 Orange Street
Sunnyside
Auckland Park 2092
South Africa
+2711 628 3200
www.jacana.co.za

ISBN 978-1-4314-0453-7

Cover design by publicide
Cover photo by Rodney Barnett
Set in Warnock 11/13.5pt
Job No. 001817
Printed by Ultra Litho (Pty) Ltd, Johannesburg

See a complete list of Jacana titles at www.jacana.co.za

Did you ever see a love that died from hunger?
Did you ever know that hunger in your heart?
And how the hell did we survive the anger
That drove us miles away and worlds apart?

Did you ever find a fire gently burning
In a part of you, you thought had turned to stone?
That's where I found a heart
In a world that's torn apart
And a life that always finds its way back home.

And I'm back in from the anger of the winter,
I've bust out of this prison called the road.
I'm caught up in the comfort
Of a small house in the suburbs,
That's my choice and where my river's flowed.

Back in from the Anger, Roger Lucey, 1995

Prologue

Cape Town, Winter 2000

FRIDAY EVENING IN THE E.TV newsroom is no time for joke calls. You can smell fear on the floor as the young staff struggle to meet the deadline. The station's only been running a few months and I'm one of the few here with any real experience in television news.

Ten minutes before we go to air the phone rings. I'm on a dangerously short fuse; my pulse thumps in my eardrums as the fingers of my free hand leave sweaty trails on the controls of the video machine.

"Roger? Sorry to surprise you. It's me, Paul Erasmus."

That voice. It's been on every radio station for the past year and a half, not to mention the dozens of times I've watched Max du Preez's weekly report on the Truth and Reconciliation Commission. My skin crawls each time Erasmus appears. But I can't talk about it, even to my closest friends. And now here he is on the phone, this total stranger who's implicated in so many turning points of my life.

"Oh, hi Paul. How's it going?" My words sound ridiculous. The chaos of the newsroom recedes to a kind of soft haze, and I look through the back window at Signal Hill getting hammered by another cold front. Nine minutes before the bulletin goes to air, and I'm gazing out at the storm. I glance back into the newsroom, a picture of confusion and carnage. Franci, the input editor, runs frantically up to me. A trickle glistens at his temple and drips onto his collar.

"Th... th... the f... feed from Bloemfontein is... isn't in yet." His stammer always intensifies as a deadline starts to bite.

"Paul, can you hang on a sec?" With my hand over the phone, I shout to the media manager. "Randall, I want that Bloem feed in two minutes, you hear?"

"Trying my best, brother," Randall whines. I give Franci a slap on the shoulder and a thumbs up. He heads back to his desk, papers flapping.

"Sorry Paul. Listen, I'm a bit busy right now…"

"Ja, ja[1], I can hear. Look, I know this might seem a bit weird, and it's probably too late, but I just want to say I'm really sorry about what happened… back then."

For a moment I'm speechless.

"It's fine, Paul, don't worry about it."

What am I saying? He fucked up my whole life. It's *not* fine, not at all.

"Bloem feed coming in, brother!" Randall's voice barely penetrates my unnerving calm. I give him the thumbs up. Franci weaves between the desks towards me. Signal Hill's almost vanished; the night and the storm have become one.

Over four years I've come to know the voice at the other end of this line – this week he was on my screen again, running his hand through his thick grey hair, recounting to one more reporter yet another abuse he'd committed. Four full years now I've been dealing with the vast backlog of pain and anger that's dogged me for so long. I'm feeling better these days.

"Look, Roger, as I said, I know it's a bit late, but things have been fucking hectic these last few years. Maybe we could have a beer sometime? You know, chat about things?"

I notice the clock. I've got to get off this call. "Ja, okay Paul. Sure. Let's do that sometime."

He chats a bit more as the newsroom implodes around me. He asks about my kids; he didn't know Sue and I had divorced.

"I know you have to get back to work, but I wonder if you could do me a big favour. My son Dylan, you know, he's fifteen already, suffers from a type of sclerosis, I wonder if you wouldn't mind saying hello to him…"

"Hello Uncle Roger. It's Dylan here." The voice is thin and shaky, like an old man's. "I just wanted to tell you that my dad gave me your album, and when you come to visit I'd like you to sign it for me. The song I like best is Thabane."

Thabane. I say goodbye, shove my phone in my pocket and head to the newsroom. That's the song I wrote for my first child.

---

1 Afrikaans for yes

There's no sense in waiting for the reaper's arrival;
There's no point in dreading the end;
There's nothing to gain from regretting your journey
Or decisions you cannot defend.

Now Is the Time, Roger Lucey, 2012

1

Grahamstown, Winter 1995

DE KLERK RAPS MANDELA

President Nelson Mandela's use of an overseas visit, when he should have been acting on behalf of all South Africans, to make highly contentious statements... was regrettable, Deputy President FW de Klerk said last night. He was reacting to statements made by Mr Mandela... that the IFP and the police jointly plotted an attack on the African National Congress Shell House headquarters during a Zulu march through Johannesburg on March 28 last year.

Daily Despatch, 7 July 1995

"Hey, china[1], you didn't need those ous[2] to close down your music career, you were doing a great job all by yourself!"

James Phillips has a way of propping up a bar that looks like he's been there all his life. The Cathcart Arms is a drab shadow of its former frontier splendour, but James can inject life into almost any pub he finds himself in.

The black taxi rank has moved from the bottom of town to the street outside the Cathcart Arms. Locals growl into their jugs about Africa encroaching on their turf. If not for his long, greasy hair streaked with grey, James could easily be mistaken for a local. He has a way of twisting his upper lip into a sneer after a few drinks, a trademark of many white South African males. Not that James is a typical white South African male, but the sneer helps him blend in.

"What are you talking about, you smelly old drunk?" I give him a hug.

There's more of him since I last saw him, especially around the middle. The locals look on with mild disgust. These ous don't do hugs.

But locals are in the minority tonight. The bar's packed with all sorts of weirdos, actors, dancers, musos and wannabes with hairstyles and clothing desperately trying to make them stand out. It's the middle of the National Arts Festival, which transforms the sleepy hamlet of Grahamstown for one week each year into the hub of the South African arts scene. James is here doing a solo show, just him and his acoustic guitar, singing songs that have made him the voice of a generation. But he's always played with bands – his early groups were the first punks in South Africa – and this is his first solo show. He's five years younger than me – our birthdays are a day apart

1 from Cockney rhyming slang, china plate for mate
2 common South African term for a man or guy

2

– but we've become good friends over the past few years. He pulls a battered newspaper from his bag and shoves it at me.

"It's somewhere about page four or five... Hey barman, bring us another Blackie, and a tequila for my mate."

James always does that – doesn't ask, just orders the damn thing and you have to knock it back. Not that I mind. I'm freezing after a long walk from the theatre where I've just finished my performance. I open the paper. There on page five is a picture of me with a beard, cradling my guitar. I'm smiling but there's no avoiding the look of quiet anxiety that haunts all men whose dreams have been left behind.

On the very same page is another face: a man of similar age with a mullet hairstyle and puffy eyes that tell of a good deal of mileage on the road – *Paul Erasmus*. The article is an excerpt from a book he's written about his time as a member of South Africa's notorious security police. The chapter the *Mail & Guardian* have published tells how, almost fourteen years earlier, he systematically set about shutting down my music career. As I scan the article, I'm learning the details of my own life story that until now I could only speculate about.

It's too much to take in right now. And anyway, the glow of the second tequila is starting to kick in. The bar's jumping, James and I haven't seen each other for ages, and there's so much kak[3] to talk... And so the night drifts into another collage of jumbled memories.

Later, in bed, fragments of the past keep playing back through my mind. I can't stop them. What the hell *really* happened back then?

I arrived in Johannesburg in the winter of 1977. Durban had become too claustrophobic; I needed a new place to ply my trade. I'd been doing gigs at beachfront hotels and bars, and only occasionally did I get to play my own songs at the local folk club.

Jo'burg was good to me. From the start I found gigs where I could play my own songs, not just the tired cover versions that Durban's beachfront drunks craved. My songs were young and angry, and boisterously attacked the state. I began to attract the attention of the local press, and then of a *Voice of America* correspondent. He recorded me live at Mangles – a Braamfontein club where I played for about a year – and combined my songs and interviews into a

_____
3 Afrikaans for shit

3

thirty-minute radio programme that was beamed around the world.

I was sure no-one would ever hear the programme. But I was wrong. South African Military Intelligence monitored all such broadcasts, and alerted the security police. And it wasn't only the authorities who were alarmed by my musical ravings. Many fellow musicians also found my approach too strident. Even James Phillips was critical. In an interview for a student documentary, he described how his band, Corporal Punishment, felt the need to reflect the world around them and condemn apartheid, "but not like Roger Lucey," he added. "He's just a communist." But out in the real world of gigs and concerts, it was all happening for me. I was recording my first album, playing all the good festivals and getting extensive coverage in newspapers and magazines countrywide. Naturally, the radio stations refused to play my songs. Radio was just another mouthpiece for the increasingly autocratic Nationalist government. But that didn't matter.

Just when it seemed I was getting serious recognition, weird things started happening. Gigs got cancelled; promoters refused to speak to me or return my calls; relations with the record company rapidly cooled. They'd vowed to stand by me through any trouble that might arise, but overnight they changed their minds.

And then in the middle of the night I was woken with my house full of armed police. I realised then that I was in a fight I had no chance of winning. My life was falling apart. It was all very confusing – and stressful.

Before long, I was hooked on Wellcanol, a powerful painkiller used on terminal cancer patients. Injected into the veins it's as powerful as heroin, and even more destructive. Yet in spite of its intense narcotic effect, I could still perform everyday functions, like driving, shopping, reading, even looking after children. Wellcanol was easy to get hold of and very effective in taking care of the mess that I opened my eyes to every morning.

In just a few short months I was transformed – from rising star to penniless junkie.

2

Durban, Summer 1969

COMMONWEALTH MEETING: ACTION URGED AGAINST SOUTH AFRICA

African fears about South Africa figured in yesterday's discussion of international affairs at the Marlborough House meeting of the Commonwealth leaders. A number of speakers mentioned the dangers of the Southern African situation and urged further action against apartheid South Africa.

Natal Mercury, 9 January 1969

"Hey, you! Don't think I can't see you, you and your little kaffir[1] friend. I know what you're doing down there. I'm telling your mother that you're smoking dagga[2]. And I'm calling the police!"

"Fuck off, bitch," Jabula says under his breath. Such sweet mutiny.

Mrs Porter is always shouting at someone: the plump Zulu men in tall chefs' hats who always seem to be late for work; the uniformed maids who sit on the pavement under the mango tree talking at the top of their voices; or the neighbourhood mutts who always choose her piece of pavement to shit on.

My family live in a large house in the middle of the Berea, a hillside suburb that rises out of what was once a huge swampland. The early settlers reclaimed the land, but somehow the swamp-like feeling remained.

The neighbourhood is thick with greenery that grows at a ferocious rate. Workers from the Durban Corporation are constantly at war with the trees that arch across the streets forming clammy green cathedrals. From 67 Milner Road, we look over the Greyville Racecourse and across the city towards Durban's natural harbour. The house sits on the edge of a triangle of parkland covered with a mass of huge tree canopies. Partially obscured in one corner of this steamy garden, Jabula and I sit smoking Durban's most famous herb. But on those dead calm, savagely humid days, the smoke rises slowly but relentlessly, straight up onto Mrs Porter's verandah.

Mrs Porter owns the Parkview Hotel, a postcolonial three-storey block across the parkland from our house, with Victorian balustrades and verandahs on three sides.

"Don't you go off like that!" Mrs Porter crows from her second-

1 derogatory term for blacks
2 marijuana

6

floor balcony as Jabula and I slope off to the other side of the park. "I know what you're up to!"

We're good and stoned now from the hits we've been taking of the small clay chillum Jabula is so expert at preparing.

"Fuck off, bitch," he mumbles again, and we take off down the road, shrieking with laughter. I'm fifteen, Jabula eighteen. We've been hanging around the neighbourhood together since I was about five.

Years later, my mother reveals that Mrs Porter did phone to report our dagga smoking.

"What an outrageous accusation!" my mother had replied indignantly. "The boy's only fifteen!"

When I first came across Jabula, he was living with his mother, a domestic worker, in the house next door to the modest one we'd just moved into in the less salubrious part of Berea. My grandparents lived over the road in an equally unassuming three-bedroom house typical of the white suburbs that sprang up around the city after World War I. Grandpa was a policeman, a kindly man with a sense of humour, but deeply conservative. He'd spent most of his working life on horseback patrolling the rural Transkei, a vast area in the southeast of the country inhabited by the Xhosa people, whom he saw as ignorant children in need of guidance by the white man. Granny was a policeman's wife, devoted and obedient, but with a dark stain on her past that later made her my ally as my life leant into its own darkness. Jabula and I were only able to maintain our friendship despite the barbaric racial laws of the land because it was the wish of my iconoclastic but violent father, Dennis John Lucey.

3

Durban, 1952

DEFIANT START TO CAMPAIGN

Fifty-two arrests were made in Boksburg, 51 in Johannesburg, 30 in Port Elizabeth and three in Durban yesterday, the first day of the non-European defiance campaign against "unjust laws".

Natal Mercury, 27 June 1952

DJ, as Dennis John liked to be known, came from a line of Irish peasants who left the motherland when the potatoes failed. Originally Celts, there was a branch of the family known as the Black Luceys said to be tainted with the seed of roving Romany gypsies. With dark eyes and flashing tempers among so many of my relatives, it's easy to see why we were reputed to be part of this sullied bunch.

DJ was a law unto himself. He wrote the rules to the games he played in life, and if he sensed he was about to lose, he simply changed the rules. He'd been a star athlete and sportsman, representing the Natal province in both rugby and track. In World War II he was a fighter pilot, serving time in the western desert. He told me once that the only time he ever fired his gun was at a Nile crocodile, which then lumbered safely into the water. He once saw a German fighter plane in the distance, but he and his mates elected to give it a wide berth. For DJ life was for living, and he wasn't about to let some German air ace spoil his weekend plans.

At DJ's wake, his friend, Jack Lea, told me that their free time in Cairo was riotous. Fucking and fighting were the order of the day, with heads broken as readily as hearts. Lieutenant DJ Lucey was powerfully built, with black hair and eyes, a strong aquiline nose and full, warm lips. Jack always said that DJ was a magnet for beautiful women, and back in Jo'burg at the end of the desert campaign he'd got a young girl into trouble. Not about to be encumbered by this sort of inconvenience, before long he was back in Durban, the child adopted, and that was the last word on the whole affair – almost. Decades later, after months of detective work, my half-sister, Margaret, finally traced her mother, who sadly had died some years previously. But Margaret continued her search and finally found DJ in the last years of his life. He embraced her as his long-lost daughter, and the two of them found much common ground over many lunches and meetings before he died. Only several years after his death did Margaret finally pluck up the courage to call me and tell me the whole bittersweet story over a cup of coffee in a Cape Town shopping mall.

Back on civvy street, DJ had met Auriol May Jonker, the daughter of an Afrikaans policeman and his English wife, who, despite being born in South Africa, still spoke of England as home. She died never having set foot on that dank, faraway land. Auriol had grown up hunting snakes and fishing for eels with her brothers in the open valleys of the Transkei. She was training as a nurse in Durban when she fell under DJ's spell after meeting him on the beach one day. His interest in photography was becoming a professional pursuit, and he would photograph my shy but stoical mother in various outfits and settings. Several of these photos made the social pages of the local newspaper, with captions like: "Miss Auriol Jonker, nursing student at Addington Hospital, relaxes during off-duty on the Snell Parade Drive. Her skirt is printed cretonne in red, white and apple-green – and she made it herself."[1]

After my mother died, her friend, Pat Bailey, told me that my parents would have sex at every available opportunity; then, being a good Catholic, mother would be consumed with guilt and resolve never to do it again. But the "never" wouldn't last long and so her dilemma increased. Finally, guilt ridden and confused, she ran to Grahamstown, five hundred miles away, where her parents lived. DJ followed her and persuaded her to marry him. According to Pat he was her one and only lover, and although they divorced thirty years and five kids later, she was the one who nursed him through his final, humiliating days.

The young couple returned to Durban to married life, but these were DJ's wild years. Nothing could stand in his way as he ripped into the world around him, leaving a trail of destruction in his wake. Over a glass of wine after his funeral, Jack Lea told me of a time when, walking along the beachfront, DJ saw a beautiful young woman sitting with a group of youths on the verandah of the Beach Hotel. He bet Jack that she would be his within the hour. By the time DJ and the girl returned from a walk along the waterside, Jack had lost the bet. But if Auriol dared confront him about these improprieties, he would fly into a self-righteous rage, often striking out at the quiet young country

---

1 *Sunday Tribune*, 26 June 1949

girl. She soon learnt to draw the veil on his philandering ways, yet he always found reasons to exercise his vile temper. Jack reluctantly admitted that the violence he inflicted on my mother started before I was born. One of my earliest memories is of my father, eyes dark with fury, flinging a glass of wine into my mother's face, then grabbing her by the throat with one hand and slapping her with the other.

"Shut up, you fucking bitch!" His voice rose to a scream. "Don't you *ever* contradict me again!"

Contradict seemed a strange choice of word while beating the shit out of someone. It was a word he used often. My mother remained silent and unflinching throughout the attack. Only when it was over did she sob quietly, wiping away the tears with the sleeve of her homemade tunic. These were parts of life that I learnt to cope with without even realising how. That was how my father was, and I learnt to steer my way around his excesses.

In spite of his wicked temper and volatile nature, his career as a photographer earned him almost legendary status. He was known to take massive risks while flying his Globe Swift, the small two-seater aircraft he owned, in an effort to get a sensational picture. One Saturday morning, just for kicks, he piled his three kids, Patrick, Kathy and me, into the cramped cockpit along with half a dozen toilet rolls, and flew over Durban city centre tossing out the makeshift paper streamers and then flying through them, turning the sky into a mess of confetti. When we landed at the airstrip a police officer was waiting. He politely asked DJ if he knew anything about the incident. DJ flew into a rage: how dare this cop accuse him of putting these precious children's lives in danger?

"I'll sue you!" he shouted. "Give me the name of your superior!" DJ stormed to his car, with us scampering behind. Then he drove out of the car park roaring with laughter.

As my father grew increasingly outrageous and eccentric, my mother became more staid and conservative. She'd always been a country girl, but as I grew older she revelled more and more in her humble origins. I'm sure it was a reaction to the many smart, talented and sometimes bizarre characters that were drawn to my father. In spite of her self-demeaning manner, she had a good business sense, and while DJ was always the flamboyant face of his various businesses, she managed the books, made sure the bills were paid and generally held the business together. She managed her home in the same efficient manner. Meals were never late and we never ran out of bread, milk or any other staple. We were taken to the dentist regularly, the doctor before anything went far wrong, and the clothing store before we started looking tatty. She also spent much of her spare time sewing, producing shirts, shorts and even stylish surfing baggies. While she was clearly utterly dedicated to raising her family, after her death I finally faced the extraordinary fact that I'd never heard her tell me or my siblings that she loved us. Maybe for her the word held too much pain.

There's a rough cliff top at Coffee Bay on the Wild Coast, one of South Africa's most magnificent stretches of coastline, that remains largely undeveloped to this day. I holidayed there in the summer of 1987 with my seven-year-old daughter, Amanda. Part of the rugged hilltop was a golf course resembling nothing I'd ever associated with that game. I walked across the lumpy terrain covered in wind-battered shrubs, trying to see where, years before, DJ had landed a single-engine aircraft. By then he'd sold the Globe Swift and would hire aircraft from the Durban Wings Club. On that little jaunt it was a two-seater Piper Cub, with Mom and Dad in front and us three kids in the luggage compartment. I walked around wondering if I'd imagined the adventure: you could barely drive a car around this obstacle course, let alone land a plane. Later that day, I recounted the story to a couple of Durban boys I met in the hotel bar. The Xhosa barman listened inscrutably while the boys laughed and said I was talking shit.

The following morning, the barman approached me at breakfast to say that an old man had come to the hotel to see me. He was waiting in the shade of a flat-topped thorn tree outside the hotel gates, knowing full well not to enter the exclusive domain of the white guests. Even with his stooped and ancient frame, he bore an air of ancestral authority. It seemed my story of the previous evening had reached him by bush telegraph. With the barman translating, the old man pulled himself tall in his ragged clothing and announced that it was he who had looked after the Piper Cub when it landed on the cliff top all those years before.

My childhood memories are checkered with my father's crazy antics, many involving small aircraft. In May 2003, I found myself in Mozambique making a documentary about the fishing industry. Maputo is a vibrant city, beautiful in its own rundown way, its population still hauling itself back from the desolation of a protracted civil war. A corrupt and top-heavy bureaucracy makes it difficult for outsiders to work in Mozambique; you need a permit just to scratch your arse. I once spent a whole afternoon hanging around waiting for permission to film in the fishing harbour. I took the opportunity to see if I could find the basement that had housed a nightclub I'd visited some forty years before, in the days when Maputo was Lourenço Marques, a place where South African and Rhodesian tourists flocked to eat massive prawns and drink cerveja Laurentina and crisp, tongue-tingling vinho verde, a wine made from slightly unripe grapes. When I was about nine or ten, maybe as one of DJ's mad initiation rites, he'd bundled me into a little single-engine Piper Comanche and flown the two of us to Mozambique.

The basement nightclub was blue with cigarette smoke, and delicious smells billowed from huge black pots of deep-frying prawns. In the far corner two musicians were playing: a guitarist and another man cradling a strange-looking cross between a guitar and a lute. The tunes they produced were unfamiliar, but pleasing to my eager young ear. DJ allowed me a small glass of the tart green vinho verde. He told me that the music was fado, a gentle, melancholic traditional style from Portugal. When a swarthy woman in a flowing floral print joined the men and started to sing, the songs were clearly those of a people steeped in hardship. Yet within the sorrowful laments and fervent melodies one sensed the hope and the fire of this passionate trio.

DJ hooked up with a couple of people at a nearby table while I sat on a barstool, listening. As the wine went to my head, a heavily made-up black woman in a tight dress sat down beside me and started talking to me in Portuguese. I had no idea what she was saying, so I smiled and shrugged. Another busty woman in black tights and a skin-tight T-shirt sat down on my other side. The first one put her hand on my thigh and immediately I felt a warm stirring beneath the zipper of my blue jeans.

I was old enough to know that back home this was against the law. In South Africa the Immorality Act of 1950 declared sex between races a crime. But this was exactly why so many South African men would visit Lourenço Marques. Not that I was about to have sex with this exotic hooker, but the sense of impending treason sent a rush of blood to my ears and other parts. A few years before in Durban, I'd once seen a Latin-looking man and a large, black woman, both handcuffed, being roughly shoved into the back of police van near our house. A fat redheaded boy called Two Bob knew the man from

13

the flats they lived in. His name, slang for two shillings, came from the British currency used in South Africa at that time.

"Fuckin' porra[2] always naais[3] kaffir girls," said Two Bob with authority. "Now he's gonna shit."

Two Bob knew everything about naaing, and once showed me the place in the botanical gardens where you could watch young Indian couples stealing sweaty, illicit moments behind a bamboo grove.

By now, the fado music was reaching a crescendo. The woman in the tight dress had her arm draped over my shoulders and without warning the second temptress suddenly put her hand on my startled member. I was frozen to my seat, DJ laughing a bit too loudly with his newfound companions. Suddenly, he saw the state I was in and rushed to the bar, shooing the ladies away with good-humoured remonstrations.

"Sheez, these fucking prozzies take a chance; why didn't you call me?"

He sat me at the corner of the table where I safely spent the rest of the evening observing him and his mates. I'd preferred it at the bar.

Over the next few weeks we flew to Inhaca Island and then up the coast to Xai Xai, João Bello and Sao Martinho. One night, in our bungalow beside a huge inland salt lake, I heard noises coming from the adjoining room. I got up and opened the door. DJ was thundering away on top of a pretty, plump Portuguese woman.

"What you doing, Dad?" I asked, through slowly lifting veils of sleep.

DJ leapt up, wrapping a towel around his waist. "This poor lady got badly sunburned and I'm just rubbing cream on her burns," he puffed. "Go back to bed."

I slunk back to bed with my heavy secret, something I knew never to mention again.

From early times, it was evident that when my parents were together, life was a long series of arguments that inevitably ended in violence. I never questioned how my explosive, violent father could become such a fun-loving gentleman in the company of others. It was just the way he was. My cousin's father behaved in much the same way to his wife, and it was something we all saw and never spoke about. At home he was dangerously unpredictable, and could fly into violent rages over

2 slang for Portuguese
3 to have sex, from the Afrikaans, to sew

something as trivial as a passing comment my mother might make. It usually ended in her getting pushed around and slapped in the face or punched on her arms and stomach. These episodes were never mentioned to anyone; it was our family secret, our family shame. My mother never considered leaving him. Although he wasn't religious, she was a staunch member of the Catholic Church, and divorce was not tolerated. We all went to Catholic schools, attended catechism classes and never missed Holy Mass on Sunday. My mother was a member of the Catholic Women's League and would arrange flowers once a week on the altar of the Holy Trinity church. The strange thing about our Catholicism is that it came not through my father's Irish roots but through my half-Afrikaans mother. My grandmother had picked up the faith by default somewhere along the way, and my grandfather – born into the conservative and protestant Afrikaans church – went along with it. Afrikaners hated the Church of Rome, and this would have alienated any relatives he had left in the world.

In spite of my fear of my father, the trip to Mozambique was good. He was calm and happy, and I felt close to him at that time. But there was the sense that this wasn't the same person I lived with in Durban. That was a man I often hated, and who stirred enormous anger in me. I found it difficult to reconcile such conflicting feelings about the same person. As I retrieve these memories, I can't help but smile as I remember this man with whom I was later to have such monumental battles, yet still make peace with before he died.

My brother, my sister and I also went on wonderful holidays with my mother, up and down the Natal coast or in the mountain resorts of the Drakensberg[4]. Then the only conflict was between my brother and me. We were like dogs in a park, always going at each other. But that was kid stuff, and when the holidays were over and we went home, the oppression of our parents' bellicose relationship would once again bear down on us.

---

4 a mountain range that runs through the middle of South Africa and separates the coastal plain from the interior

Durban, Autumn 1962

HURLEY LAMBASTED

The Roman Catholic Primate of Durban, Archbishop Denis Hurley, was yesterday attacked by Dagbreek *and* Sondagnuus, *the Afrikaans newspaper of which Dr HF Verwoerd is chairman, for sending out what the newspaper describes as "subtle propaganda against the South African government". The attack was sparked off by an appeal for financial aid from overseas countries, launched by Archbishop Hurley after the South African Government had withdrawn its subsidies for private schools.*

Natal Mercury, 6 August 1962

JIM REEVES, CHET ATKINS AND FLOYD CRAMER AT THE DURBAN ICEDROME

Natal Mercury, 6 August 1962

Nelson Mandela is arrested outside Pietermaritzburg. The incident goes unreported in the Durban newspapers.

5 August 1962

I WAS EIGHT WHEN DJ STARTED Durban's first self-service liquor store, selling – apart from the standard fare – a range of exotic wines, spirits and liqueurs from around the world. The Strand Bottle Store was in the Golden Mile on Durban's beachfront, and we moved into a penthouse apartment across the road. At about this time the government had rescinded a longstanding law governing the sale of liquor to blacks. Until then, the only alcohol legally available to the black population was iJuba, a high-nutrient, low-alcohol beer brewed from sorghum. The scrapping of that law opened up a new and thirsty market, and DJ was quick to see the potential. Even though I was only eight years old, DJ insisted I work in the store on busy Friday afternoons and Saturday mornings. My main job was to manage the endless flow of empty bottles to be returned to the breweries for refilling. The neighbourhood hobos would collect empties and return them for the small deposit they earned. DJ always tried to pay these poor bums less than their due, something he'd never try with his more upmarket customers. I hated his petty meanness, and when he wasn't around I'd pay them the full amount. On the few occasions he caught me he'd scream and cuff me over the head for cutting into his profits, all in full view of customers and staff, leaving me embarrassed and humiliated.

The liquor law under our righteous and Calvinistic government also stipulated that stores close at midday on Saturday, in preparation for a total dry out on Sundays. Understandably, the rush to stock up for these sober Sundays was intense and highly profitable. I would deliver small orders to residents in apartments around the neighbourhood. Like any Golden Mile in a tourist town, the city's ugly underbelly wasn't far away. Just two blocks from the pristine beaches, Point Road could have been in another country. Backing onto the side

17

of Durban's busy harbour, it was the territory of prostitutes, thugs, nightclubs and all-night bars. My deliveries often took me into the heart of this dark district, and I quickly became familiar with a world I never mentioned to my parents. DJ must have known what I would encounter in the back alleys of The Point, and probably thought of it as some sort of initiation.

But it was my mother who ran the show. Her hands full with this new business, she was unable to keep a close eye on the kids. DJ still had his photographic business, and when school was over, I was free to do as I pleased. Of course, there was hell to pay whenever my report card arrived, but DJ's whipping would soon wear off as we played our games around the neighbourhood. I'd spend occasional weekends with my cousin Leonard at their crowded house, and he and I would extend our home range to other suburbs, always on the lookout for mischief. Leonard was a master at recycling. He once found a bent and buckled bicycle on a scrap heap, and after a few weekends of hacksawing and hammering in his father's garage, had it up and running. With me on the crossbar, we could now go greater distances and get into deeper trouble.

Leonard's mother, Aunty Leonie, was DJ's youngest sister, and from an early age she showed huge talent as a painter and musician. She was headed for a career in the arts until she met Len Downing, a large, handsome British seaman with a voice that could sing like an angel and roar like a devil. He was tall with strong features, bushy eyebrows and one raffishly lazy eye, which I later discovered had gone blind after an accident in his youth. Leonard had inherited the best of both his parents: besides his practical and mechanical skills, he was also a wonderful musician. He was equally at home on the guitar and the piano, and at summer youth camps he could sing a girl into the bushes with ease. He looked like his father with his black hair, strong straight nose and generous mouth, and even from an early age he was never short of women – old and young, regular and casual – with whom to exercise his blossoming sexuality.

But Leonard wasn't the only gifted one among my cousins. His three sisters, Franny, Miranda and Trish, had all inherited their mother's fine-chiselled, beautifully balanced features and flashing dark eyes, and like her they all sang, danced and played the piano. Franny and Miranda were older and would sing Joan Baez songs on the guitar, their faces etched with all the pain and pleasure of those sweet, sad songs. They were also rebellious, and had boyfriends who were beatniks, ducktails, hippies and surfers. Miranda dated a man called Tommy Felleen from the bad part of town. Youth culture at the time was divided into beach boys and bullets. The beach boys rode surfboards and wore floral shirts and faded blue jeans; the bullets rode motorbikes and wore black denim and leather. What both had in common was that they were all a bunch of thugs, always bristling for a fight. Tommy was a bullet. He was also a rock and roll dancer and a legendary street fighter, battling every weekend with the meanest and most fearless from other neighbourhoods. He'd never been beaten, and he looked and spoke like a psychotic desperado, but in Miranda's pretty little hands, Tommy Felleen became a doe-eyed, Old World gentleman. She had the blood of the Black Luceys. She had those black eyes.

By the age of nine I was picking up the local slang from my streetwise cousins, so DJ sent me off to the Mavis Wayne School of Speech and Drama to learn to speak properly. Miss Wayne was a large handsome dowager with a voluminous bosom into which was always stuffed an embroidered handkerchief. She was relentless as I red-lorry-yellow-lorried and lallary-lallary-lolled my lazy tongue into submission every Wednesday afternoon. Her efforts paid off, and soon I was winning prizes at Eisteddfods and speech and drama festivals. When I wanted to, I could switch on the accent of a little toff from the expensive side of town, while still behaving like a delinquent. I was learning to live on many levels, change like a chameleon, and slip and slide between the many inconsistencies that growing up in South Africa was throwing at me.

5

Durban, Winter 1963

TERROR ARRESTS IN VAAL
The arrest of six whites and 11 non-whites including the former secretary of the banned African National Congress, Walter Sisulu, in Rivonia, Johannesburg, yesterday was a major breakthrough in the elimination of subversive organizations, General JM Keevy, Commissioner of Police said in Pretoria tonight.

Natal Mercury, 13 July 1963

I DON'T REMEMBER IF IT was announced or just filtered into my consciousness, but with some disquiet I became aware that my mother was pregnant with her fourth child. Having already learnt about naaiing from the rough and redheaded Two Bob, this meant that in spite of the hostilities between my parents – I can't recall a glimmer of affection between them – they were still at it. My father seemed pleased enough at the news, but he didn't behave any more kindly towards her. Nor did her condition give her any respite from her daily workload. The bottle store had done well, and this is when my parents decided to buy the big house at 67 Milner Road. It was a move that shot us up the status ladder, although DJ grew ever wilder and more erratic. My mother decided to have a home birth, so a midwife was brought in and a room prepared for the arrival of our new, somewhat unexpected, sibling.

One humid, steamy day at the beginning of December, my sister finally arrived. A small group of us – friends and kids from the neighbourhood – stood in the garden listening with discomfort and embarrassment to the sound of my mother moaning, wailing and shouting at the arrival of our pretty little curly-haired sister. DJ was elsewhere at the time.

Louise was breastfed for about two minutes, so that my mother could leave her with our faithful maids, Gertie Mshali and Matilda Mbele, and get back to running the bottle store. After all, her husband might wake up on any given morning and announce that he was off to Mozambique or Russia or any other damn place he felt like going to. On one occasion he literally gave my mother a day's notice that he was leaving for Greece. Rumours began to circulate that he had more than a passing interest in that country.

Around that time, DJ decided that my brother Patrick and I

21

should take piano lessons with Aunty Leonie. We'd sit at the piano while the always beautiful, calm and mystical Aunty Leonie tried to impart the mysteries of this terrifying instrument amid the chaos all around. Uncle Len would be shouting at Leonard as they banged and sawed and did God knows what else in the garage. Miranda and Franny would be shrieking with laughter in the kitchen, with little Trish crying at her exclusion from their adolescent secrets. Although Patrick became an accomplished musician, I struggled. After two months, it became evident that I had neither the concentration nor the aptitude for classical music, and while I knew that music was *somewhere* in my blood, I was content to live in secret awe of Leonard's extraordinary abilities.

6

Durban, 1964

MANDELA TELLS COURT HE DID PLAN SABOTAGE
Nelson Mandela, the no. 1 accused at the Rivonia treason trial, admitted yesterday that he had been one of those responsible for the formation of Umkhonto We Sizwe (Spear of the Nation). He told Mr Justice de Wet, the Judge President, that he would also admit planning sabotage, not through recklessness or a love of violence, but because he felt there was no other course open to the African people.
Natal Mercury, 21 April 1964

AFRICAN'S SENTENCE WAS SHOCKING AND EXCESSIVE
The Judge President of the Free State, Mr Justice AJ Smit, yesterday described the sentence imposed on an African by a Bloemfontein magistrate as "shocking and excessive". Mr Justice Smit and Mr Justice HJ Potgieter allowed the appeal of Martiens Mochochoko against his sentence of 10 strokes with a cane on a charge of wearing a button off a police uniform without being a member of the force.
Natal Mercury, 21 April 1964

DJ ALWAYS SURROUNDED HIMSELF with social misfits, people he could dominate and get to play his bizarre games. There was Roy Hunt, a buck-toothed, popeyed idiot who did anything DJ asked of him. His manic laughter around the house drove my mother mad, but she soon learnt not to criticise DJ's cronies. She once commented on his presence and was rewarded with an explosion of slaps and invective. DJ and his cronies would go hunting in the rural forests of the Natal Midlands, a group of fired up, bloodthirsty jocks blasting at anything that moved. Occasionally I'd be allowed to tag along. Aubrey Marchant, a tailor, once fired at something moving which turned out to be Roy Hunt. The bullet whizzed past Roy's ear and the forest erupted with shouts, shrieks and crashing branches as the motley bunch rushed around trying to work out what had happened. DJ gave Aubrey a mighty slap across the back of the head, and they all skulked off back to the car.

Cliff Matchett was an ex big-game hunter who'd spent time in the Serengeti. Uncle Cliff and DJ once flew to Europe in the Globe Swift, a craft with a range of five hundred miles. They set out from Durban not really knowing what the next destination might hold. They flew up the east coast of Africa, through Mozambique and on to Dar es Salaam, then inland to Nairobi and up the Nile until they reached Cairo. From there they went through Israel, Lebanon, Turkey, Greece, Italy, France and finally to England. The trip home was much quicker, more or less straight down over Sardinia and Corsica, through Tripoli into the western Sahara and then down to South Africa. The journey took twenty-two days with thirty-one fuel stops. There's a photograph in one of my mother's albums of DJ and Cliff sitting in the shade of the tiny aircraft wing in the middle of the Sudanese desert. Beside them is a Bedouin boy with a donkey, and a group of Bedouin youths gathered around the wing. There has to be some crazy story to go with that picture, but I never got to hear it.

Some years after this epic journey, Uncle Cliff took a room in my grandparent's house. We'd moved into the big house up on the hill, and my grandparents found the extra money useful. On the occasional Friday night we'd have dinner at my grandparents, and Uncle Cliff would sometimes take his elephant gun from its canvas case and let me hold it. He had thrilling stories of his time as a big-game hunter and I dreamt of the places he spoke about. He'd hire a 16 mm projector and we'd all squeeze into the small living room and watch American TV series like *Hawaii Five-O* and *Perry Mason*. One night my parents allowed me to sleep in Uncle Cliff's room on the camp bed he kept folded on top of his cupboard. When everyone was asleep in the house, he gently coaxed me into his bed. He fondled my hairless little penis for a while and then kneeled beside the bed and put it in his mouth. All the time he was giggling in whispers and telling me not to tell anyone what he was doing. He pushed his erect penis between my thighs and after a few hushed shoves and grunts gave out a deep sigh. My legs were covered with a warm, sticky fluid that he quickly wiped away with a towel he had hanging over a chair beside the bed. The following morning I woke up and ran up the hill to my parent's house. I knew that what had happened in Uncle Cliff's bed must be written all over my face, and tried to stay away from my parents for the day.

After that, Uncle Cliff would take me for driving lessons in his Alpha Romeo Sprint. Through the sugarcane fields outside Durban, the smart red car was rapidly swallowed up by these massive green thickets: me, all of ten years old, on Uncle Cliff's lap taking control of the steering wheel as he changed gears and slipped his hand into my little red shorts. He'd find a deserted spot among the sugarcane and fondle me as he masturbated, eventually coming into his neatly folded handkerchief. With that done, we'd drive back to the city as if nothing had happened. There was a certain strange pleasure in the feelings I experienced during these encounters, and while I knew I'd probably get killed by my father if caught in the act, I felt complicit in Uncle Cliff's manoeuvrings.

I don't know how he managed to single me out, but these trips to the sugarcane fields happened regularly over weekends. At that time Uncle Cliff worked at a photographic shop in the centre of town. One Saturday afternoon, after the shop had closed, he took me into the darkroom and snapped some Polaroid pictures of my taciturn, naked body, keeping my face out of the picture. Using a long, flexible cord attached to the camera, he took a shot of himself standing behind me with his penis poking between my legs. It was all couched in jocular conspiracy, but thoughts of these episodes kept me awake at night, the anxiety and fear of being found out by my parents drilling deep into my young consciousness. This pattern was entrenched for several years: drives to the cane fields, sleepovers in his camp bed after Friday night films, and the occasional after-hours visit to the photographic shop. I never mentioned these encounters to anyone. I was implicated and trapped by a shameful secret, along with this man who was such a jolly friend of the family.

At school my teacher would rap me across the knuckles for daydreaming, but these daydreams were more like a whirling vortex of conflicted, illicit thoughts, far too perilous for me to make sense of. I had become a good sportsman, but despite winning all the school swimming prizes, I was plagued by a lack of confidence. By the time I reached my early teens I was able to avoid Uncle Cliff, and after a while he disappeared from our lives. I often wonder what DJ knew or suspected about his creepy friends. One thing was sure: I knew I couldn't rely on my father to protect me from the world.

Durban, Autumn 1966

TWO MINUTES AND DR VERWOERD WAS DEAD
Dr Hendrik Frensch Verwoerd died within two minutes of being stabbed by his assassin, Dimitrio Tsafendas, a temporary parliamentary messenger, in the House of Assembly yesterday afternoon. Dr Verwoerd was cut off at a time when he was riding the crest of the political wave – the embodiment of republican South Africa. A staunch supporter of separate development, he extended the hand of friendship to independent black African States on the republic's borders and to the north.

Natal Mercury, 7 September 1966

SIX YEARS GAOL FOR PAC MAN
A Durban magistrate said in the Durban regional court yesterday that he was shocked to hear that four years after the Government has banned the Pan-African Congress, the organization was still operating in South Africa and envisioned the violent overthrow by means of force of White rule in the country. Mr SM Rossouw was sentencing to six years imprisonment an African, Mandleni Ephraim Mbele, for being an office-bearer in the Pan-African Congress after it had been declared an unlawful organization.

Natal Mercury, 9 September 1966

IF ANYTHING WAS CONSISTENT throughout my early years of domestic pandemonium, it was the constant bombardment of Catholic dogma. It started at junior school with the nuns of the Holy Convent. Before I'd even discovered the sins that would later torment and tantalise me, I was taught to confess to them and prepare for my first Holy Communion, which all Catholic boys undertook at the age of twelve. I was given the traditional gift of a rosary for the occasion, and used the beads to count off the endless prayers of contrition I hoped would forgive me my sinful thoughts. I became an altar boy in a black cassock and flowing nylon surplice. After Mass, Father Kelly would hold his head in his hands. "My nerves are shattered," he would intone. "When will you learn, boy, that the bell is rung after Kyrie Eleison, not during the Angelis?"

My big moment of shame, however, came during Midnight Mass. This high point of the church calendar would begin at eleven on the night of December twenty-fourth. Sitting with all the other altar boys like a row of penguins, I started feeling a discomfort in my stomach. The boy beside me elbowed me in the ribs as rumbles and squeaks churned uncomfortably through my belly. I shifted slowly, as Father Kelly had ordered us to keep dead still and look pious. Archbishop Denis Hurley, swathed in purple, gold and silver robes, held the sacred chalice high as I lifted one numb bum cheek from the cold marble altar stairs. Suddenly, without warning, a massive wind thundered from beneath my cassock, echoing through the eaves and arches of the Holy Trinity Church. I sat staring straight ahead in surprise and shame as the boys on either side of me shifted quickly and quietly away, leaving me isolated and conspicuous just moments before the birth of Christ.

Despite my inability to ring the bell at the right time, I was deeply affected by the dogma of the church. It would take years to undo the shame and guilt imposed by that mighty institution for simply having the feelings of a normal boy. Yet the courageous stand Archbishop Hurley was starting to take against the government wasn't lost on me. After all, he had conducted my first Holy Communion and was a great, warm, friendly presence in my life. He was also extremely accessible, and whenever I ran into him, he called me by my first name. My feelings for the Church, however, left me in a quandary.

At school, the Catholic education wasn't having much success in getting me to understand the mysteries of maths. St Henry's was run by the Marist Brothers, an educational order of monks with roots in early nineteenth century France. The holy brothers used the cane incessantly to try to instil a better learning ethic in me, but to no avail. Mr Siraaj was a maths teacher at an Indian school in the nearby suburb of Sydenham, and also worked as a driver at DJ's bottle store on Friday afternoons and Saturday mornings. Mr Siraaj displayed the type of politeness I came to associate with Mahatma Gandhi, and my mother decided he was the one to help me. Every Tuesday afternoon I went to his apartment where he patiently but unsuccessfully tried to get those mysteries into my impenetrable brain. In the background he always had a radio playing Indian music, and one day, while wrestling with some theorem or other, he heard a flash announcement that Prime Minister Hendrik Verwoerd had been assassinated. Mr Siraaj turned up the radio and listened grimly to the news.

"Ooh, this is a very terrible thing, very, very terrible indeed!" But his eyes didn't follow what his mouth was saying. Although only twelve years old, I already knew that Verwoerd was not the saint my grandfather claimed him to be. While he continued to intone "terrible, terrible, very terrible indeed", I knew Mr Siraaj was saying it for the benefit of the small white boy whose father gave him part-time employment, and that, like Mr Siraaj, many other South Africans would have little sadness at this news.

In 1967, when I reached standard six, I left the Marist Brothers school for Durban Boys High School. For the first time I was out of the Catholic education system, and it was a very different world. DHS was modelled on the British public school system with its rigorous discipline and ridiculous social affectations. We had to wear woollen blazers throughout the hot, humid Durban summers and stiff straw boaters to all public places, including the beach. The list of petty rules was lengthy, and contraventions were punished by caning.

AJ Human, the science teacher at DHS, had a great, wicked devil up his bum. His was the first class I attended at this new school. He started the lesson by furiously whacking his cane on the desk, screaming that his class would not be a place for slackers, malingerers or imbeciles. By the time he was halfway through his venomous welcome speech, the veins of his neck were standing out like cocktail sausages and his eyes looked about to explode. He seemed to have some sort of speech defect as well as a strange tic in his cheek. Suddenly he turned on one of the boys at the back of the class.

"What's so funny, boy?" he bellowed. "Share the joke, boy! Tell the rest of the class what you find so funny!"

"Nothing, sir," whimpered the shocked boy, eyes on the floor.

"Laughing at nothing, are you? Come here, boy!" The boy walked nervously to the front of the class. "Bend!" screamed AJ. "Touch your toes."

With a swift ferocity that drew a collective gasp, AJ's cane struck the boy's bum with a sickening sound. The boy leapt, his face twisting in pain.

"Down!" screamed AJ. "Touch your toes." The boy hesitated. AJ grabbed his neck and pushed him down, landing another vicious blow squarely on the now trembling buttocks. "Anyone else with a joke for the class? Sure? Right, then we'll get on with the first lesson."

AJ proceeded to talk about the table of elements, but the more I tried to concentrate, the more my mind drifted out of the classroom to some dreamy, peaceful place. Not even fear of the dire consequences I faced helped steer me towards an understanding of these alien concepts. It was like trying to stick photographs in a scrapbook without glue. The information floated freely around my head and then wafted off at its own convenience to a place I would never again visit. It wasn't long before AJ's cane started landing on my own startled bottom, but as painful and humiliating as it was, it simply didn't help to get all those facts into my head.

AJ was probably the most extreme of all the teachers, but the general principal applied by most was that the cane should be used liberally to support the acquisition of knowledge. So, as my dysfunctional brain struggled with the abstract concepts of maths, the mysteries of science and humankind's tortuous march through history, I resigned myself to an endless succession of detentions and canings.

My good friend at this time was a pimply kid called Kevin

Humphrey. Kevin's parents were an English working-class couple with thick accents and a sense of humour that was totally new to me. Mr Humphrey worked for the Durban Corporation, the body that kept the city running, while Mrs Humphrey ran an ice cream parlour at Mini Town, a tourist attraction on the beachfront. Because of his weight, Kevin was teased by the jocks-in-training at DHS. I was also an outsider. I suffered from chronic hay fever: I never stopped sneezing and always had a raw, red nose. So with my funny looks and girly surname and Kevin's pimply plumpness, we two misfits formed a strong and happy bond.

Kevin was good in class but also streetwise. He subscribed to the British music papers, *New Musical Express* and *Melody Maker*. He knew everything about the underground music scene, a genre shunned by Springbok Radio because of its subversive nature. Through this awkward but trenchant boy I discovered a world of radical thinkers, intellectual songwriters and avant-garde musicians. Kevin introduced me to the British rock group Jethro Tull, and after listening to frontman and master flautist Ian Anderson, I desperately wanted to play the flute. Kevin was also funny and irreverent, questioning my slavish obedience to the rituals of the church, which started questions blossoming in my own head.

Even at that early age, Kevin had opinions about the politics of the land. Under the influence of his clear but youthful observations, I was able to start putting into perspective my own disillusionment with what I saw around me. But we were on our own. All around us, boys of our age were buying into the ideology of Christian National Education, a new and repressive system being pushed into public schools by the Nationalist government. At its core was the ideology of racial segregation.

Durban High School, while an English-speaking establishment, was nonetheless a bastion of the ideologies that propped up the Nationalist government. Its traditions were from another time and another country. Small boys had to endure humiliating initiation rites. They had to fag for senior boys: running errands, doing chores, fetching and carrying their books and sports kit, picking up snacks and drinks from the store down the road – anything the seniors wanted. Punishment for disobedience or dissent was to have your testicles "polished" with black boot polish. Prefects were allowed to cane younger boys, and you'd get beaten for anything, from not knowing the name of the first rugby team players to not knowing the

31

cricket team's war cry. Endless caning was going on. Teachers and prefects had pet names for their canes, and the process of receiving "cuts" was carried out with pomp and ceremony. Cuts for hair touching your collar, talking in assembly, untidy blazers, dirty shoes, missing song practice… and a hefty share of these cuts ended up on my poor arse.

Every Friday afternoon we'd have to kit out in khaki military uniforms, belts and shoes polished to a glossy shine, then line up on the rugby field to march up and down in preparation for the communist invasion. Seventeen-year-old sergeant majors would yell about the need to defend our beautiful land against the kaffirs. Kevin and I weren't fooled by this onslaught, and our friendship alliance was strong. What started to disturb me, however, was a growing awareness that I didn't identify with many of the jokes and references he and his family used, or the comics and magazines like *Beano* and *Boy's Own* he got in the post, where the language was in colloquial Liverpudlian, Geordie, South Country[1] and other far-off accents. This was Kevin's culture and identity, not mine. Much of the cultural influence surrounding me was imported from faraway lands, and I was beginning to realise that I had little to do with that distant place called England.

Back home on the Berea, my mother announced once again that she was pregnant; number five was on the way. By this time I'd begun to wonder what the hell was going on with my parents. They spent their lives engaged in mortal combat, and then to everyone's surprise and disbelief, my mother would suddenly be pregnant. Dennis Michael "Mikey" James was born with a smile on his funny little face and a special place in my mother's heart.

The bottle store was still going strong, but DJ now had a new interest. He bought a whole pile of film equipment, cameras, editing tables and sound recording machines, and converted one of the big rooms in the house into a film studio. While my mother continued to run the bottle store, he played with his new toys and started making commercials for the cinema. For me, I had a new holiday job. While I still had to do my tours of duty at the bottles store – deliveries and empty bottles – I also had to start learning the basics of the film business, especially the laborious task of editing. My incompetence would enrage DJ, who'd lash out with tongue and fists. He'd bellow at

---

1 various British dialects

the top of his voice, punching and slapping as I covered my head until the assault ended. I hated that studio, and vowed never to go into the film business.

8

Durban, Summer 1969

SOUTH AFRICA AT PEACE, SAYS VORSTER
Order, calm and lack of tension was the hallmark of the South African scene during 1968, the prime minister, Mr BJ Vorster, said in his New Year broadcast from Johannesburg last night.
Natal Mercury, 1 January 1969

There you stand
At the edge of the desert at the end of the war
There you stand
In a world I could never look into
There you stand
An old Don Quixote with your eyes on the floor
There you stand
In a bubble I tried to break into
My Son, My Father and Me, Roger Lucey, 1994

THE ROAD AROUND THE EDGE of the racecourse is lined with acacia trees that spread like veins above the melting tar. In summer they're covered with bright orange flowers and little pods that squirt a clear liquid when you squish them. I pump furiously at the pedals of my Raleigh three-speed bicycle. The acacia pods pop and burst under the spinning tyres. I'm barefoot, wearing shorts and a short-sleeved cotton shirt. My heart is pounding, not only from the effort on this hot-as-hell day, but also because of the risky mission I'm on.

The broad road runs past a series of narrow alleys in the rundown area of Greyville. This is an area of ducktails and drunks; of warehouses and dark, seedy shops. There are no white people around, and as I cycle up the dingy alley, I stick out like the balls on a bulldog. Where the alley ends, I turn and ride through a gap in a huge metal door into a massive steel shed. Its huge, windowless walls are blackened by dozens of braziers and wood fires glowing in the bleak interior of this almost mediaeval-looking place. The floor space is divided into hundreds of little compartments and cubicles formed by corrugated iron sheets, old car doors, plastic milk crates and pieces of jagged and splintered timber. There are windows fashioned from broken glass panes and beds made from old doors and paint cans. There's an overpowering smell of umqombothi, a pungent milky sorghum beer. Large plastic barrels of the stuff are propped in nooks and shadows around the cubicles. This place is the rickshaw shed, teeming with sweaty, gleaming, half-naked Zulu men, the rickshaw drivers. Some work the tourist pitch wearing ornate headgear, all feathers and horns and bits of mirror and plastic reflectors. Others, dressed in rags, cart fruit and vegetables from outlying market gardens for the Indian traders.

I know where to go; I've been here before. The old Zulu pulls a huge sack from under his bed, stuffed with the finest dagga from the deep rural area south of Durban. "A rand a hand," he says. I pass over a scrunched up one rand note and stick my hand into the bag. He passes me a piece of newspaper, in which I wrap my big handful of sticky vegetation. He waves with a toothless smile, and with my shorts pocket bulging like a tumour, I mount my bicycle and head back around the racecourse to the large house on the edge of the open piece of land. I'm fifteen years old.

While there were white boys from school and the neighbourhood that I played with, Jabula was my favourite. He and I were getting bolder and more reckless in seizing control of the streets. It was he who introduced me to the sweet pleasures of zol[1]. I was already familiar with the reputation of this vilified weed. Grandpa had been working in the law courts processing the accused, and it was always a story of disgrace when he came across a "European" who'd been caught smoking the dreaded dagga. At that time the term "European" was used to describe whites, and the city was littered with "Europeans Only" signs on buses, public toilets, cinemas, beaches and everything else denied to the vast black population. According to Grandpa, only kaffirs, coolies[2] and the scum of the earth smoked this morality-destroying drug. Not surprisingly, our relationship took a nosedive years later when the police arrived on his doorstep looking for me after I'd been busted for possession of this very weed, and then contravened the terms of my bail conditions. But that's another story.

Jabula taught me the ceremonious process of preparing the sticky green buds for smoking in the small clay pipe or chillum. Chillums were sold at a store in the Indian shopping area of Grey Street, and had to be burned in before use. A small stone or gerik was placed in the neck of the chillum, and shaped to allow maximum flow while keeping the zol from falling through. The zol was crushed in the palm of the hand, taking care not to let any of the precious plant fall while throwing out all the stalks and seeds. It was then mixed with a small amount of tobacco and loaded into the pipe, not too tight, not too loose. A small rag or sulfie was wrapped around the neck of the pipe as a filter. It was now ready for smoking. Using two hands, one person would hold the pipe and the other would light it, taking care to knock off the sulphurous tip of the match before applying it

1 dagga, marijuana
2 a derogatory term for Indians

to the pipe. Jabula would puff away until the pipe was glowing, then pull a huge draught into his lungs, coughing and spluttering as he did so. As he exhaled through nose and mouth, his entire head would almost disappear in a bluish cloud. This ceremony had become highly ritualised and was practiced by zol smokers all over the province. It was a ceremony that united zol smokers in their daily underworld.

Then it would be my turn. The effect went straight to the eyes, turning them red and languid. In minutes, the whole world looked softer and gentler. But what I loved was what it did to my brain. My mind slid into a warm, comfortable zone no unwanted person could enter. All the trouble at home and at school became a distant aggravation, all the fear and anxiety, the racing heart, the waking in the middle of the night with mother weeping, DJ shouting, and my brother and I trying to pull him off as he slapped and punched and banged her head against the wall. Only when DJ was exhausted would he stop, often morphing seamlessly into a state of apology as he saw the damage he'd inflicted. All this would disappear in the warm comfort of the smoke, although the real world always loomed just around the corner. In the bristling aftermath of these battles nothing was ever said. My mother never said a word to us kids, and we never mentioned it among ourselves; it was as if it never happened. By morning, in the rush to get to school, my mother's bruises and my father's remorse were just further clutter in this already chaotic, emotional quagmire.

9

Durban, December 1969

INDIANS' FATE IN THE BALANCE
The fate of more than 25 000 Indians in Durban, Umkomaas, Park Rynie and Umzinto is still hanging the balance as the Government decides the future zoning of the areas in which they are living. And Indian leaders have predicted that there will be many, many "heartbreaks" if they are uprooted to make way for other race groups.
Natal Mercury, 1 December 1969

The Bantu Homelands Citizenship Act (National States Citizenship Act) No. 26 of 1970, passed on 26 March, required that all South African Blacks become citizens of one of the self-governing territories.
"No Black person will eventually qualify [for South African nationality and the right to work or live in South Africa] because they will all be aliens, and as such, will only be able to occupy the houses bequeathed to them by their fathers, in the urban areas, by special permission of the Minister."
Connie Mulder, South African Information and Interior Minister, 1970

DURING THE SUMMER HOLIDAYS of 1969/70, I spent a good deal of time working at the bottle store – in disgrace after failing standard eight.

"I've had a gut full of you and your attitude," my mother never failed to remind me.

I was on a very short leash, but with Jabula around it was often a lot of fun. If a delivery was too big for me, Jabula and I would head off together on large, unwieldy bicycles with wicker baskets attached to the front, loaded with all manner of booze. Jabula could always explain the anomalies I saw around me – the white sailors with black prostitutes, the huddles of men desperately smoking broken bottle necks in dark alleys – he knew everything, and more.

Jabula's part-time career as a petty thief scared the hell out of me. By this time he had a fulltime job at the Strand Bottle Store and lived in one of the servants' quarters at the bottom of the garden. Many years before, I'd been caught slinking out of the Portuguese shop up the road with a large packet of Liquorice Allsorts bulging ludicrously from the pocket of my boxer shorts. I was so shocked when the thickset Madeiran shop owner grabbed me by the collar that I was unable to lie about my name or phone number. As I sat in my bedroom after a thorough whipping from my mother's wooden spoon, the shame, as a policeman's grandson, of being caught committing such a heinous act was permanently branded into my psyche. Now, here was Jabula committing these crimes with righteous self-assurance. I was disapproving. Of course, we who lived in the big house, while not spoilt brats, wanted for nothing. Jabula, even though he was DJ's favourite employee, earned a pittance and lived in squalor in the khaya[1] at the bottom of the garden. The room was dark and unpainted, with a single small window high up on the wall. It always smelt of paraffin, which he used in the Primus stove to cook his meals. His clothes hung neatly from a piece of rope strung between window and doorframe, and his shoes, polished like patent leather, stood under the rusty iron bed.

"The thing is, you see," he'd instruct in his gravelly voice, "money doesn't grow on trees, like. That's why a man must look after his things. And you must always aim at quality, you make out what I'm saying? Me, I never steal a cheap pair of shoes, you make out? And a woman will always go with the man with good shoes."

The small cubicle beside the room is both the toilet and shower. It's a hole in the concrete floor with a black cast iron cistern that clunks like a farm implement when you pull the chain. The cold water shower hangs off the end of a rusty pipe, high in the gloom of this squalid indignity.

It was inevitable that Jabula and I would view shoplifting differently. But dagga smoking was different. By this time it was becoming part of a conspiracy of lifestyle that separated us from the black-hatted, short-haired, sanctimonious prigs that formed the pillars of society: teachers, doctors, policemen, salesmen and even bus drivers, all seemingly the custodians of this God-ordained society that I was starting to deeply distrust.

Some of the maids in the neighbourhood made extra money selling dagga and iJuba, the traditional Zulu beer, they would brew in plastic barrels hidden in the corners of their khayas, or in parts of the walled compounds that housed these itinerant workers. The dagga would often come from their traditional homes in the rural areas – small, round thatched huts where they were often forced to leave their children with an ancient grandmother while they came to the city to work. Jabula got me exclusive passage into these tidy, transient sleeping quarters. We'd use the dark to cover our illicit journeys, knocking softly on small frosted glass windows and slipping quickly into the tiny rooms. The beds were always placed high on paint tins or bricks for fear of the mythical Tokoloshe, a small evil beast that attacked at night. Once inside, there was always a lot of muffled giggling as Jabula charmed these lonely servants of the white elite. It was customary to offer a drink of iJuba. He'd hunker down on his

1 Zulu for house, but denoting the small, one-roomed servant's quarters of most white homes

haunches and after giving the plastic bottle a good shake, take a long slow pull on the sour, milky brew.

"The thing is, you see, this beer is full of stuff that keeps you alive like, you make out? If you had no food you could live on it." That was hard to believe. It smelt lethal, and after a few agonising tries, I gave it up for good.

One of the maids was young and pretty, and used to tease me relentlessly. She was the darkest shade of black and wore her uniform tight, showing off the shape of her compact breasts. She had buttocks like boulders, small, round and hard, and when I did finally get to touch them, I thought my heart would pound itself to death. She'd say things about me to Jabula in Zulu, which would get him belly laughing, but he wouldn't say what she'd said. I never did get to learn his language – just another symptom of the inequity of our lives. She was about eighteen, called Florence because the madam couldn't pronounce her name, and she'd rub petroleum jelly on those smooth inky legs as we sat there. She'd wink at me and then say something in Zulu, which made me coy but lustful. Later, Jabula would regale and taunt me with stories of the intricacies of black women's bodies.

"Between their legs," his voice dropped to a hoarse whisper, "they've got these things called malebes, you make out? And the thing is, when you put your pipe inside there, the malebes are like worms and they grab onto your thing and you can't get it out. I'm not giving you a bullshit speech, s'true's Bob, but those malebes, if you're not careful, they can make you mad."

His stories electrified my imagination; I had only once seen one of those mysterious organs. With my head under the tepid water of the neighbour's swimming pool, I'd shown her mine and she'd shown me hers, pulling down her bikini bottom while keeping an eye out for her mother.

I can't remember how it came about, but sometime later, Jabula contrived to get me into Florence's room alone, just her and me – a white boy just turned sixteen. She sat and smiled and didn't say much, and then told me to come and sit with her on the bed. She put her finely toned jet-black arms around me, and with a mouth tasting of maize meal, kissed me hard and relentlessly. I suddenly became aware that I'd had some sort of accident. My virgin member was on fire and there was a small sticky stain creeping through my denim jeans. I jumped off the high bed and told Florence I had to go home. Her forthright approach had taken me by surprise, but it was

41

the thought of the malebes that put the fear of God into me. I often wonder how it might have been if only I'd been more courageous.

St Charles College was run by the Marist Brothers in Pietermaritzburg, a small college town fifty miles inland from Durban, and it was here that I was sent by my exasperated parents to repeat standard eight. My mother hoped that these holy brothers could put me right.

On the evening before the start of each term, boys would arrive from all over the country and as far afield as Mozambique and Mauritius. Some would lie around the musty dormitories on foam mattresses set on iron frame beds; others would walk around the sports fields or sit in groups on the steps leading to the refectory, waiting for the first meal. Behind the junior dormitory was an old boiler room where all the smokers would meet up. Through the gaps in the walls you could detect any approaching Brothers from quite a distance, and make a quick duck through the bushes and back to the senior dormitory. The misfits hung around here or a number of other secret smoking hideouts, telling tall stories about their sexual and other conquests during the holidays. I never uttered a word about what had happened with Florence, not because of my failure of courage, but because even among the more open-minded boys, the idea of sex with a black girl was total taboo. Instead, like most other boys, I made up the occasional story.

I suppose I only have myself to blame for not endearing myself to my new teachers. On my first day at St Charles, our class teacher, who also taught science, asked each boy in the class what he wanted to be when he left school. Mr Granger was a neat but gormless man who looked like he needed his self-importance challenged. By the time he turned to me, I was ready.

"I want to make films that show the positive aspects of communism," I stated with authority, "and how it can improve the lives of common people."

I'd learnt quite a bit on the subject from Kevin's older brother and father, who were dyed-in-the-wool socialists. Mr Granger looked like he'd swallowed a large dollop of wasabi paste. His face turned red, his eyes looked like they were boiling from the inside and his bottom lip trembled as if he would burst into tears.

"Do you *understand* what you've just said?" He could hardly get the words out.

"Yes sir, I do." I spoke the words like a bridegroom.

Some of the boys shuffled around giggling, others looked ahead in shocked silence. The teacher launched into a tirade of anti-communist rhetoric, pro-government exaltation, and why boys of sixteen had no right to speak their minds. Needless to say, we didn't hit it off, and I thought I was doomed to scholastic damnation. But Mr Granger was only one of the teachers I had, and a few were to become allies.

Rob Tate taught English, and while not subversive, showed signs of not being the typical fascist acolyte brand of teacher I'd come to know. He was urbane and cosmopolitan, and approved of the poetry I was reading at the time, even though my favourite was the work of a black poet, Oswald Mshali. His anthology, *Sound of a Cowhide Drum*, had resonated deeply within me, and I read his earthy lines so often that I could recite them by heart. Rob Tate encouraged this type of pursuit. I'd also show him my own painful efforts at this erudite art form, and he'd tactfully try to point me in the right direction.

But the most influential person I came across at the time was a young student teacher named Tim Dunne. Tim and a group of students from the nearby university lived in an old cottage on the school grounds. In lieu of rent they performed duties at the school. Tim taught the occasional maths class in which I was his most dismal pupil. These students were all young men of Catholic background – Tim had studied for the priesthood at the nearby Cedara Seminary – who had discovered Liberation Theology, and they were the most radical people I'd ever come across.

One of the most famous old boys of St Charles was Archbishop Hurley himself, and his nephew, Jeremy, was among this group of firebrands. While there was an overriding conservatism among the Brothers and teachers, the archbishop was already challenging the government in a big way, and was a pillar of strength and inspiration to many leftists. Jeremy's duty at the school was to look after one of the dormitories, but one Sunday he chained himself to the altar of the nearby Catholic cathedral, demanding to be allowed to talk to the parishioners about the evil of the government's policies. For many this was a deeply shocking act; for me and a couple of likeminded schoolmates, it was heroism. Tim had been picked up and interrogated by the security police, but was still a respected member of the teaching staff. I now knew adults who were on the right side, and Mr Granger could go to hell.

The seeds of my rebellion didn't germinate in a vacuum. In America the hippie movement was in full swing, and in all the big cities of South Africa its influence was being felt. During the summer holidays at the end of my first year at St Charles, my cousin Leonard and I sneaked into the Palm Beach Hotel on Durban's beachfront to listen to Franny's new boyfriend, Dave Marks. I'd never heard anything quite like it. Dave was famous, he'd written the song Master Jack, and he and another well-known singer, Richie Morris, were down from Jo'burg for a season at the Palm Beach. I was captivated and amazed by these two talents. They sang songs by Bob Dylan and Phil Ochs, they poked fun at the government, but above all they sang their own songs. I'd never heard anyone sing their own songs, and these were brilliant.

Dave was a serious and complex man, not given to suffering fools. His father was an American merchant seaman whose ship was sunk by a German U boat off the South African coast before the war even started. With third degree burns over much of his body, he ended up in hospital in Cape Town where Dave's mother was a young nurse, and they married before he left the hospital. But two years later, after he'd recovered, the military recalled him to the USA. His young wife never heard from him again, and he never knew that she already had a bun in the oven, which was David. In due course she married a Greek immigrant, Gerrasimo Markantonatos, who raised David as his own, along with a string of other children who arrived on an annual basis. David was working as a gold miner when he started his singing career, and started going by the name Dave Marks.

During the winter holidays in 1971, I watched the Woodstock movie three times. Here were people openly challenging the mighty US government over the war in Vietnam. But we had our own war, and boys of my age – seventeen – were already registered with the South African Defence Force. The songs of Bob Dylan, Richie Havens and many others that banged the drum for the peace movement resonated with our own growing rejection of what was happening on the border[2]. Music had become more than just a pastime; it was now the vanguard of the cause. So when my mother gave me a flute for my birthday, I started on my journey as a voluntary flag bearer for the Good Guys. I couldn't read a note of music, but what I lacked in theory I made up for with enthusiasm and an ability to improvise. Before long I was playing with a small group of boys in school Folk Masses, doing songs like Kumbaya and We Shall Overcome. It was

---

2 the Angolan border, where the conflict with South West Africa's liberation organisation was increasing

an effort by the school to get us reprobates back into the Flock, while for us it was a way to avoid the study session.

The Marist Brothers were a mixed and motley lot; some were old and twisted by years of their strange half-life with the outside world, while many younger ones wrestled with their vows as young girls flocked to the rugby field on Saturdays to support the players. Occasionally they could be gentle and sympathetic, like Brother Gerard. He loved literature and poetry, and we'd sit in his little office during school counselling sessions and listen to music like Stravinsky's Rite of Spring.

Brother Francis, on the other hand, was a weird, antisocial snake of a man who'd obviously never had a friend in the world. His nickname was Stinky because of a rare skin disorder that blocked his sweat glands. His skin really was reptilian, and would even slough off every so often. He was our housemaster in my second year there, and his cell-like cubicle at the end of our vast dormitory stank like an adolescent sock festival. François Mayer, a six-foot-three kid from Curepipe, Mauritius, who was always in trouble for smoking cigarettes, hated Stinky. One night, as this lonely man's torchlight drifted from bed to bed making sure the boys were asleep, François unleashed the plan he'd been hatching.

We were all prepared and feigned sleep as the fetid, robed servant of the Lord wafted through the sixty beds lined up in the huge hall. When the torchlight reached François' bed, it revealed the francophone giant in full tussle with his enormous, erect penis. The torchlight flailed around the room for a second and then went out as the ghostly form of Stinky fled to his cubicle, banging into beds along the way. Stinky's nightly inspections were less resolute after that, which made it easier to occasionally slip out to listen to live music at the Arab coffee bar in town.

Jose de Oliveira was a short bull of a boy who lived in the Mozambican coastal town of Xai Xai. He was tough and funny, violent and compassionate, as well as radical and talented. He was also a vociferous supporter of the Frelimo guerrillas who were fighting the Portuguese administration in Mozambique at the time. The majority of the boys at school referred to blacks as kaffirs, but they soon learnt not to use that sort of language around Jose. By this time a small group of us were generally regarded as lefties and liberals.

Jose never hid the fact that at the end of every school holiday he'd get his father's driver to detour via the shantytown outside Lourenço

Marques airport, where he'd engage in an hour or two of hired lust to last him through another term with the holy brothers. About a week into one of the terms, Jose started walking like he had a large root vegetable rammed up his poop-chute. Eventually he admitted that all was not well in the penis department. He let us all take a look. The poor thing was swollen and discoloured, the foreskin like an over-tight polo neck strangling the life out of his wretched whanger. Eventually he got to a doctor who sorted the problem out, but our first sighting of the dreaded gonorrhoea struck the fear of God into us.

For all Jose's robust rhetoric and violent threats against anyone who challenged his political views, when he picked up a Spanish guitar he became a gentle, romantic Latin troubadour. He tucked the gentle curves of the wood beneath his stocky arms as his fingers flew with flamenco elegance across the fret board. He'd raise his head and open a mouth filled with crooked, tobacco-stained teeth – he'd smoked since he was eight – and let loose a voice that croaked and cried through the laments of generations of poor, impassioned lovers. Jose taught me a few chords and a couple of simple songs. The first time I got one of them half-right I felt a pleasure unlike anything I'd ever felt before. It stirred my blood.

Years later, when I bumped into Jose again in Durban, that mouth that had once broken so easily into laughter was twisted and bitter, his eyes in a permanent scowl as if looking into the sun. He'd left Mozambique, shattered by the Stalinist excesses of his beloved Frelimo. I don't know exactly what happened, but that once animated face transformed by pain and desecration still haunts me.

During school holidays, I was required to work again at DJ's bottle store, doing deliveries and running the empty bottle storeroom. It was hard work, but I was developing a manly strength. I could toss a wooden crate containing two dozen empty beer bottles onto the top of a ten-foot stack. Jabula still worked at the bottle store and during our free time we'd still get up to mischief. There was nothing like a good hit on a chillum to relieve the boredom of packing bottles.

One Saturday afternoon, after failing in our quest to buy a couple of kaartjies – thin pencils of dagga wrapped in brown paper – we got on a bus for KwaMashu. Blacks weren't allowed in white buses, but a white kid in a black bus just raised a few laughs and pointed fingers. Jabula's mother lived in KwaMashu, so he knew his way around this shabby mass of matchboxes. It was my first time in a township, and my mind and heart were racing. If the police spotted me we'd have to run for it, but it was the overwhelming sense of poverty that burnt into my idealistic young mind. I'd only heard about these places, but now the sight, smell and abject misery of it all stuck in my throat as I breathed. Jabula didn't seem to notice; he called out loudly to other young men on the streets and had boisterous conversations from fifty metres away.

We went to a shebeen[3] to buy a roll of kaartjies. The place was full of merry men and women clutching quarts of Castle and Lion lager. They danced to the distorted blare of township music, sticking their bums out and making swift, natty movements with their feet. We then went to have tea at Jabula's mother's house, a single room with an outside toilet. We were ushered in with a formality that made me feel a little awkward. The precious little she had was kept immaculately, her high bed covered in white linen embroidered with icons and motifs from the church of Zion, which she attended every Sunday. She sat me down on a rickety, high-backed chair and gave me strong, sweet, milky tea and a thick slice of white bread smeared with apricot jam. I'd never felt that welcome anywhere in my life. Whatever the arguments at St Charles about the pros and cons of our government's policy, I knew then that it was terribly wrong.

---

3 an illegal tavern selling alcohol and dagga

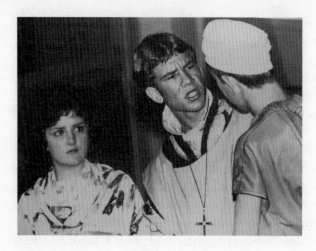

10

Durban, Winter 1971

SUICIDE AFTER SEX LAW CHARGE

A railway policeman committed suicide after being charged with contravening the immorality act, according to inquest papers filed with the Durban Magistrates court yesterday. Det. Sgt Willem Jacobus van Dyk (55) committed suicide by gassing himself in his car on February 25 this year. He had been charged with contravening the immorality act with an African woman on February 2.

Natal Mercury, 7 May 1971

Students to be tried by Students Representative Council for producing pamphlets protesting black wages.

Dome Special Issue (Natal University student newspaper),
17 June 1971

THE SHOPS IN GREY STREET are stacked to the rafters with shoes and jeans, T-shirts and jackets, all at half the price of the smart department stores downtown. Young Indian men with neat clothes and fancy hairstyles trawl the endless stream of humanity, touting to make a sale. The sidewalks are packed with people from the other side of South Africa's cynically crafted social divide: blacks, Indians, coloureds[1], and every shade in between. The few white faces are welcomed by the smiling touts, an opportunity to pull a good deal. Jabula walks through the crowd with a pronounced swagger. He smiles at the touts, his ample lips revealing an immaculate row of white teeth. He wears a checked jacket a size too big and puffs out his chest and shoulders like the lifesavers at south beach. He's just turned nineteen but looks anything between twenty and thirty. He walks into a shoe shop, its display window a nest of Jarman, Florsheim, Clarks, Stateside and other American fashion brands. The walls are stacked deep and high with shoe boxes.

"Howdy," says Jabula, giving the salesman a thumbs up. "Just came from stateside, US merchant marine. Swell shoes you got here, pardner." He speaks with an American accent, but not the black American version; there's no Harlem or New Orleans here, no drawl from Kentucky or Mississippi. He talks – and walks – like John Wayne.

But the salesman, running up and down the ladder and showing off dozens of the latest models, doesn't know this. He doesn't know the shrewd lessons this young man has learnt in the cheap, stuffy cinema reserved for non-whites watching reruns of John Wayne, Richard Widmark and Kirk Douglas movies. Jabula thanks the exasperated

---

1 the official apartheid racial category for people of mixed race, distinct from black and Asian

salesman, gives him another thumbs up and swaggers off down the road. A closer look reveals lumpy creases in the folds of his jacket. Beneath it, nestling safely in each armpit is a shiny new shoe.

One good thing had happened to me at DHS. At age thirteen I'd won the under-14 hundred yard hurdles on sports day and broken the school record. Like DJ, I was becoming an athlete, and this pleased him. I continued to win this event, and by the time I got to St Charles, I was up to provincial standard. One of my deceptions at interschool competitions was to sit in the changing room, smoking loutishly just before my race. My competitors would rule me out; meanwhile, I was fired up and hungry to win. It was always a pleasure to see the surprise of those serious athletes when they were beaten by the lout with the cigarette in his mouth. For the first time in my life I was achieving something. It was amazing how a little sporting achievement could raise your status among the in-crowd. While I enjoyed the success (I was no longer the odd geek who got picked on), I still didn't view athletic achievement with the respect I accorded to poets, musicians and actors.

During the championship when I was seventeen, I hit a hurdle and fell hard, twisting my knee. The damage was bad, and the surgeon removed my kneecap and stuck me in a plaster cast from toe to groin. Despite several months in this plaster cast, I tried to carry on with normal life, never imagining that this would be the end of my athletics career. My friend Martin had a sister who quite fancied me, and sometime earlier I'd kissed her in the orchard of the agricultural college where they lived. In the holidays after my knee op, they came to visit. Because the college was far from Durban, they stayed the night.

We hung around listening to Led Zeppelin and Pink Floyd albums, and at some point in the evening Martin's sister and I wound up on the sofa in DJ's studio. It was clear she wanted to carry on where we'd left off in the orchard. So, after a period of manic face sucking and breast kneading, the time came for striking out to home base. This was my first time, and all common sense now resided firmly in the tip of my aching member. I tried to get my trousers off, hopping around tugging as the denim spitefully attached itself to my plaster cast, all the while trying to keep watch for intrusions from siblings or parents. Finally, both in the buff and ready for action, we realised there was no condom, and made a frantic final negotiation to extract the now delirious beast before it could deliver its poisonous payload. Between the passion and plaster and puffing and panting, when we finally docked it lasted about a second and a half before it was time for an emergency exit, anointing DJ's white patent leather sofa in the process.

Sometime later my mother got a call from the girl's mother to say she was pregnant. I eventually discovered that this was untrue. The girl's mother had seen the guilt in her eyes and forced her to confess. The rest was simply grandstanding, but not before my poor mother had reached the end of her tether with me. I was lucky to be getting away, back to St Charles.

When Rob Tate invited volunteers to audition for the school production of The Royal Hunt of the Sun, I saw my chance to be a performer. The senior boys got all the main parts, but I had a few lines and was determined to get noticed. I immersed myself thoroughly in books by the famous Russian actor, Constantin Stanislavski. His Method School of acting had inspired many of the greats, like Marlon Brando and James Dean, and I devoured the theory. After two weeks of rehearsal, Rob was at his wit's end. Among all the matric boys with the major parts there wasn't an ounce of talent, and Rob watched his production turning into a huge embarrassment. After one particularly atrocious rehearsal he finally lost it.

"You're useless, every one of you! You couldn't act yourselves into the matron's infirmary. Get out, and if I never see any of you again it'll be too soon."

The matron was about ninety and it was the easiest thing to skip a maths class by feigning a headache or rubbing the thermometer on your shorts until it read 114 degrees. I was devastated as I saw the chance to express my true self disappearing in the cloud of Rob Tate's rage. The following day he took me aside during lunch break.

"Listen Lucey, there's only one way I'm going to get out of this mess." He'd clearly taken the collapse of the previous effort to heart. "There's a mediaeval morality play called Everyman. It's basically one long monologue with a few bit parts here and there. Since you're the only one with any acting ability, I want you to do it. We can get Boyd, Hughes, Stewart and so on to play the other parts, but I need you to play Everyman."

With this affirmation, it felt as if a huge piece of a puzzle had just fallen into place. I'd been recognised as an artist, and my life was starting to have meaning. My father had little patience with my creative aspirations. "Whadya wanna go get involved with odd buggers for?" he'd ask without a hint of irony. But with this newfound success his attitude didn't matter; I was swimming with pride and confidence.

I worked hard at the part, and my exalted position led to a few extra privileges as well as some unexpected encounters. One of Rob's master strokes was to set the play in the school chapel instead of the hall. It was perfect. After running through our lines in the evening, I'd slip into the sacristy, the small room behind the altar where the priest prepared for Mass. It was like my personal change room, and I'd sit with my feet on the table, smoking away without fear of being caught. It was during one such quiet moment that I had a run-in with the most eccentric boy at St Charles.

Bernard Hughes wore his hair slicked back and plastered flat with heaps of Brylcream, the exact opposite of the fashion at the time, but he didn't give a dog's bollocks. His nickname was Smoothy, and the constant, often vicious teasing with slaps and punches did little to deter him from his quest for individuality. At sixteen he had the voice of a seasoned old queen and a sense of humour to match. He played one of the bit parts, and one evening after rehearsal I waited for the others to leave, and then slipped into the sacristy to smoke my peaceful, solitary cigarette. Suddenly the door swung open and in came Bernard.

"Well, well, what have we here? Everyman all on his own, smoking." He was as camp as a row of pink tents.

"Fuck off, Smoothy." It wasn't hostile; I really liked what he stood for, though I never imagined he was actually a "queer". Homosexuality was illegal and gay men were regularly beaten up for being gay.

"Come along now, *Roger*," he said it like Sir Lawrence Olivier, "no need to be rude."

Without warning he walked up behind me and put his hand firmly on the lump in my tights. Everyman's outfit was black tights and a cotton smock, tracing the stark outline of my adolescent body. It must have piqued Bernard's hormones, because by this time he had his own equine organ out of his tights and in his hand. In the dormitory, boys showered communally, displaying their pubescent appendages with jock-like pride, but this was a monster. I'd never seen such a dick on a person before. I was surprised into a compliant silence while he quickly and professionally got to work, on his knees, with his head beneath my cotton smock.

When Bernard finished, I left the chapel hurriedly, my ears and other parts burning. For a Catholic boy, this was about as sinful as it could get. I was now well on the path to the fires of hell. Bernard and I saw each other every day, but never said a word about the encounter.

A few nights before the opening performance, a few of us had just finished rehearsing and were preparing to leave when the huge chapel door creaked open and a robed figure came stumbling into the gloomy light. On instinct we ducked behind a pew in the side chapel. Peeping through the gaps in the straight-backed benches, we saw the principal, Brother Benedict, or Beak, go berserk. Whether drunk, crazy or both, he was falling around the altar, shouting and swearing and calling for forgiveness. Eventually he lay down on the steps to the altar, face in hands, and sobbed. We slipped out of the chapel and back to the dormitory, where in hysterics we all took turns imitating him. But despite our bravado and laughter, what we'd just witnessed was disturbing. Our headmaster was clearly in a tortured state and our laughter and jibes couldn't cover the disquiet we all felt.

The play was a triumph. There were standing ovations, extra performances and even an invitation to perform at the cathedral in town, where it was seen by the legendary head of Natal University's drama school. This grand dame of theatre, Elizabeth Sneddon, proclaimed it the best school production for years. I was on a roll and loving my success. Yet somehow my self-confidence remained fragile, and the threat of failure never seemed far away.

11

Valley of a Thousand Hills, 1971

WE'LL CATCH KILLERS, OVER BORDER OR NOT
South African security forces have been ordered to track down a band of terrorists – over the border if necessary – in reprisals for two landmine outrages in the Caprivi Strip. A senior police officer was killed in an explosion yesterday and four constables were hurt on Monday. Two of the men come from the Durban area.

Natal Mercury, 6 October 1971

SOUTH AFRICA IN S.W.A. ILLEGALLY
The Government of South Africa "has not only continued its illegal occupation of Namibia (South West Africa) but has also persisted in the application of the criminal policies of apartheid to destroy the unity and territorial integrity of Namibia and to consolidate South Africa's illegal presence in the territory."

Natal Mercury, 6 October 1971

IN A PLACE CALLED MONT AU CIEL, overlooking the Valley of a Thousand Hills, there's a cave where climbers like to rest. It's approached from an escarpment down a steep, rocky path leading to a battlement of cliff faces that loom over the endless valley below. Dotted over the myriad hills stretching into the distance are huts and kraals[1], arranged in neat circles and linked by narrow footpaths. Here and there a dusty road winds around the steep inclines of this magnificent terrain. From the cave one sees only dots on a distant landscape, not the hunger and daily trials of these desperately impoverished people. It's a Friday evening, and I'm sitting on a large rock at the edge of the cave, looking out across the valley. The sun has just set behind the hills towards Pietermaritzburg.

I've spent the afternoon with a group of musicians who've set up home on a nearby farm. They call themselves Freedom's Children and are preparing to record their new album, Tribal Blues. We smoked a lot of dagga before I left them.

I'm on a free weekend from boarding school in Pietermaritzburg. My mother thinks I'm at school, gated. The school thinks I'm at home. I slipped through the school fence at the edge of the grounds that border the main road to Durban. I hitched a ride to Cato Ridge and walked the rest of the way to the band's smallholding. Now I've come to the cave to be alone. I'll sleep here, freezing, in a blanket on the ground. Recently, my mind has been impossible to control, taking me to strange places: deep wells of loneliness, or sudden black storms of fear and despair. I went to Addington Hospital once, but by the time I saw a doctor I was feeling better and couldn't explain what was troubling me. But here in the cave I feel at peace. I wander around

---

1 common usage for homestead

the rocky outcrops, occasionally shouting into the valley to hear the echo of my voice.

I have two cans of Vienna sausages, some beans and a loaf of bread. The milk is starting to turn but there's a spring near the cave. By Sunday morning the climbers will start arriving, so I'll slowly make my way back to school.

At St Charles, many of the boys were now openly at war with the Brothers. Gervais Morel, a Mauritian from Port Louis, had threatened to beat the shit out of Stinky. Caught smoking in a classroom, Gervais calmly flicked the fag out of the window and denied the accusation. When Stinky asked to smell his breath, Gervais went ballistic. He squared up to Stinky, screaming and swearing, the veins in his neck standing out like sausages. The fact that he'd been caught red handed didn't seem to bother him at all, as he vented his rage at the hated celibate. Stinky seemed genuinely intimidated, and didn't even attempt to stop Gervais's tirade. But eventually, at the end of a term, Gervais was told not to return from Mauritius.

One issue the boys from other countries didn't have to worry about was conscription. The South African boys in our class were all starting to receive their dreaded call-up papers in the post. Compulsory conscription was introduced in August 1967, and every white boy in the country received his call-up papers from the military. Like Vietnam, it was because of a war we should never have embarked on in the first place. South Africa had taken over the administration of South West Africa, later renamed Namibia, after World War I. With the collapse of the League of Nations, the newly established United Nations gave South Africa trusteeship of the country, which South Africa regarded as a fifth province. What started as minor insurgency by SWAPO[2] on the country's northern border with Angola in 1966 had, by the early seventies, become a very nasty and damaging war. Namibia, then called South West Africa, had become a German territory in 1890 through a treaty between England and Germany. The Germans wasted no time making clear to their new Ovambo, Herero, Damara and other native subjects who now ruled that dry country. All dissent was viciously crushed and some even hunted the natives for sport. After Germany's defeat in World War I, the territory was handed to South Africa to administer, and by the late

---

2 the South West African People's Organisation

56

1950s its apartheid policies were being enforced there.

The Ovambo People's Organisation emerged in the late 1950s and became SWAPO in 1960, intent on achieving independence for the country. But for the South African government, South West Africa was a crucial bulwark against a much anticipated Soviet-led invasion[3] from Angola and other newly independent neighbouring countries, and Namibian independence was just a communist plot. Initially the South African police dealt with the insurgency, but by the mid-1970s, young South African soldiers "on the border" were dying in droves defending the country against the so-called red peril.

Every able-bodied white boy in the country was called upon to serve, and very few managed to escape the clutches of the defence force. Black youngsters were not called up. After all, the state was trying to ensure that all blacks lived in their own countries – "the homelands" – which were increasingly being created in the driest and most inhospitable parts of the country. Blacks were to have their own armies to defend their own miserable pieces of dirt. Compulsory conscription had a huge impact in further entrenching the racial divide that apartheid laws had already inflicted on the country.

But the army was still a way off for us, and we continued to push the bounds of discipline under the Brothers' noses. Pat Lambert sneaked out one night to meet his girlfriend who was spending the night at the Central Hotel. In the bar lounge he saw Brother David in slacks and sports shirt, dancing with a woman. Pat ducked behind a curtain, but the story hit the dormitory that same night. Some nights later, Brother David disappeared, leaving his robes, a few pictures of saints and sportsmen, and his small dog, Pushkin. It was the last anyone saw of him. Brother Patrick had been reported for trying to fondle a couple of younger boys, but nothing happened. Ripples of discontent grew steadily in our dormitory. A few senior boys had started smoking dagga, and the atmosphere at St Charles was growing dark and rebellious. The food that emerged from the huge kitchens grew intolerable, and I decided to agitate and arrange a boycott of our shitty conditions. One evening when the dinner bell sounded, not one boy arrived to eat the greasy, sloppy victuals, except for Brian Boyd, a youthful nihilist who wore a black armband to protest Charles Manson's imprisonment. Stinky's reaction, according to Brian, was spectacular. Enraged, he demanded to know where everyone had

---

3 Among the many MPLA, Cuban and Soviet documents subsequently released, no evidence has emerged of a plan to invade South Africa.

disappeared to. He headed down towards the cricket field, whacking his cane against his cassock, but turned back and returned to scream at the only boy who had come to the dining hall. I was fingered as the ringleader of the insurrection, but I felt it was justified. But for Beak it was the last straw, and my parents were summoned from Durban. I sat in the passage during twenty minutes of hushed conversation in Beak's office. Then I was called in and told that I'd been expelled, and also failed the year. With nothing more to lose, I was glad to be getting out of there, albeit under such hapless circumstances. Rob Tate wrote in my end-of-year report that I'd "achieved my objective. He set out not to pass and has succeeded."

I didn't quite see it like that. I'd lost the ability to concentrate on schoolwork no matter how hard I tried. My failure further damaged my self-confidence, but it was also a time of finding my individuality. I'd taken the few chords I'd learnt on the guitar and was writing words to simple melodies that popped up in my head. My flute playing was proficient, even if I couldn't read a note of music; I'd even jammed with some serious musos in Durban during the holidays. I'd discovered the power of music and drama, and, significantly, made friendships based not on the athletic power of our bodies, but the power of ourselves. Growing up in a hierarchy that rewarded the physically strong, I was conscious that this patriarchy was deeply flawed. My friendships with Jose and François and even Bernard had exposed me to ideas free of the constraints increasingly gripping the minds of young South Africans. I was discovering my own voice. Angry, confused and rebellious though it was, it was *my* voice – and I liked that. I was starting to sense that what I really wanted to do was play music, and I wasn't going to learn those ropes at this school.

At the beginning of the new term, I wasn't the only one who didn't return to St Charles. Word slipped out that Beak had checked into a mental institution.

12

Durban, 1972

VORSTER TALKS ON RED THREAT
The most important motive of the South African government in wanting dialogue with the rest of Africa is eventually to arrive at a common front against Communism in Africa, says the Prime Minister, Mr Vorster.

Natal Mercury, 27 January 1972

BAD, BAD BEATLE BEAT
Psychedelic music as inspired by the pop group the Beatles is a serious attack on the youth, Church and State and a direct influence from Communism, it is stated in an article by Dr HG van der Hoven in the latest issue of the "Kerkbode", the official organ of the Ned. Geref. Kerk.

Natal Mercury, 27 January 1972

In the early 1970s, Durban witnessed an explosion of musical activity. Every weekend, church halls, sports clubs and empty warehouses across the city were transformed into noisy destinations for teenagers. Every neighbourhood had their own bands, jamming away in garages trying to sound like the Beatles or the Beach Boys. Although most bands played popular British and American hits, there was a growing trend towards original music. Bands that could claim their own songs in the repertoire were seen as a cut above the rest. Durban was also the country's premier holiday destination, which created a ready market for live music. Every beachfront hotel had a club with a resident band or an open-air venue with duos, trios and combos playing background music. At the same time, a folk music movement was gaining followers. There was a lively circuit of venues, with musicians from Johannesburg and even Cape Town regularly coming to do gigs. The Flames, a coloured group from the poor suburb of Mayville, had found great success in the USA recording and working with the Beach Boys.

This was a time when kids from different race groups had nothing to do with each other. We went to separate schools and churches and lived in neighbourhoods far removed from each other. The coloured neighbourhood of Mayville was closer to the white suburbs than the black townships of KwaMashu and Umlazi, but we were still raised to keep our distance. Coloureds were seen as lazy alcoholics who couldn't be trusted. In 1958, an act of parliament had removed the coloured population from the voters' roll. They'd been socially demoted, but were still seen as a cut above the blacks, who weren't even regarded as citizens. This was the South Africa The Flames left in the mid-1960s in search of recognition. Before long they were being feted in both Britain and the USA. In 1970, they returned briefly to South Africa for a triumphant tour of the biggest venues around the country. Their concert at the Durban City Hall inspired me beyond belief. The place was packed as Blondie Chaplin and the three Fataar brothers, Steve, Brother and Ricky, took the audience on an unprecedented musical journey. Sporting the latest in bohemian US fashion under that colonial, proscenium arch of carved marble and teak, they stood out like icons of a future multiracial, free South Africa. As Steve started the soft-spoken introduction of their huge hit, For Your Precious Love, the building erupted. Meanwhile, planted throughout the audience, plain-clothes members of the vice squad were on duty to make sure that no love erupted between these coloured boys and their white groupies.

The racial mixing taking place among the young musical fraternity kept the police increasingly on their toes. The country's most famous rock band, Freedom's Children, had embarked on a loose musical association with afro jazz pioneers, the Malombo Jazzmen. When they played together at the Durban City Hall, the black musicians dressed in overalls with buckets and mops ready offstage; in case of a police raid they could pick up the mops and claim to be cleaners. The day-to-day realities of how apartheid affected people were often bizarre. The Separate Amenities Act of 1953, which enforced racial segregation in all public premises, transport and other amenities, made it impossible for blacks and whites to play or listen to music together. While the rock bands gave the police headaches, it was the folk scene where the real voices of dissent were heard.

On Sunday evenings, the Totem club was the destination for all famous musos. Here, in the basement of the Palm Beach Hotel, white South African musicians were pushing the boundaries hard. Colin Shamley sang Song for the Children of the Revolution; Dave Marks's spoof Jolly John had us hooting and jeering at Prime Minister John Vorster; and Brian Finch's searingly emotional Curries Fountain recalled the rally for Mozambique's liberation movement, Frelimo, where police let loose with dogs and truncheons before detaining twelve black student leaders under the Terrorism Act. Dissent was in the air, and this music was the mouthpiece of an alternative generation.

In 1972 at the age of 18, I was admitted to the Thomas More College, a boys-only, but nonetheless progressive, boarding school started by Chris Hurley, brother of Archbishop Denis Hurley. Chris Hurley was a liberal who based his school's philosophy loosely on Summerhill, the school started by AS Neill in 1920s England. Although the education laws prohibited black pupils from attending the school, he nonetheless attempted to break out of the repressive mould that personified South African schooling at the time. Despite my dismal record, Jeremy Hurley, the student activist I'd got to know while at St Charles, had put in a good word with his uncle, and I'd been reluctantly admitted to the Matric class (Grade 12), on condition that I did extra lessons and worked my arse off. It was a beautiful place, on top of a hill covered in trees in the village of Kloof, about twenty kilometres from Durban. If their parents consented, senior boys were allowed to smoke, and rules were generally less rigid than at other schools. Most weekends I was free to go home. The whole setup was much more geared to my real educational goals, the discovery of popular music. I'd work the Saturday morning shift at the bottle store, which set me up with money for the various gigs and concerts around the city. Cousin Leonard and I had been playing together and we'd got a couple of songs together, with him on guitar and me on flute. After much pleading, wangling and coercion, we persuaded Brian Finch to let us play at Totem. In spite of my inept tooting, Leonard carried us through with his rich voice and competent guitar playing. It was all I needed to confirm my ambition of becoming a musician.

Of the 160 seats in South Africa's parliamentary assembly, only one was occupied by a liberal politician. From 1960 to 1974, Helen Suzman was the lone parliamentary voice of dissent in those white male halls of power, which pretty much reflected the balance of political power in the country. Even in the progressive atmosphere of Thomas More College, many boys were conservative and racist. When I first arrived at the school, I was placed in a four-bed dormitory with two of the school's worst racist bullies. On my first night they decided to treat me to an initiation ritual which involved polishing my testicles with boot polish. DJ's early lessons in using fists came in handy, and the matter was swiftly resolved, though not to everyone's satisfaction.

My first friend at Thomas More was Titch James. He was a small, wiry boy with a doleful expression that belied his wacky sense of humour. He was also a provincial judo champion, and many local toughs had learnt to respect him the hard way. His father had owned an earth moving business and made a fortune. At the bottom of their large garden, his father had built a dojo where Titch ran a judo school.

More recently, he'd started playing the guitar, and was also regarded as the most talented boy in the art class. The art teacher said Titch had the potential to make his mark on the art world.

We soon became firm friends along with another of Titch's mates, Robin Downing. Robin was a champion waterskier, his father was a successful builder, and they lived in a big house on the hill. Kloof was a strange mix of old and new, known for its nouveau riche inhabitants who'd made fast money in property development and speculation. Robin's and Titch's fathers were both of this ilk, but their sons were searching for more meaning than the crass materialism on offer. They were deeply moved by the writings of the Lebanese sage, Kahlil Gibran, and despite their own physical competence they rejected the macho values dominant among schoolboys. Not surprisingly, when these two discovered the whacky weed, they took to it like warthogs to a mud puddle. Robin had his own car, a red Ford Capri, and Titch was allowed to use his father's VW bus. My early resolve to get through the academic year soon started unravelling as our home range grew wider and the sound of music louder. Titch took up the bongos and was getting more and more competent. I started writing songs, and we'd sit together at night in the middle of the Kloof golf course in his father's VW bus, lost in our newfound creativity amid plumes of blue smoke.

Titch was friendly with some neighbourhood girls, including Glenda, the girlfriend of the school bully. She was a bright, ethereal girl whose school was the nearby convent. She'd hang around at our school sports events and other social functions, and one day she arrived with her even more celestial younger sister, Sheila. Sheila had long blonde hair and pale skin, and in long flowing clothes she seemed to float through the mists that swept through this hilly terrain.

In spite of my patent lack of academic success, I was popular. I was elected chairman of the school council, a representative body for pupils to interact with teachers and staff, unheard of in other schools. The patron of the school board was Chief Mangosuthu Buthelezi, the leader of Inkatha, a Zulu cultural and political organisation firmly opposed to apartheid. Buthelezi later become tainted as a collaborator of the Nationalist government, but in the early 1970s he had credibility. As chairman of the school council, I would welcome the chief to the school on his frequent visits and chat with him over tea.

I also met up again with Archbishop Denis Hurley, who visited the school from time to time. My trust in Catholicism had by this time taken a serious nosedive. The whole experience with the Brothers at St Charles had left me disillusioned with the church, but meeting the archbishop was always a great experience. His opposition to the government was becoming legendary, and he took the battle against apartheid into the church even though it threatened the unity of his flock. He was a big, gentle man, whose goodness and charisma always left me feeling like I'd been in the company of true eminence.

I was in a strange and uncomfortable position: one foot firmly in the real world and the other just as firmly in the conspiratorial underworld of the dagga smoker. I'd become an organiser of several music events, one being a series of weekly lunchtime concerts of aspirant school boys, often featuring original songs and music. The school had several musicians, and we formed groups, playing at events and parties. For my efforts I was awarded the school music prize. By this time I'd recovered sufficiently after my kneecap removal to be chosen for the first rugby team. But the team wasn't much good and hovered near the bottom of the log. I returned to the athletics track and, despite not making the provincial team, won the Victor Ludorum, the school's highest athletic award. It was a dangerous balancing act, especially since Titch, Robin and I still bought our weekly supply of zol deep inside the nearby black townships. New legislation carried harsh mandatory prison sentences for possession of dagga, yet we continued undaunted, sure that we were on the *right* side – the side of the oppressed who grew and sold the dagga. The propaganda machine at the Christian Education schools warned young white pupils about "blacks, communists and hippies" who wanted to subvert the "God-given system of apartheid". The oppressed majority – the politicos and the dopeheads – were all lumped into the same category of "traitors to the cause". In any other country we'd probably have simply been young criminals, but here we were part of the broad wave of resistance to the state. It's interesting that throughout the period of apartheid, the politicos who were incarcerated with common criminals were often protected by these very criminals from the many abuses most prisoners suffered in jail.

In the meantime, my adolescent testosterone compass was pointing directly at the sprite-like Sheila, and before long we were seeing a lot of each other. Her father was a successful builder in the area and they lived in a large, comfortable house near the school. He was a man of few words but tolerated my presence around the house.

Her mother was a jolly, contented woman who liked me, making it easy for my relationship with Sheila to flourish.

Life was busy and filled with adventure, love and excitement, but things at home were getting worse, and my relationship with DJ was at an all-time low. My brother Patrick was showing great talent as a classical guitarist, and would spend hours in his bedroom practicing. For some reason, this irritated DJ, driving him to into irrational fits of temper.

"Why're you always sitting there playing your fucking guitar? Get out into the open air for a change!" His voice would rise an octave with rage.

"Look at your fucking shoulders, all hunched like some fucking sissy; jeez, straighten up and fly right, for fuck's sake."

During one of these episodes, he grabbed the guitar from Patrick's hands and smashed it across the back of the bed, shattering my brother's prized instrument into tiny pieces. Patrick, a mild-mannered and studious sixteen-year-old, went berserk. He lunged at DJ, fists flying, but DJ had the upper hand and left Patrick bruised and beaten. I wasn't around during the incident, but this event made me realise that my father would stop at nothing to enforce his rules. For me the destruction of that instrument was tantamount to murder. What little respect had been beaten into us was now well and truly gone. Late one night, a short time later, we were woken by the sound of DJ's voice in my parents' bedroom.

"You fucking bitch, I'll fucking show you not to contradict me in public!" That weird word again, so formal and out of place! The sound of slaps and punches was much louder than the muted groans and whimpers from my mother. Her refusal to react to his attack seemed to drive him even more crazy, and his voice soared to a shriek.

Patrick and I knew the time had come to end this abuse. We went into their bedroom and attacked DJ from behind. He was sitting astride my mother, his hands around her throat. He lashed out at us, screaming at us to get out of the bedroom. But Patrick and I had reached a new and empowering level of anger. We would never again take instructions from this madman we called our father. The three of us tumbled off the bed and onto the floor in a storm of shouting and writhing. I had my arms locked around DJ's neck and Patrick was punching furiously at his face. The fight lurched out of the bedroom and into the corridor, the three of us like a twelve-limbed monster crashing into the walls and ending up at the top of the stairs. My father had done everything he could to subdue Patrick and me, but he was now breathless and running out of steam. Suddenly the three of us were rolling down the stairs, a furious ball of fists, feet and teeth. Patrick and I kept up the assault, knowing we'd gone too far to let him take control. Suddenly, to our amazement, DJ surrendered. He lay on the floor of the entrance hall, shock and surprise on his swollen face. I remember being instantly overcome with pity and sadness for this defeated old warrior. The balance of power would never be the same again. It was also the death knell of the marriage: my mother knew the time had come to terminate this cruel and vicious relationship.

In the years before they separated, my mother had quietly been planning her escape. She'd bought an overgrown and rundown property adjacent to our house, and demolished the old wreck of a house that was hidden among the banana trees. She'd sold a third of the property, and with the proceeds had built a duplex on the remainder. Once both halves of the duplex were earning a rental income, she built a rambling bungalow-style house on the remaining portion of land, which she also rented out. When she finally left my father, she took my sister Louise and brother Michael down the road to my grandparents. It wasn't long before she moved back into the rambling bungalow she'd built, right beside DJ's house. And there they remained, at the edge of each other's lives, performing a strange dance of dependence and disdain until years later, when he passed on, wasted and afraid.

13

Durban, Summer 1973

NEW WARNINGS OF STRIFE IN SA

Two influential magazines warn South Africa that "bloody violence and anarchy" may be sparked off by labour injustice.

Natal Mercury, 23 January 1973

AFRICAN TELLS OF SEX AT GUNPOINT

Police are investigating an African woman's claim that two Army trainees in an army truck had raped her at gunpoint on Durban's Bluff last weekend.

Natal Mercury, 13 January 1973

ONE OTHER BURDEN IN MY life loomed ever larger as the year drew to a close: the South African Defence Force. I was to report for duty early in January 1973. The boys who qualified to enter university could apply for a deferral, but I already knew I wouldn't be among this group. By this stage my schoolwork had fallen too far behind for me to pass the exams. There was endless discussion about ways of avoiding this inescapable sentence. A few boys had British passports and were going to live and work in the crowded island of their forefathers. Others were planning elaborate ruses to convince the army doctors of their insanity. For me, going into exile wasn't a possibility. A white male with a South African passport straight out of school had very few alternatives. Having just had another operation on my knee, my big hope was that with my missing kneecap and my leg still withered from a couple of months in plaster, I could get medical exemption. My parents couldn't understand why I'd want to shirk such an honourable duty so necessary for the safety of our country.

The writing of final exams at Thomas More was an exercise in futility, and when the results arrived they were predictably catastrophic. I'd tried my utmost to study, to read, to understand the mysteries of maths and implant the facts of history in the shifting sands of my memory. I embraced the task with the best will I could muster, only to find myself hours later staring at an open book, my mind returning from some distant journey. The realisation that I seemed to have no control over my wandering thoughts threw me into states of anxiety and panic, which I covered with a show of macho disinterest in my schoolwork. The fact that I desperately wanted to succeed and pass the exams didn't help to get the necessary information into my head. I had failed the year, and as a result I was left with only a standard eight (grade 10) certificate to face the world.

The Junior Certificate, or JC as it was then known, qualified one for entry into an apprenticeship in a trade or a job on the South African Railways and Harbours. These were looked down on as lowly pursuits by those on their way to university and the higher professions. But I already knew that I wanted to be a singer and songwriter, and all the maths, science and history in the world couldn't prepare me for that journey. Meanwhile, the army was calling my name.

My mother drives in silence, the windows of her little green Austin 1100 open to the dripping humidity of the Durban summer. The road that runs through the middle of the racecourse is lined with vivid beds of canna lilies in full bloom, each bed a different colour. A few nights ago I fell into one of these beds while walking home, drunk and giggling from Totem. I'd gone to listen to Abstract Truth, where Kenny Henson played a twenty minute guitar solo, in the middle of which George Wolfhaardt put down his bass guitar and went to the bar for a beer. No-one seemed to notice that he was gone. I lay in the canna lilies looking at the night until the dawn oozed through the high white fence around the race track. I walked past the drill hall, headquarters of the Natal Carbineers where I have to report for duty now, inside the race course where the canna beds ended. Then it was quiet and dark, the guard asleep in the small wooden guard hut.

But now the whole area is thick with cars and pedestrians, and my mother nimbly parks her tiny vehicle in a little space between two canna beds. We have to step into the freshly turned soil to get out of the car. We say nothing to each other; not out of hostility, but quiet resignation. The drill hall is packed with young men, tanned and happy, still living the last memories of their summer holidays. The crying mothers and girlfriends are comforted by these self-conscious recruits, determined to show their manliness. My mother shows no such emotion; she's satisfied that I'm finally going to get some discipline drummed into me. I hug her. We look at each other and smile; I know she's run out of patience with me, but has nonetheless found the time to pack a box of biscuits, dried fruit and other delicacies for my journey.

"Okay men, time to go!" The corporal has a huge rasping voice and the smile on his face is not one that brings comfort. I don't want to be here, but there's no escape. I know from other older boys what to expect, and I have a hollow, sick feeling in my stomach. We're herded into the back of large Bedford trucks and then driven to the railway station in the centre of town. I have my medical certificate from the orthopaedic surgeon safely in my bag: my last weapon against this invasion of my life that's causing me such anxiety. The train journey only serves to fuel my fears, as the now drunken youths started hurling abuse, then bottles and cans at the black men, women and children we pass along the way. The blind hatred and derision twisted into the faces of these young patriots leaves me feeling powerless, voiceless and hopeless.

We arrive at the Fourth Field Regiment in Potchefstroom early the following morning. The first queue I stand in is for the army barber. What kind of person ends up being a barber in the army, I wonder. They use this first opportunity to fire the opening salvo at the city boys who're about to become men. They shout and swear, making sure their snow white scalps get a good spread of nicks and razor burns. With my skull stinging and dignity reeling, we line up for the second rite of contemptuous abasement, the medical examination. No doctor I've ever met behaved like these young men. The arrogant and pompous surgeon who operated on my knee still always spoke softly and was gentle in his examinations. It shocks me that these young men who've gone into this most noble of professions, who have taken the almost mythical and all abiding Hippocratic Oath, could become such lackeys of the regime. Their manner towards the recruits is no different from that of the barbers.

"What's this fucking shit?" The young doctor is careful not to meet my eyes as he flings my envelope on the ground.

"It's a medical certificate about my knee," I reply meekly.

"Don't try that shit with me, you scab." He has the neat moustache allowed as a privilege of ou manne[1], those who've finished their basic training.

He makes no eye contact as he goes through the routine check-up: heart, lungs, tongue, eyes, ears, nostrils and finally testicles. He orders me to lie down on a stainless steel examination table, like those in a veterinary hospital, and starts tugging and bending my ailing leg. I let out a few sharp yelps and then he sits back at his desk.

"Pick it up, scab," he says, pointing to the medical certificate still on the floor.

I place the envelope on his desk and he tears it open with aggressive flicks of his wrist. After reading the contents, he fills out a form and

---

1 literally old men, meaning those who've been in the army longer than six months

tells me to report to the transport officer.

I've been given a reprieve, a six-month deferment until my knee recovers. The train back to Durban is almost empty. I share the six-bed compartment with a silent old railway worker who thankfully has nothing to say. My mind's in overdrive, planning my next move. I have six months to come up with a way to get out of this obligation for good. I barely sleep as the train rocks and sways through the South African hinterland. The following morning I'm back in Durban. My parents are madder than a pair of army barbers at the prospect of having me back in the house, but I'm overjoyed at my stay of execution from that savage army.

Until the late 1970s, Durban was Africa's busiest harbour. The first European settlers landed there in 1824, the only natural harbour along the country's otherwise potentially treacherous east coast. The Portuguese explorer Vasco da Gama had named this territory Natal in honour of the nativity while sailing past on Christmas day in 1497. The narrow entrance to the broad, shallow estuary is protected from the Indian Ocean by a long, narrow strip of land known as the Bluff. Before international sanctions against the apartheid state started crippling the South African economy, almost all the country's imports and exports went through Durban's well-situated harbour. Once the National Party was voted into power in 1948, the South African Railways and Harbours became a refuge for poor Afrikaners. These descendants of the early Dutch settlers had lost much of their land and power after their defeat by the British in the second Anglo-Boer war in 1902, and a major platform on which the Nationalists were voted in was their pledge to look after these Afrikaners. In a policy known as "job reservation", Afrikaners were favoured as employees in huge state institutions like Railways and Harbours.

But it was also a place where an English-speaking boy like me could get a job, if you were prepared to work long, hard hours and take the verbal abuse from the Afrikaans bosses. One of the available jobs was stoker, which entailed keeping the fire burning on the old steam trains and making tea for the train driver. It was hard work and the pay was terrible. Instead, I decided to apply for a job as a crane driver on the docks. This job required more skill than being a stoker, and a longer training period at lower pay. Once the training was over, the pay wasn't much better than for stokers, but with overtime and weekend work you could come out with a fair amount of money in your pocket. I was apprenticed to a kindly old Afrikaner called Hennie who showed me the ropes. The official training period was three weeks, but within the first week I became adept at hauling those four-ton loads in and out of the deep holds of a multitude of foreign freighters. Hennie would sit in the back of the crane's cabin smoking long dagga joints, and then go to sleep, leaving me to carry on. The majority of crane drivers were middle-aged Afrikaans men, and many were regular dagga smokers. Given the zealous vilification of the weed by my Afrikaans grandfather, this surprised me. These hard-bitten, often virtually illiterate men were at the bottom of white South Africa's social ladder. It was the promise of these types of jobs that got the National Party voted into power in 1948.

The westerly winds were always a welcome respite, bringing rain that would stop work, which meant days of smoking zol and sleeping on the long wooden benches in the crew room at full pay. There were always scams going on at the docks: shady characters sneaking on and off ships with parcels and bags. The railway police appeared the most stupid of all branches of law enforcement and never seemed to notice, but I later found out that they were paid to look the other way. There was also a flourishing trade in prostitution in the docklands. While the rest of the country was sexually segregated by laws like the Mixed Marriages Act[2], Immorality Act[3] and others, visiting sailors banged their way across the colour bar until their knees grew weak. One early afternoon, loading large wooden crates from a Greek freighter, I saw a sailor and an enormous, shiny black woman climb the steel steps past the bridge and up to the funnel. There, on the narrow deck behind the funnel, she lifted her dress and placed one leg on the railing. Within seconds the sailor had dropped his trousers and was thrusting away like a steam train. The crane drivers were all hanging out of their cabins hurling racial abuse at the couple, who carried on unperturbed. The abuse and taunts grew louder as the stevedores and workers on the quayside became aware of this lascivious exhibition, and added their voices to the raucous chorus. Without missing a beat, the sailor looked around and gave the jeering audience a royal wave and a broad smile. Back in the crew room I told Hennie about the incident. He scratched his balls and smiled.

---

2 the Mixed Marriages Act of 1949 prohibited marriage between people of
   different races
3 the Immorality Act of 1950 prohibited all sexual relations between people of
   different races; severe prison sentences were prescribed for breaking this law

"They can shout, but they're the first to naai a Bantu maid[4] when their fat vrou[5] closes her legs."

So here was this group of staunch Afrikaners, firmly behind the Nationalist government, yet smoking the dreaded dagga and sleeping with black women. I was already well aware of the duplicity and hypocrisy entrenched in our fractured society, but here in the harbour it played out like a textbook on the subject.

I scraped together enough to buy a little car – an old, barely roadworthy Renault Dauphine – and my newfound mobility meant that my precious free time could be used more efficiently. Sheila and I used every possible opportunity to exercise our libidos in the back seat of the car, the forests around Kloof and Botha's Hill, the swimming pool, the sea and on the beach. But the Renault died a few months after I bought it. There was always DJ's Mini Minor delivery van, and I'd learnt how to get it in and out of its garage without my parents noticing. The tiny van was a blaze of gaudy green and red, with Strand Bottle Store written from one side to the other. Many quiet streets and cul de sacs saw the van rocking and bouncing as a flurry of arms and legs entwined in youthful exploration.

Robin had been exempted from the army because of a heart murmur; they didn't mess with things like that. It seemed ironic that this healthy, strapping boy was declared medically unfit for the army. Titch had been called up for the July intake, but that was months down the road. In the meantime, life was a party, but beneath the fun and games I was constantly aware of the very fine line I walked between darkness and light. In minutes I could veer from happy and carefree into darkness, where the world around became strange and hostile. My thoughts would spin out of control and nothing would make sense. I saw myself as pretending to be who I was with nothing beneath my skin, like a life-sized doll made of real flesh but devoid of all other substance. I felt alienated from those around me, even those who were closest to me, like Sheila.

I was aware that these feelings were irrational, but unable to get rid of them. I was often paranoid that others would realise there was nothing to me, that I was all make-believe. I had two recurring dreams: one of slowly falling off the edge of a cliff into a black nothingness, and another of stealing an old Tiger Moth – like the one we'd sit in as kids at the Durban Wings Club – and flying off up the coast of Natal.

---

4 literally an African maid
5 Afrikaans for wife

The only solution was to be on my own. I was aware that my copious use of cannabis had become a problem, but was not ready to face the fact head on. Smoking would take me away from the many harsh realities I faced: my violent father, my unavoidable commitment to the army and my bleak future in the job market through lack of education. It would also give me some relief from the dark moods; a deep lungful of smoke would wash over me like the warm ocean of the north coast.

I couldn't help noticing the frightening dependence I'd developed for the drug over the past five years or so. Occasionally, the police would make a big bust and supplies would become scarce in the city. Titch and I would go to excessive lengths to find even the smallest bit of zol, just to keep the jitters at bay. "I'm hanging for a skyf," we'd say to each other as we headed off into the dark roads in search of zol – and hanging was how it felt. We were edgy and volatile, and we took risks we were lucky to survive. We went deep into the black townships late at night – sometimes for miles on foot – into areas with some of the highest crime and murder rates in the country. But then supplies would resume and the problem would go away, although darkness would still descend on me without warning and take me on a whirlwind tour of hell.

The first time I laid eyes on Big Bertha, I knew she'd one day be mine. Leonard discovered her in a carpenter's workshop close to where he lived. The carpenter was a rather eccentric old Englishman who made peculiar musical instruments in his spare time. Big Bertha was the biggest guitar anyone had ever seen, modelled loosely on the large bass guitars of Mexican mariachi orchestras, but with six strings instead of four. The carpenter gave it to Leonard after realising that this strange, unruly beast was of no use to a real musician – it was effectively unplayable. But that detail didn't stop Leonard and me from embracing this great, plywood mother of music and coaxing it into song. Even with your arm over the narrowest part of its body, you could still barely reach the strings. So, with legs splayed to balance her excessive weight and arms spread in a cumbersome imitation of a guitar player, Bertha and I sailed into the first heady days of a vocation that would dominate my life: song writing.

My early songs were loud, raucous and angry, and Bertha was the perfect partner for these explosive outbursts against society, state and Church. But it was more than simply blowing off steam. Songs and music were becoming a major part of my new voice. I now could speak where before I felt incoherent, I could express myself where before I'd only felt frustration and rage. The biggest reward of this newfound form of expression was that it brought an enormous sense of satisfaction and a feeling of belonging to a musical fraternity that, despite its antisocial image, earned the respect of my peers. Leonard, in the meantime, had joined the Baptist church, and was spending a lot of time in prayer and getting laid at church outings. He was the musical inspiration of the church, and for his efforts they gave him a beautiful new Yamaha guitar. With this new plaything now dominating Leonard's musical life, Big Bertha came to live with me.

In the third month of my crane-driving career I hit a bump in the road. I was loading palettes stacked with bags of mica powder into the hold of a large Korean freighter. The hold of a ship is a very deep place, and when empty, the black workers load and unload cargo seven and eight storeys down in these steel mausoleums. The division of labour during apartheid was clear cut: blacks did the dirty work and whites did the rest. The palettes on which the bags of mica were loaded had rings on each corner. Attached to the end of the crane's cable was a device consisting of four steel cables with a hook on each end. The hooks would be inserted through the rings on the palette, which was then lifted into the hold. It would take several days to fill a hold with the hundreds of thousands of bags packed onto palettes, four tons at a time. A good long spliff always helped to relieve the tedium of this humdrum process, but could also affect one's judgment and faculties.

Soon after starting the loading process into the Korean freighter, I was lowering a load through the hold's narrow entrance on the deck when a corner of the palette bumped ever so gently against the side of the steel framework. Eight storeys below, twenty or so bare-chested Zulu labourers watched as the palette started rocking unsteadily from side to side. One hook became detached, but the other three remained connected. I shifted the boom of the crane slightly from side to side, trying to steady the load, but this only made the delicately poised cargo even more unstable. I went into a mild panic. Hennie was no longer around to help, and I could feel sweat between my fingers and the control lever. The whole episode started playing out in slow motion as I noticed a second hook become detached. The palette was hanging in calamitous indecision above the now shouting voices out of sight, deep in the hold. Slowly, first one by one and then with increasing acceleration, the bags started falling from the doomed palette into the dark belly of the ship. I thrust my head in disbelief out of the window of the cabin and my dark glasses, which I'd bought with my first pay packet, flew off my face into the filthy water below. Mica powder is pure, white and extremely fine, more feathery than cake flour in texture. For what seemed like several minutes, I watched in shock as the stricken palette hung, now without its load, over the hold. Then, like a mushroom cloud, a huge blossoming of mica powder came billowing out of the hold, followed a short time later by twenty snow white Zulu's, shouting, pointing and threatening in the way only a Zulu impi[6] can. I retired to the little space at the back of the cabin, my ears burning from the humiliation of such a spectacular catastrophe. No-one was hurt; the labourers had plenty of time to get out of the way of the falling bags, but I was shaken and very aware that this would cost me my job. Eventually I climbed down the ladder and headed for the crew room and my final pay packet.

Popeye Hattingh was a pig of a man. Everything he did, said and wore was affirmation that he'd only recently crawled out of the swamp and was beginning the long haul up the evolutionary ladder. He wore the same pair of shorts every day for all the months I knew him: green tartan crimplene shorts so tight you could see the contour of his balls as he sat, legs apart, behind his large grease-stained desk. Below his hideous shorts, his stubby thighs squeezed achingly out, forcing him to waddle like a duck, swaying his fat bum from side to side as his shorts seams threatened to explode. His tight, round paunch strained over the waistband.

Popeye's face was twisted into a permanent sneer and his nose, reshaped by many a barroom brawl, was underlined by an aggressive, bristly moustache. His crowning glory was a wig that he wore at varying angles, which appeared to be made of recycled broom bristles; it looked more like a piece of West African ceremonial headgear than a head of hair. Despite his grotesque appearance, when seated behind his desk, feet up and hands behind his head, Popeye was The Man, Chief of the Hellenic Taxi Company. The traffic official who'd issued my public service driving license had put me onto him.

"Who you gonna draaive for?" he'd asked economically.

---

6 a traditional Zulu fighting regiment

"I don't know yet, I'll try at Aussies Taxis."

"Traai Popeye Hattingh, he's looking for a draaiver raaight now," He handed me a scrawled phone number.

I started on night shift, and the first time I slipped behind the wheel of that Chevrolet Impala, brightly painted in the national blue and white of Greece, I felt that once again I was driving my own destiny. The Chevy had automatic transmission, so that night I drove out of the taxi bay with one arm resting casually out the window.

My beat was the Monte Carlo nightclub a couple of hundred metres from the main harbour entrance. Standard fares were hookers and sailors, and as the name suggested, Hellenic Taxis catered mainly to Greek seamen. We'd line up our cabs in the taxi rank outside the club and take turns carting these lonely and desperate men back to their ships. The Monte Carlo was rough and a fight was always brewing, in full swing or being cleaned up. I got to know a couple of the members of the band, mainly coloured boys who learnt the knack of playing their repertoire without missing a beat, even while blood and guts were being spilt all over the dance floor in front of them. The Zulu guitarist could switch between the funky dance styles of the time and traditional Greek music without batting an eyelid. He made his Fender Stratocaster sound exactly like a bouzouki, the distinctive lute-like instrument native to Greece, while teary-eyed sailors linked arms and danced their traditional dances and hurled plates. But it always ended in a battle when it came time to take their hired loves and try to relieve their unquenchable loneliness.

One steamy night, a furious mess of fists and feet came tumbling down the long flight of stairs from the club to the street. The warriors untangled themselves briefly, long enough for us cabbies to see that one was a local pimp and the other a hard-faced, overly made-up woman with a reputation as a fighter. They faced each other for a moment and then started exchanging blows with a ferocity seen in the fiercest of seamen. We cabbies just watched; we knew this wasn't the type of battle in which to intervene. They kicked and punched and bit each other, and as blood started staining their faces and clothes, neither showed any sign of retreat.

Suddenly a police van screeched to a stop in front of the battle and a large, fresh-faced young constable jumped out. His black colleague took his time, making his way very slowly towards the skirmish – he plainly had no appetite for this. The constable, arms swinging with macho stride, walked straight up to the pimp and grabbed him by the collar, towering over the wiry little man who hung helplessly as the cop shook him about. The woman wiped her face and without a word, picked up a beer bottle from the gutter. Looking about to give her adversary a killer blow, she stepped instead behind the cop and smashed it over the back of his close-cropped head. He dropped to the pavement like a sack of potatoes, legs quivering involuntarily. Then she leaned over him. "Nobody touches my man!"

We cabbies watched in astonished silence as she and her pimp walked off, arm in arm, down the road.

A few weeks later I changed to day shift, and started to realise that Popeye was more than just a taxi boss. The shift started innocently enough with my arm-out-the-window cruise around the city centre, hoping for the odd fare. Later in the day I'd move onto the dockland beat, picking up sailors from the rusty freighters that steamed in and out of Durban harbour. It was all normal taxi business, until the morning Popeye called me to the office and tossed a huge bunch of keys at me.

"Okay, gerra paper 'n pen 'n take this down," he drawled.

I found a scrap of paper and a pencil on his desk among the mess of greasy car parts and empty wrappers.

"Ten thirdy, number 67 Malibu Heights," he yawned, not looking at me. "Up to the sixth floor, use the keys marked Malibu Heights. Once you open the door, shout *taxi*. You get no reply, go in 'n wake the cunt up. Take him to Pride of Piraeus moored at T jetty, 'n make fuggin' sure he pays you in dollars, you got that?"

"No problem, Popeye." I headed for the cab.

Malibu Heights was an ugly lump of concrete one block back from the ocean, but obscured from all sides by bigger, uglier, more modern apartments surrounding it. I used to deliver cheap wine to an old alcoholic on the eighth floor, and often had to walk up when the lift wasn't working. Although the eighth was the top floor, it was dwarfed by the fifteen- to twenty-storey buildings crowded around it. I'd once walked up while water rushed down the stairwell. I'd found the old alcoholic's door open, and him in his underpants in the tiny kitchen, watching the water pour from the kitchen tap into the overflowing sink and over the kitchen floor. I walked in and turned off the tap; he smiled and thanked me for the delivery. Standing outside number 67 now, I thought back to that day with a chuckle.

Getting no response to my knock on the door, I tried various keys from the huge bunch until one opened the lock. I called into the darkened apartment. No reply. Remembering Popeye's instructions, I cautiously walked in to "wake the cunt up". He was lying on his back, his greying head twisted uncomfortably to one side, a trace of dry drool on his heavy black moustache. His face was scarred and his large hooked nose at an unnatural angle. A massive scar glowed like a pink ribbon from his shoulder to his elbow, partially covered by a black satin sheet. I'd never seen a black sheet before. The woman beside him was in her early thirties with dyed blonde hair – the dark roots already quite long – and a fine-featured but hard face with bad skin. One leg poked out of the black sheet, slung across his thigh. Both were snoring. It was a bachelor apartment and smelt of smoke, beer and other things I didn't have the stomach to identify. I shook him, softly at first and then vigorously. He slowly opened his eyes and lifted a calloused hand to an evidently throbbing head. Then he climbed out of bed, releasing a long, squealing fart. She didn't move, just lay there snoring – one tattooed breast exposed as a shiny thread of saliva slipped across her sullied lipstick. He hauled on his clothes, peeled several notes off a wad from his back pocket, tossed them onto the bedside table and followed me out of the apartment.

As I drove towards the harbour, it started dawning on me that I'd just become implicated in a prostitution racket. This was obviously Popeye's real business, and Hellenic Taxis just the transport department for his trade in human flesh. As we drove down the pier towards the sailor's grimy freighter, I looked in the rear-view mirror and suddenly felt an enormous sadness for this battle-scarred old sailor whose doleful eyes told the story of a thousand faithless fucks.

As the weeks went by, I picked up several other sailors from different apartments in the area around the dockyards, and finally got to asking Popeye about the situation.

"Listen pal, you don't like the job, then fugoff." He was a man of few words.

The taxi bay was two blocks from The Strand Bottle Store, and one lunch time, Jabula came by to visit me. Occasionally we'd go up onto the rooftop of the building and smoke a quick pipe. As we were walking up the ramp towards the rooftop parking bays, Popeye came out of his office and saw us sloping off together.

"Yey, warrafuck you doing with that kaffir boy?"

I told him he worked for my father and was delivering a message, but from then on Popeye referred to me as a kaffir boetie[7], which at the time was one of the worst insults possible. For me it was a badge of honour. I wanted to be a kaffir boetie; I knew I was on the right side and that people like Popeye were wrong. For Jabula, being called a kaffir boy was just part of the endless litany of verbal abuse black people suffered daily in every corner of the country. For the two of us it didn't even warrant comment, except a quick "fuck you" under our breath.

One morning I walked into the taxi bay and heard a strange noise coming from Popeye's office. There was no-one else around and immediately I got the feeling something was wrong. It sounded like a dog choking on a hairball, and I feared that maybe Popeye was being attacked. Dead scared, I crept up to peep through the thin frame of clear glass around the frosted pane in his door. It took some squinting to work out what was going on. Popeye had a huge black hooker on his desk and was plunging furiously, all the while making that weird choking sound. I knew her from the neighbourhood; she was a friendly woman in her twenties with traditional scarification on her cheeks, an easy smile and enormous buttocks. Jabula had told me she was a farm girl who'd come to the city and fallen into bad company. Her skirt was up above her waist and his filthy green tartan shorts around his ankles. As I ducked from the window, Popeye saw me and let out an enraged roar. "You fuggin' kaffir boetie... fugoff, cunt!"

As I ran down the ramp and into the street I could hear him screaming after me. A few days later he fired me, but I wasn't unhappy about it. It was only a few weeks before I had to return to the army, and I hadn't managed to save any money or devise a way of escaping, so I welcomed this last bit of free time.

---

7 Afrikaans for brother of blacks

14

Voortrekker Hoogte, Winter 1973

THREAT TO S.A. BORDER
The Mozambique terrorist movement, Frelimo, plans to send hit-and-run groups to within striking distance of South Africa by next year, Portuguese military intelligence reported in Lisbon yesterday.
Natal Mercury, 5 July 1973

SWAZI LIFE FOR YUKO
Mr Chris Butler plans to go dairy farming in Swaziland so that he can live with his Japanese wife, Yuko. But the 57-year-old Hillcrest farmer, who married Yuko Gejima in Manzini on Tuesday, has no hard feelings against South Africa, whose Nationalist government continually refused the couple permission to marry.
Natal Mercury, 5 July 1973

My toes were completely numb from the pre-dawn Highveld frost that crept up through my thin sneakers from the dusty parade ground. Thousands of us from all over the country stood in long lines, young corporals shouting and shrieking at everyone and no-one in particular. We'd arrived in Pretoria the previous evening on a troop train from Durban, and had spent a freezing night in tents pitched on an arid field between army barracks. This was Voortrekker Hoogte. The previous evening as we drove in large trucks from the station to this mighty military fortress, I couldn't believe how it just continued stretching out in front of us. At one point, from the top of a hill, all I could see all around, mile after mile, were military buildings. This epicentre of South Africa's military establishment was the size of a large town. By the time we got to the Services School, where I'd been reallocated, we'd driven past miles of grey prefabricated and red brick buildings, cheerless barracks and vehicle parks stretching further than the eye could see. Pretoria is situated in the middle of the Highveld, a vast inland plateau covered by grasslands and thorn trees, very different from the sub-tropical east coast that was my home. Winters here are cold and desolate, the grass turns brown and the days are short and dry. Lips crack and noses bleed easily, the air is thin and the dry winds make the eyes water.

The deeper we drove into this grim citadel, the more I lost hope of talking my way out of it. By the time I saw the doctor who was to decide my fate, my heart fell through the soles of my flimsy trainers. His long thin face was stuck on a wrinkled neck covered in red blotches and peeling skin. Beneath a nose that must have been punched often and vigorously was a thin, tight mouth partially covered by a narrow moustache. Both his nose and mouth were twisted as if he had something rancid stuck in his moustache. He took one look at my knee and medical certificate and hurriedly filled out my medical report. As I moved to collect my uniform, rifle and steel trunk, I saw I'd been declared unfit for combat and placed on light duty permanently. I was elated, and with this sliver of hope, I started making plans to escape this implacable nightmare of place.

I was to spend six weeks at Voortrekker Hoogte and then be sent elsewhere for the remainder of my conscription period. More than anything I wanted to be sent back to Natal's military headquarters in Durban, which was known to be the most relaxed base in the country. It was right across the road from the beach and a twenty minute walk from our house on the Berea. Natal Command was jeeringly referred to as Hotel Command by those rugged young South Africans who believed manhood could only be achieved through deprivation, derision and degradation. For the less rugged, like me, Natal Command was first prize for redeployment. The problem was that it was a very small camp, with little opportunity of getting a posting there. I had to find a way to secure my passage back to Durban, and quickly got to work on the problem.

One young lieutenant in our detachment was Chookie Retief, a kid I'd known at Durban High School. Chookie and I had never really been friends, but he was a good kid, and was friendly towards me even though he'd been in camp for six months. The military encouraged the system of hierarchy, where those who'd been in the force for a while would abuse and humiliate the younger troops. Chookie didn't buy into that iniquitous system, and I decided to try to use him as an ally in my attempt to get back to Durban. I told Chookie a massive lie about a pregnant girlfriend and potential suicide, and a lengthy tale of other strife I needed to attend to back home. Chookie believed me and made a recommendation to the camp commander. Within weeks I was on a train bound for Hotel Command. I felt bad about lying to Chookie, but this was about survival. In time, though, the lie would come back to haunt me, as much of it came true in a kind of karmic retribution.

I was immensely grateful to Chookie for this break, especially since at school he'd been a high achiever, both on the sportsfield and in the classroom, and I hadn't been part of his A-group circle. Among that group had been a handsome, talented kid called François de Villiers, whose father was Durban's leading gynaecologist. François was good at absolutely everything. He played rugby for the A team, was the best swimmer in the school and a champion surfer. He was sun bronzed and muscular and no-one at school ever dreamt of picking a fight with him. His strong features and clear blue eyes ensured a constant gaggle of schoolgirls around him at sports events. François was destined for great things, and his mother, who was friendly with mine, didn't encourage any friendship between us. I was an underachiever and a bad influence. In later years, after the army, I'd bump into François around town, and watched as he gradually sank into alcoholism and then drug addiction. One evening as I walked past the balcony of the Beach Hotel, I saw him drunk and roaring, challenging a large tattooed man who was sitting drinking with a group of people. François had kicked off his shoes and ripped off his shirt as he hurled challenges and abuse at his startled victim. I moved on quickly to avoid being seen by him. I had my own problems with alcohol and drugs, but François always seemed to be spinning out of control. Each time I saw him he was dirtier and more ragged. He once threatened to "fuck me up" when I addressed him as François, unaware that he'd changed his name to Frank. He got into frequent fights, and within a short time his youthful, aquiline face became misshapen and scarred. He often lived rough and the last time I saw him I couldn't understand what he was saying. He rambled and raved, drifting between quasi-religious epithets and streams of invective. As I walked away he threatened me again and told me he'd find me and "fix" me. He ended up moving into a squatter camp or "informal settlement" with a Zulu woman on the south coast of Natal. A few months later I heard he'd been stabbed to death in a drunken brawl. The anomalies of South African life showed up shockingly in the most unexpected places. It seemed that for all those like Chookie who made success of their lives, Durban High produced as many tragedies, like François. And there was no way of telling who'd draw the short straw.

While I was making plans to get to Durban and the easy life, Titch had got himself into deep, deep trouble. We'd both planned to get ourselves sent back to Durban where we could go through our military commitments together. Neither of us had any intention of doing more than was absolutely necessary to get through this ordeal. But on the train on his way to camp on the first day of his call-up, the military police caught him with a stash of dagga, and sent him straight to the notorious detention camp, Greefswald. Situated in the north of the country on the border with both Botswana and what was then Rhodesia, it was where drug addicts and homosexuals were sent

84

to get "straightened out". Here young deviants were put through the most humiliating and tortuous training imaginable. They were forced to run for hours over that hot, rugged terrain carrying telephone poles. If they slowed down or collapsed they were locked in tiny, airless cells without rations. Their days started at three in the morning and ended late at night after endless inspections and parades. Several weeks after I arrived in Durban I got a letter from Titch telling me what had happened. I was devastated. I knew all about Greefswald and the torture its inmates were subjected to. Knowing it would be a long time before he got his first pass made my easy life difficult to swallow.

Colonel Aubrey Levin was the psychiatrist in charge of the rehabilitation programme at Greefswald. During the Truth and Reconciliation Commission hearings his name came up often, especially among young gay victims, who described his cruel experiments performing secret, enforced sex change operations on these young soldiers. Dozens of young men committed suicide, either during their training or afterwards while trying to reintegrate into society. Doctor Levin now lives in Canada, and has consistently refused to comment on or return to face these accusations. Despite being a physically tough kid, Titch was an extremely gentle soul, and while I was making all sorts of plans to evade my military responsibilities, he was going through a life of hardship and pain in Greefswald. It was almost a year before he was allowed out, and when we finally met up again I was shocked to see the damage inflicted on my gentle, creative friend. When I flung my arms around him the way we'd always greeted each other, he remained stiff, arms at his side. His easy smile had become a cynical sneer.

My moods continued to swing irrationally, and now more frequently, from light to dark and back again. At times I could barely distinguish between being awake and dreaming; the world seemed so unreal and alien. Titch and I often shared our secret experiences with each other, which gave us a measure of support, knowing that we weren't alone with our craziness. A few years after getting out of the army, during one of many episodes of what became recurring depression, I went for a consultation in the psychiatric ward at Durban's Addington hospital. I'd become desperate with this condition that I was unable to share with anyone but my closest friend, and which caused me so much pain and anxiety. The doctor I saw was a fat, crass, unsympathetic man who made no effort to help me. It was only when it dawned on me that his name was Doctor Aubrey Levin that I got out of there and sought other ways to ease my troubled mind. His experiments at Greefswald had caused too much controversy for the army, so he'd been transferred to Addington Hospital to unleash his psychiatric talents on the general public.

When I started my time in the army, it was to be a one-year tour of duty, followed by annual camps lasting anywhere between three and six weeks for the next ten years. Towards the end of my first year we were offered a deal whereby we could do an extra year and then be finished for good. I chose to do another year and get my commitment over with. I'd been assigned to a small depot that supplied spare parts for obsolete army trucks, and had worked out a way to disappear off their radar screen. The military was an inefficient establishment, and as long as I appeared on the parade ground every morning, I could then take my clipboard and walk quickly and purposefully to the back of the camp, climb over the fence and walk home. For the second of my two years in that camp, I only ever appeared at the morning parade. After that I was over the fence in civvy street.

One of the first people I met at the depot was a slight but cocky anglicised Afrikaner called Charl Phyfer. He protected me from much of the initiation that new recruits often suffered at the hands of the ou manne who'd been in the army more than six months. On my first night in the barracks, a group of ou manne, seeing that I had a guitar, ordered me to entertain them. I hauled out Big Bertha and launched straight into the virulent anti-war classic by Bob Dylan, Masters of War. I'd never been shy to wear my political heart on my sleeve, and saw this as an opportunity to make a clear statement about who I was and what I thought. Charl, who also played the guitar, was mesmerised, partly at the sight of this huge instrument and partly at hearing this powerful song in the middle of the army barracks. The rest of the ou manne gave me a half-hearted round of applause and drifted back to their beds. Charl and I soon became firm friends, and when the local bully, Wayne Donkin, ordered me to shine his boots, Charl threatened him with "shots to the head" if he didn't leave me alone. That was the end of my being ordered around by ou manne. Wayne Donkin would glower at me menacingly, but Charl was my guardian angel and Donkin's teeth had been pulled. I also fell in with two young ruffians who came from the tough side of town, and before long we'd worked out all the safe places to hang out and get thoroughly stoned.

The army was a joke, and the big challenge was to see how much you could gypo[1] your way out of work or any other responsibility. But all that was about to change. In June 1974, word went around the camp that the defence minister, PW Botha, had announced that the army was taking over the military operation on Namibia's northern border. The South African police would still be active, but it was now a full military operation. We all knew there was trouble on that distant bit of desert, but now it was suddenly a lot closer.

I was still jumping the back fence every day. My cousin Leonard had finished his military service and had a job singing on the balcony of the Beach Hotel. During the day we'd hang around together playing music and smoking dagga, and every so often I joined him at his gig, accompanying him on the flute and an ancient saxophone he'd borrowed. I was writing my own songs, and occasionally got onto the guitar and sang these angry, naïve offerings to the crowd of boozy beach bums who hung around the insalubrious hotel verandah.

I still have some handwritten copies of these songs. I read them like a clue to a mystery that I still haven't fully solved. They describe a young, tortured mind seeking some sort of relief through trying to understand the world he lives in. These days it's hard to imagine that I was ever in such desperate straits or that things would get even worse. But then my songs were all I had to give voice to the inner conflict that growing up in South Africa had stirred in me. In the middle of one of my anguished performances, a scruffy drunk lurched up to the stage and stood looking at me unsteadily.

"Play Tie a Yellow Ribbon Round the Old Oak Tree," he slobbered.

"Sorry, I only play my own songs," I replied with youthful disdain.

He pulled a huge knife from under his denim jacket and looked at me with bloodshot eyes. "Play Tie a Yellow Ribbon Round the Old Oak Tree," he said again.

I launched into a hearty rendition of the song, making up the words as I went along, while my attentive fan stood in front of me, clutching his knife and swaying drunkenly to the music. When I finished he put the knife back under his jacket.

"Thanks, pal, that was lekker[2]."

I realised then that I had to find a more discerning audience for my songs.

---

1 derogatory for gypsy, implying lazy and unwilling to work
2 Afrikaans for nice

15

Durban, June 1975

4-POINT PLAN FOR MIXED AUDIENCES
The Cabinet accepted a four-point plan to open certain cinemas and theatres to all races.

This was officially confirmed in Nationalist circles yesterday and it is understood that the government will make known its decision within a few weeks.

Natal Mercury, 19 June 1975

DURBAN'S WHITE HERITAGE DEFENDED
What belongs to whites should stay white; it is our heritage, says Durban Councillor Lew Phillips, talking about the Durban bus service.

Natal Mercury, 19 June 1975

THREE WEEKS BEFORE I WAS due to finish my time in the army, my scam was discovered. Corporal Lewis was a nasty piece of work. An Englishman in his late sixties, he was employed by the army to run the camp's transport pool, a job he'd done for the British military. He had the nominal rank of corporal, and was constantly trying to outdo the other non-commissioned officers in the camp. He never spoke but shouted in a shrill Lancashire accent, and was constantly having drivers do press ups for some or other infringement. He happened to be driving down the road behind the camp when he saw me go over the back fence, and the next morning at parade I was summoned to the Commandant's office. He told me I'd be court marshalled the next morning, and that I'd better prepare myself for another year in the army.

The Commandant was old and not very bright, and when I appeared in front of him the following morning with my hair cut very short and my uniform neatly pressed, he seemed to have forgotten what I was there for. I told him a long story about a death in the family and how, in my grief, I'd made a bad decision and gone over the fence. The fact that I'd been making this bad decision daily for the past two years got lost in my skillful storytelling. Corporal Lewis tried to interject, but the Commandant, a staunch Afrikaner who clearly hated the little Englishman, told him to be quiet. I was given a fine of one week's pay and his sincerest condolences, and told to enjoy my life in civvy street. Three weeks later I was free.

The first thing I did was start a band with my cousin Leonard, Titch and a friend of Charl's called Michael Green. We started doing gigs at the university and other venues around Durban, and called ourselves the Rancid Dwarf, a nickname I'd given one of the Brothers at St Charles, a nasty little pervert. It seemed a fun name for a band at the time, and has since entered Durban's musical folklore; to this day people regale me with memories of our few performances. Michael was a brilliant songwriter, and went on to become an acclaimed author and poet as well as one of the country's leading literary academics. He recorded several collections of his songs in later years, but never received the acknowledgment he deserved.

It was while doing these gigs that I met the famed Steve Fataar. Here was the guy whose voice and guitar playing had such an enormous influence when I first heard him with the Flames at the Durban City Hall. They'd been playing with the Beach Boys and were doing very well in England and the USA. They even did a Royal Command Performance for the Queen at the Royal Albert Hall. Steve had returned to South Africa after the death of his brother, the bassist for the band. Brother, as Steve's brother was known, had succumbed to the pressure of the road – the drugs and mental illness – and died in Paris. For Steve it seemed that the bubble had burst. Blondie Chaplin and Steve's younger brother Ricky continued playing with the Beach Boys, but Steve was back home where he started. I often wondered why he made the decision to return to the dead-end, prejudiced world he'd come from. Looking back now at the way we sat around stoned, unable to get even the most basic of acts together, I wonder if the decision had been made for him.

I was becoming increasingly politically motivated in my music, influenced by the protest songs of Bob Dylan, Phil Ochs and others. Frelimo had recently won independence in Mozambique, and it was an inspiring time for a young "cultural revolutionary" like me. At that time we knew it was only a matter of years before we won our own revolution. I started doing gigs with Steve, but he was never keen on the political angle of my music. He'd returned from a certain amount of turmoil when the Flames had finally broken up, and the dangerous world of politics was the last thing he needed. But the simple fact that coloured and white musicians were playing together was enough to attract the attention of the security police. And it didn't help that we smoked spliffs from morning to night, giving Durban's notorious drug squad reason to raid and harass us at will.

In spite of the unquestionable fact that I was far from a perfect son, my mother was always a solid pillar in the centre of my very uncertain life. She made her disapproval of my lifestyle clear, but never denied me a place to sleep or a good meal. She'd bought me a saxophone on my twentieth birthday, and for my twenty-first in

January 1975, she gave me an air ticket to London. In spite of my earlier realisation that I was South African, not British, I nonetheless had a craving to visit the country that was home to so much of the music that had inspired me. But England was an expensive country to visit, and I needed to earn money to be able to survive there. Playing gigs to penniless student hippies wasn't going to crack it.

Fraser & Chalmers was a company contracted by the big oil refineries to do their annual maintenance clean-ups known as shutdowns. The entire refinery would close down and hundreds of lowlifes, ducktails, Australian surfers and recovering alcoholics – anyone who could wield a spanner and a four-pound hammer – would swarm over the hundreds of kilometres of steel piping that made up the oil refinery. Technically, only qualified fitters and turners were allowed to be recruited, but it was dirty, heavy work, and they often waived the rules just to get the job done.

Old Charlie Watson did the hiring, and as long as you had a toolbox and a good story about why you didn't have your papers, you could get onto the crew. Fraser & Chalmers was a magnet for bums and down-and-outs, and earned the nickname Farmers & Chancers among the scores of youths who flocked to the refinery to earn quick money. Situated on a strip of land at the edge of town close to the ocean, the refinery was right in the lee of the Bluff, that long, low hill parallel to the ocean that prevented the cooling ocean breeze from blowing over its matrix of pipes and boilers. Durban summers often reach the mid-thirties (95 ºF) and humidity regularly reaches ninety per cent. Conditions on the refinery were physically demanding, and while working those fifteen-hour shifts, I came across people I never knew existed. Andy Cotton always sat at the back of the bus that took us from Point Road to the refinery. The journey lasted only twenty minutes, but in that time he'd down a half bottle of rum and smoke two or three chillums of dagga. That was before six in the morning. When I first encountered him, I avoided his manic gaze, fearing for my life if I accidentally pissed him off. He was thin and sinewy, his face like a cross between a chopping block and pack of pork chops. He smoked dagga at every break, but was amazingly energetic and hard working. The refinery had an area of about ten football fields, eight or ten storeys high, and all sections were connected by a network of steel catwalks and staircases. During shutdowns, extra networks of scaffolding were erected around the boilers and tanks that were to be opened and cleaned out. I once got into a potentially disastrous situation while trying to weld a bracket to the side of a massive tank. I was stoned at the time, and as I welded, I didn't realise I was busy burning a hole right through the side of the tank. When I saw the extent of the disaster, I asked a fellow worker for help.

"Only one who can fix a fuck-up that big is Andy Cotton, my china," he replied with deep satisfaction. It was the type of fuck-up that if not repaired correctly could set the entire refinery on fire. I steeled myself and went to where Andy was working, suspended like a spider high in the maze of pipes.

"'Scuse me, Andy, sorry to bother you, I was wondering if you could help me out with a balls-up I made on the side of the tank," I said cautiously to this man who looked like he killed for kicks.

Andy listened without looking at me, continuing the job he was busy with. I stood silently, getting more and more nervous, when he finally looked up at me with hard, snake-like eyes.

"No problem, boetie, I'll be down in a seccie."

His voice was soft and kind and I couldn't believe it came from this tough bastard I was so afraid of. When he finished fixing the hole, he sat down on the steel walkway beside the tank and pulled a roll of kaartjies out of his overall pocket. "Calls for a skyf, boetie, whaddaya think?"

I felt ashamed that I'd so badly misjudged this sweet, kindly, but dangerous looking man. As it turned out, the worst on the crew were the Englishmen from Liverpool or Newcastle, who were often racist and violent, and more than once I came close to an all-out fist fight with these "kaffir haters".

One miserable Liverpudlian who worked in my section constantly shouted and swore at his black handlanger[1]. One steamy hot day he punched his handlanger for a minor infringement. I ran at him in a fury and grabbed the collar of his overalls. He grabbed mine and we stood pushing and shoving on the narrow catwalk high above the mass of pipes below. If it had broken out into an all-out fight one or both of us could easily have fallen to certain death, but instead we turned away, cursing each other. After that altercation he was more restrained; maybe he simply hadn't expected a white person to object to his racist outpourings.

Charl, Robin and I were all working on the shutdowns, and we rented a small, smelly flat together near Point Road, Durban's red

---

1 Afrikaans slang for an assistant or helper

light district. We were earning good money, but it was tough and tiring, and every so often we'd take a break from the work. During one such break, along with Titch, we decided to combine business with pleasure and take a trip down the coast, selling a bit of zol while we were about it. The bit of zol ended up being a huge cardboard box full of kaartjies of the finest Durban Poison. We knew of several hippie communities in places like Knysna and Plettenberg Bay where we were assured of a captive market. We headed off in Robin's VW camper, the box nestled between the two front seats disguised as a third seat. The first leg of the journey was through the "independent homeland" of Transkei, and we entered the country via a little-used dirt road to avoid the border post.

We stopped at many idyllic spots along that magnificent coastline, dipping into the box like it was chocolates. When we realised we were in danger of depleting our inventory, we decided to take our box and head for the hippies of Knysna. Once again we left the homeland using a back road to avoid the border guards, but after only a few kilometres back on South African soil, we came over a rise to discover a roadblock bristling with policemen in the dip ahead of us. Robin, Charl and I were in the front, me sitting on what was suddenly a very hot box. Titch was in the back having just lit an enormous spliff and there was nothing for us to do but keep driving straight into what was clearly going to be the last day of our free lives. Titch dumped the spliff and we opened all the windows as nonchalantly as possible. The cops were silent and menacing as they looked in the glove compartment, under the fold-out bed, in the ice box, between the suitcases, on top of the cupboard, next to the spare wheel and through the box of fruit and vegetables. When they finally waved us through my bum felt like it was on fire, sitting on enough dagga to keep us in jail for too many years to contemplate.

We sold the stash as quickly as we could after that, keeping just enough for our own consumption during the rest of our journey. We also traded some for tiny dots of LSD. We'd never taken the stuff, but knew all about it from the writings of Ken Kesey, Aldous Huxley and others. What we didn't know was that these acid trips might begin as journeys that were fun, crazy and insightful, but often end in complete madness.

16

London, February 1976

5000 SA TROOPS ON BORDER
South Africa is holding various points across Angola up to 50 km deep and stretching from the Atlantic Ocean to the Zambian border, the Minister of Defence, Mr PW Botha has disclosed.

Daily News, 4 February 1976

NO GUARANTEE OF TORY ARMS SALES TO S.A., WARNS VISITOR
The return to power of the Conservative Government in Britain would not automatically mean that South Africa would be able to buy British arms again. This was made clear by Sir Geoffrey Howe, the British shadow chancellor, in an interview in Cape Town yesterday.

Daily News, 5 February 1976

WHAT I THOUGHT WAS A DECENT AMOUNT of money, saved from those long hours of labour on the oil refinery, failed to impress the steely eyed immigration officer at Heathrow airport. I had just turned twenty-two and was learning that the world beyond South Africa wasn't as easy to negotiate as I'd thought. After a thorough interrogation, he stamped my passport and I made my way into the cold, inhospitable streets of London. I made contact with an old friend from Durban who allowed me to sleep for a few days on the floor of his tiny Hampstead apartment. For the next few days I walked around looking for a room to rent. One evening I saw a group of people gathered in the living room of a house just off the high street. A massive communist flag was draped across one wall, and from out on the street I could hear the speaker talking about Marx and Lenin. In South Africa, these people would have been locked up and charged with treason, but here they were speaking freely. The repression of my upbringing was thrust into sharp contrast by this very different world. At one house with a sign advertising a room for rent in the window, my knock was answered by a young Indian girl. I was flabbergasted when she spoke with a north London accent. I'd somehow expected the lilting tones I'd come to know from Durban Indians; this wasn't the first time I'd be forced to face my own prejudices and stereotyping. My world view was rapidly being challenged by the ideas, attitudes and opinions I was getting exposed to. I saw myself as streetwise and well informed; I'd been to the army, driven cranes and taxis and worked on the oil refinery. But here in this great metropolis I felt like a farm boy, and a very small one at that.

Life in London was expensive and unforgiving, and no-one seemed to care a hoot for anyone else. I went to visit some guys I'd

95

known in Durban who lived in a squat in Camden Town, where a group of militant young Londoners had taken over a council-owned building that had been condemned. At the time, a loophole in the law allowed squatting to happen, and literally hundreds of buildings and apartment blocks around the city had been taken over by squatters. You entered the building through a hole in a barbed wire fence. The passages and courtyard were lined with garbage bags, many torn open by stray cats and dogs, spilling their stench like colourful entrails. The Durban boys lived in total squalor, which seemed to have rubbed off on their approach to life. They were suspicious and hostile, even of me, as if I was there to get something from them. Mike Mullins had been an altar boy with me at the Holy Trinity church, and here he was in a room with boarded up windows, boiling a potato and an onion in a small aluminium pot on a single-plate gas burner. He was now an anarchist and held forth about the necessity of a total world revolution; everything had to be destroyed in order to start again. His lifestyle seemed a pretty good start towards total destruction, and I got out of there as soon as I could and never went back. The other Durban boy was even more nihilistic, and to top it off he was shooting heroin. At the time, the idea of sticking a needle into my arm was abhorrent, but it's funny how circumstances can change your thinking. It was depressing to see how these homeboys had somehow lost the plot, and I was determined to have a better London experience than this. London was the centre of the world for so many young South Africans and I continued to search for what created this perception. I bought a copy of *Time Out* to see which artists and groups were playing where and when. My excitement about seeing my favourite musicians faded when I saw the ticket prices.

After a week of sleeping on the floor, I managed to rent a room not much bigger than a cupboard in the building next door. I had enough money to buy a guitar, but that was it, so I started looking for a job. Mrs Black was a tough, middle-aged woman who owned the Coffee Cup in Hampstead, and after hearing my South African accent hired me immediately as her short order chef. South Africans weren't allowed to work in Britain, and Mrs Black knew she could pay me a sinful pittance without any problem. Mrs Black was part of a much larger network of illegal employers. All over London, young men and women from every corner of the globe worked illegally for appalling wages and the "privilege" of living in that great city. Hampstead was home to many famous actors, and both Peter O'Toole and Alan Bates regularly had breakfast at the Coffee Cup. The closest I got to these great men was a quick glimpse from the top of the narrow stairs that led to the cramped, grimy kitchen where I spent my twelve-hour shifts. I'd start preparing breakfasts in the tiny kitchen at six in the morning and only break for half an hour after the lunch rush. The rest of the day would be spent preparing lasagne, shepherd's pie and other dishes for the next day's lunch. I worked literally double the hours of the English waiters for half their pay. Mrs Black wouldn't have been out of place in a Charles Dickens novel, and used any opportunity to complain about my performance, yet held me up to the local lads as a shining example of one who worked tirelessly for a fraction of what they earned. Needless to say, the waiters never invited me for a pint after work.

Aside from buying a guitar, my other main mission in London was to audition at the East 15 Acting School. I'd heard that they admitted students on the basis of an audition, and might overlook my lack of academic qualification. I'd prepared a monologue from *King Lear* and one of the wonderful speeches from the Athol Fugard classic, *Boesman and Lena. Boesman and Lena* is the story of a homeless coloured couple who live a transient life, scratching a meagre living in the depressed areas around the city of Port Elizabeth in South Africa's Eastern Cape Province. With my rough features and intrinsic understanding of that peculiar accent, I slipped easily into the role. The school was situated in a large house in Essex and was known to be "socially committed". When I walked in, the head of the school, Margaret Walker (nee Bury), was sitting at a table in a small room with a young man and an older woman. They were surprisingly pleasant and welcoming, and I set about my performances with confidence. The audition went extremely well; they were clearly impressed with my ability to switch between the majestic but faltering Lear and the desperate Boesman. When they started talking about my study visa and how the course was to be financed, I realised I hadn't done my homework; I had no way of meeting the requirements. On the tube back to Hampstead, I realised that even if I raised the money, because I hadn't completed high school, getting a study visa would be impossible. On top of that, something else had crept into the equation and started to influence my world view: a cheap and steady supply of LSD.

LSD can be a lot of fun. The only problem is that if you're a bit unstable, it can turn on you suddenly and take you on a trip so horrifically mind-bending that it's hard to come back to earth. In fact, I know people to this day who are still out there on some cosmic plane they never returned from. Taking LSD while riding the London tube is not a good idea…

The man staring at me from the other side of the compartment sends shivers up my arms and into my already rigid jaw. He's wearing black leather from head to toe, with huge boots covered in chains and buckles. On his shaved head sits a shiny leather cap, the type worn by Nazi SS officers. I keep looking away, but every time I glance in his direction he's staring straight at me with hard blue eyes. The hallucinations fired by the LSD accelerate my fear and panic as I try to breathe steadily and stay calm.

It's the last tube of the evening and by the time we reach Belsize Park station, he and I are the only ones left in the compartment. My heart feels like it's pounding through my head and out of my ears. When the train pulls into Hampstead station, I leap off and to my horror, he too disembarks. The lifts to the street aren't working and I start up the long spiral stairwell, my murderous stalker close behind. When I reach the high street I keep up a brisk pace, trying not to show fear. Every time I glance over my shoulder, he's there. I cross to the other side of the high street and he follows. I pass the street where I live and carry on towards Hampstead Heath.

This is a mistake. I don't want to be cornered and hacked to death in the quiet entrance to my building, but now I'm heading towards Jack Straw's Castle and the darkness of the Heath. I cross from one side of the road to the other a few times; he remains on my trail. When I realise that I'm heading into the darkness, I panic and take off at full sprint. I veer off into a bushy area to the side of the road. After a short distance of thrashing though undergrowth and shrubs, I dive under a large bush and, in spite of my frantic panting and pounding heart, keep as still as possible. I can hear him slowly walking through the undergrowth, backwards and forwards, until eventually silence resettles over that terrifying corner of the Heath.

The following day I take a detour on the way to work past the Place of Horror. As I enter the thicket close to my hiding place, I'm approached by a man with a desperate look in his eyes, rubbing a large, swollen lump in his trousers. I keep my eyes straight ahead and hurry on to the Coffee Cup.

Years later I went to the King William IV pub on Hampstead High Street to enjoy a pint of English ale. As I entered, the hair on the back of my neck stood up as I saw the same murderous Nazi who'd almost dispatched me in the dark of the Heath several years earlier. My heart started pounding and I resisted the urge to get the hell out of there. Then I noticed several other men dressed in the same leathery attire as my perpetrator. I ordered a pint of "heavy" and slowly made my way over to where this group of villains stood drinking. It finally dawned on me that these parodies of the Village People were just that, a group of gay men in very butch clothing. Giggling to myself, I realised I could no longer tell my story about how I'd almost lost my life on Hampstead Heath. The pub's website describes how "The Willie (as it's commonly known) turned discreetly gay in the late 1930s, specifically to cater for men visiting the Heath, the publican in those days being a woman known as Mumsy".

While all this was going on, the winter gave way to one of England's warmest and most beautiful summers. But news from a cold and cruel Johannesburg was deeply distressing. On the sixteenth of June 1976, thousands of Sowetan school kids had taken on the might of the South African police. The riots had quickly spread to other centres around the country, and made it onto the front page of most British newspapers. The BBC news was filled with images of my home country in flames, kids with stones and petrol bombs in fierce battles with armed cops in armoured personnel carriers. The revolution was finally happening, and I felt homesick and alienated. I once asked directions from a group of Indian youths near Camden Lock. When they heard my South African accent, they told me to "fuck off". I wanted to tell them that I wasn't one of the bad guys, that I supported the ANC. But I knew it would be fruitless, and walked on, ears burning with shame.

I finally found the guitar I'd been looking for. It belonged to a cabaret singer/comedian who had once worked the circuit in South Africa.

"Ooh yeah," he enthused. "I looved Jooberg, shagged me'self silly, I did. Too bad aboot all them fookin' kayfirs takin' over the place." I just couldn't win. I handed over the two hundred pounds and walked out with my Martin D-28 Dreadnought – still my main instrument all these years later, although I'd need to be a wealthy man to try and buy it today.

I was now armed and dangerous. I'd had enough of Mrs Black's exploitative ways and had fried, scrambled and poached enough eggs in that grubby little kitchen to last a lifetime. It was time to exercise my musical skills.

My first performances with my new guitar were on the streets and in underground stations in central London. Buskers could make a good living if they landed a good pitch. A pitch was a strategically demarcated area of the underground or street where an escalator ended or a series of tunnels joined. They were always just out of earshot of the next pitch. In busy areas of central London, like Green Park and Trafalgar Square, the management of pitches was overseen by a loose hierarchy of buskers, as I discovered the first time I took out my guitar and started singing at Green Park tube station. No sooner had I launched into one of my impassioned songs about freedom and revolution in my homeland that a grisly old bloke with a guitar case approached.

"'Ere, matie, better fook orf if you don't want yer guitar smashed over yer 'ead."

He looked like he'd seen more than his fair share of barroom brawls, so I unceremoniously packed up and made way for his ghastly wailings. I soon learnt to wait in line to sing my songs, as waves of humanity swept past like an endless, faceless army. I also found that my own songs didn't bring in the small change. So I walked around and listened to several of the buskers at work. The one who seemed to be earning the most was singing Bob Dylan's Blowin' in the Wind. It didn't take long to realise that he was singing just the first verse, over and over, for the entire half hour he was on the pitch; in fact, just the opening lines:

'Ow many roads must a man walk down
Before you can call 'im a man?
An' 'ow many roads must a man walk down
Before you can call 'im a man?
An 'ow many roads must a man walk down…

And so he went on, occasionally emphasising the "call 'im a ma-an" part.

Hell, I'd already discovered at knifepoint how people crave familiar tunes, so when my next turn came, I droned out the same endless cycles of Blowin' in the Wind, and my earnings were instantly respectable. I could see them coming – those who were going to fish for loose change – as they hummed, mimed or sang along to my endless repetitions of that great song. They never made eye contact or acknowledged me in any way, but simply tossed their coins into my guitar case and strode by, careful not to snarl up that colossal human serpent winding its way to and from work. But this wasn't enough to change my ideal of being a songwriter. My songs, unpolished and naïve as they were, were already a part of my life, providing a deep satisfaction I couldn't get from any other pursuit. Reason enough to keep seeking my own voice.

Bagshaw, a good friend of my father, owned one of the most beautiful yachts on the island of Hydra. He'd started building it in his backyard in Durban and one day he packed the half-finished vessel into crates, left his sad, bitter wife and headed for Greece. Bagshaw was cut from the same crazy cloth as my father. Once, while driving through Durban with me in the back seat, they started arguing, and the next thing they were out on the pavement, punching, yelling and kicking each other; the next day their friendship continued as if nothing had happened.

Bagshaw had invited me to visit him on the island if I were ever in the area, and when I finally decided that London held no future for me, I got on a bus and headed for Athens. It was hot and humid and I spent a couple of days sightseeing, sleeping at night in a large untidy park near the city centre. It was a time of political upheaval in Greece and although I couldn't understand a word, I was struck by the large groups of people gathered in squares and cafés to discuss the situation. A military coup, the "Regime of the Colonels", had ended two years earlier, and politics had now taken to the streets. I'd never known such a thing, and the prospect of real democracy was thrilling to my idealistic young mind. I was convinced that a similar thing was going to happen back in South Africa, that the black majority would push the apartheid regime out of power. I wasn't sure what the fate of the white population would be, but felt fairly confident that they wouldn't be "driven into the sea". More and more I saw my role as using songs to reflect the situation back home. Seeing a production of *Mother Courage* by the legendary German playwright and poet, Bertolt Brecht, at a small independent London theatre had left a huge mark on me. His philosophy of didacticism, of letting his plays and songs comment on what was going on in society, made so much sense. *Mother Courage* spoke against the rise of Fascism and Nazism, and it inspired me to speak out against the apartheid regime.

I took a ferry from Piraeus to Hydra, a tiny, beautiful island that had only one motorised vehicle, a three-wheeler used to cart bricks and heavy goods from the ships to destinations on the steep hillsides. All other merchandise and provisions were transported on handcarts along the narrow cobbled paths between whitewashed houses. The stone wall of the harbour looked thousands of years old. Once on dry land, I asked a thickset man with a mane of curls where I might find Bagshaw. He pointed to an exquisite wooden-hulled cutter that a pirate might have sailed, moored between dozens of sleek, fiberglass yachts crawling with sun gods and goddesses in miniscule swimsuits, expensive sunglasses and designer shorts and T-shirts. A few of them cast contemptuous glances at me. Hippies with rucksacks were clearly not part of this social milieu. I felt utterly out of place as I walked down the jetty surrounded by the playthings of so many millionaires. It was a hot summer's day without a hint of a breeze. Colourful bottles were crammed onto drinks carts under pastel beach umbrellas.

As I approached Bagshaw's vessel, the only wooden boat in the harbour, I heard anguished cries from inside. A woman was whooping, panting and wailing in a foreign language. Interspersed was a deep and feral grunting forming a syncopated symphony so loud that I stopped in my tracks. Surprisingly, the beautiful people on the neighbouring boats seemed indifferent to the commotion. Only when I heard an orgiastic crescendo of *yes, yes, yes* did I put my rucksack down and tactfully wait for the cries to subside into sighs and finally silence.

Eventually a slightly bedraggled man in his mid-forties appeared on deck. I hadn't seen him since my early teens, but I recognised Bagshaw instantly. He recognised me too, despite being all grown up with curly blonde hair well below my shoulders.

"Dear boy, how absolutely delightful to see you! My God, you look exactly like your bastard father. How is the darling man? Yvette darling, come and see who's come to stay. It's DJ's boy, the black bastard. Come in, dear boy, let me get you a glass of retsina."

He poured three glasses of pungent, green wine from a five gallon cask as the petite, smiling Yvette emerged, wrapped in a towel. I spent several weeks on the boat with them. The only inconvenience was the incredibly noisy sex they had several times a week, which had reached legendary status on the island. On still afternoons it was said they could be heard as far as the mainland. Bagshaw's friends were all artists, writers and academics, or people hiding from ex-lovers or tax collectors in other countries. I met some of these eccentric refugees over lunches that lasted until dinner and dinners that ended when the last man stopped singing. Bagshaw's specialty was singing songs from Shakespeare while doing mediaeval jigs. He encouraged me to sing my songs, and for the first time I had an attentive and critical audience as well as the attentions of the occasional young beauty who passed that way.

Bagshaw was friendly with an American man who owned a sparsely furnished, rambling house at the top of the hill. He needed to return to the USA for a few months and asked me to housesit for a couple of hundred drachmas a day. It was enough to keep me going, especially since the small rocky garden was full of tomatoes, onions and cucumbers. It was an idyllic existence, and for the first time in many years I was completely free of the numbing effect of dagga. It wasn't a conscious decision, but dope was in short supply in that part of the world and with the sea, sun and daily doses of that delicious, pine resin-flavoured wine, I hardly noticed its absence. But I was also well away from the madness and anxieties of my country and home life. It couldn't last, of course, and as the cool autumn breezes began, I said goodbye to Bagshaw and began the long haul back through Europe and finally home.

17

Durban, December 1976

FIRST SIGN OF ANC ACTIVITY FEARED: URGENT BORDER TERROR ALERT CALL

Yesterday's hand-grenade attack on two policemen near the Mozambique border is being suspected as the first sign of an African National Congress terrorist thrust into South Africa. The Minister of Police, Mr JT Kruger, made an urgent appeal to Eastern Transvaal farmers near the border to go on full alert for any unusual happenings or the presence of strangers.

Daily News, 1 December 1976

TO A BETTER LIFE

If the Government seems to have no sense of urgency about the unrest in the townships, at least businessmen do. Meeting in Johannesburg this week more than 100 of the country's senior executives decided to form a foundation to improve the quality of life of urban blacks. It is the most positive and encouraging step to be taken since the trouble began in the townships five months ago.

Daily News Editorial, 1 December 1976

IN THE FEW MONTHS I'D BEEN away, South Africa had become a different place. The newly introduced medium of television was full of the coarse, heavy-handed propaganda vilifying Black Nationalism, Communism and any other -ism that stood in the way of God's chosen people carrying out His divine instructions. The townships were on fire, but when I spoke to Jabula about the situation, he would come down heavily on the teenage revolutionaries, saying they needed a good beating to straighten them out. I found it odd that I, the middle class whitey, supported the agitators while he, the young black outlaw, was all for them being crushed by the police. It was a time that stretched and confused the consciences of so many South Africans and would end up dividing families and alienating friends. I later came to better understand Jabula's viewpoint as I watched many of these young soldiers discard the discipline of the organisations they represented and turn to crime and mayhem. The irony was that Jabula always saw himself as an honest criminal.

Even though there was pressure on me to get a real job, I easily slipped back into the routine of doing whatever gigs I could get or reporting for duty on the shutdowns. Before I'd left on my journey, my relationship with Sheila had been in decline. She was talking about marriage and kids while I was thinking about freedom and adventure. As I became more interested in politics and the world around me, she became more introverted and unwilling to move beyond our small social circle. We started seeing the world very differently, and the gap between us was widening. Nonetheless, when I returned we resumed the habitual ebb and flow of our dysfunctional relationship, breaking up and making up, never quite knowing the difference between love and comfort.

I was living at my mother's house next door to DJ, and the tension between him and me threatened to spill over into full-scale war. The fact that I was trying to be a musician and not working for his film company was the catalyst for our conflict, and we'd regularly hurl abuse at each other across the garden fence for all the neighbours to hear. My relationship with my mother was also tense, and she made it clear that my stay at her house should end as soon as possible. Nonetheless, she tolerated me and fed me without too much complaint. Once, when my mother was away on vacation with her cousin, DJ and one of his girlfriends walked into her house, sat down and turned on the TV. His girlfriend tried to engage me in a conversation about the futility of being a musician. My response was short and not very sweet.

"Why don't you just stop talking shit and fuck off?" I surprised even myself.

DJ flew into a rage and ordered me to apologise at once. Instead, I grabbed him by the collar and walked him backward up the stairs from the TV den and out the front door.

Throughout this conflict there was one person who was a quiet yet resolute ally, my grandmother. She still lived down the road with Grandpa, but was always understanding and sympathetic about my reckless life. Grandpa had been a prisoner of war in Italy for several years, and during that time, rumour went, Granny had sought out other comforts, and hadn't been entirely faithful to Grandpa. With me she was never judgmental or critical, and often came to my aid in times of need.

As the months went by, my mother became increasingly irritated with my inability to get a proper job and become a respectable member of society. At one point, along with my younger brother and sister, she went to visit family in Zimbabwe, but wouldn't trust me in the house alone. I didn't blame her; I was being joyfully irresponsible and loving every minute of it. My grandparents were also going on that visit, and although Grandpa was also infuriated with my attitude and appearance, Granny slipped me the keys to the vacant maid's quarters behind her house. When she finally died a few years later, Grandpa was not the only one who grieved deeply. I too had lost someone who had quietly, but tacitly, supported me in spite of my wild ways.

A decade-and-a-half later, while driving from Durban to Cape Town through the Wild Coast, my young daughter finally coaxed the true story about Granny out of my mother with innocent manipulation. While Grandpa had been locked up in Italy, Granny had lived with my mother and my two uncles in the small town of Butterworth in the Transkei. During these barren years Granny had started seeing a man who lived alone in a large house overlooking the hamlet. It was a known secret, and the scandal was discussed in whispers around the conservative, repressed little town. My mother either didn't know or wouldn't tell the real nature of Granny's relationship with that man, but when Grandpa returned from the war, she walked quietly away from the big house on the hill and resumed her role as dutiful wife and mother. What had happened never got in the way of the dedicated and loving marriage they shared until Granny died. As I saw it, my grandmother knew what it was to be an outlaw, and so was sympathetic to her outlaw grandson.

Granny's sister Aseneth, or Seny for short, had an ancient orange VW Beetle. She was a spritely woman in her sixties with a trim figure and short grey hair, who played bowls several times a week and was never short of suitors. She'd moved in with my grandparents after we bought the big house and was always a happy and invigorating figure in our lives. She was active in her social life and discreet in her love life, easily playing her suitors off against each other. One day she announced that she'd met a new man she planned to marry. Lew was pleasant enough and clearly dedicated to her. But after they married she discovered the possessive, mean streak he'd managed to conceal. Aunt Seny told Granny she'd made a huge mistake and that in a few short months of marriage, Lew had become intolerable. One evening a fisherman angling for rock cod on the north pier – a long, manmade breakwater that juts into the Indian Ocean – saw Aunt Seny walk towards the end of the pier in the dim light, then jump into the waves that were crashing into the rocks below.

My mother inherited the old orange Beetle, and having no use for it, gave it to me. Once again I was mobile, and I used that old car in the same spirit of adventure that my great aunt had lived her life.

My Martin Dreadnought was loud and robust, perfectly matching my loud, robust voice. My songs were now becoming more structured, and I'd actually been invited to the Natal Folk Music Association's annual festival. It wasn't so much a case of being recognised by the music fraternity as their inability to ignore me any longer. Owen Coetzer, a journalist and art critic, was on the committee at the time, and when we met up more than twenty years later, he confided that my "abrasive and argumentative" songs had really "got up their noses".

We laughed about how far we'd all come in this crazy country and he arranged for me to write an article for his newspaper about the road I'd travelled. It felt good to have built yet another bridge across one of the many chasms that had ruptured our lives. A few weeks later Owen died from a heart attack.

18

The Road is Much Longer

A Story by Johnny Rogers, illustrated by Andy Mason

Durban, Summer 1977

GLOOMY TIDINGS

There is precious little for our comfort in Mr Vorster's gloomy New Year's message. Deserted by the West, who generally will not even sell us arms to protect Western interests, South Africa has to go it alone, says the Prime Minister. He sees no hope except in ourselves.

Daily News Editorial, 3 January 1977

VIOLENCE WILL GO ON WITH APARTHEID, LABOUR PARTY TOLD

South Africa was a violent society, with violent laws defended by violence, Dr Allan Boesak, student pastor at the University of the Western Cape, said last night.

Daily News, 4 January 1977

CATTLE THEFT: MAN HELD

Ubombo police are holding a 26-year-old man on charges of stock theft after a spot check on his vehicle revealed the skins and carcasses of two cattle allegedly stolen from a Zululand farmer.

Daily News, 14 March 1977

RAPSON ROAD, A HUGE, turn-of-the-century colonial house, had become a commune for arty types and intellectuals. Steve Fataar got me a room there and introduced me to these young hotshots. There I was most impressed by the young cartoonist, Andy Mason, who was studying at Natal University. He lived with his beautiful but demure girlfriend, Deanne, in the back corner of the house. Andy had a regular strip in the student newspaper, *Dome*, and was just starting his new comic series, Vitoke in Azania, based on the residents of Rapson Road. His unbridled imagination created a hilarious world of maladjusted young South Africans living through those turbulent years. Deanne, Andy and his mate Spectro were true intellectuals who discussed South African politics in a way I'd never heard before. They read books by political scientists and theorists with names like Gramsci, Althusser, Foucault and others I'd never heard of. I tried reading them too, but couldn't get past the first chapters. It was as if they were written in a language I didn't speak. Until then my reactions to my environment were all heart and balls; now I was expanding my head and exploring theory – distant concepts that seemed aloof from the sweat and blood of street politics. From this young intelligentsia I heard about people like Rick Turner and Steve Biko. Although banned by the state, Andy and Spectro had copies of their writings and I glimpsed a South Africa far removed from the one I'd grown up in. A new breed of young black radicals was espousing Black Consciousness, in which whites had little or no role in changing the shape of the future society. These were new and frightening ideas, ones that forced me to start looking at our country far more critically than before. The country was now in a state of constant conflict and trouble was never far off.

Dave "Plod" Tarr was an eccentric, warm-hearted violinist who played in the Silver Creek Mountain Band at a hotel a few blocks away. One night Charl and I went to hear them and were having a beer when Plod arrived pale and shaken. While walking to the gig he'd been accosted by a group of soldiers from the nearby military barracks, who'd dragged him into the building and roughed him up. One stuck a gun up his nose and told him to "fuck off back to his hippie friends". Incensed, Charl and I set out the next night for vengeance. We stacked Robin's van with rocks and petrol bombs and pulled up at the barracks after midnight, where we loosed our projectiles on the sleeping soldiers. As flames licked through the foyer we got out of there smartly. This was one of a few acts of "terror" I took part in. Andy was critical when he heard, as random acts wouldn't help bring about change in the country. Right as he was, it still felt good to get back at those soldier boys, if just for the satisfaction of making them pay for terrorising my friend. Plod and I went on to enjoy many musical collaborations, both in studio and on stage. He remained beautifully eccentric, but died of melanoma in 2003. His last words were "Christ, I'd do anything for a beer".

Friends of Steve Fataar in Swaziland occasionally arranged gigs for him and his band there. It was always a pleasure to go and play in that small but fertile mountain kingdom. Despite its proximity to South Africa, it was worlds away from the repression and conflict that defined our existence, and life there was peaceful and agreeable, at least until the South African Defence Force started their brutal raids on ANC operatives. The only signs of the neighbouring police state were the men in their smart cars and bakkies[1] who came to gamble at the casino and consort with black prostitutes. On weekends, the smart hotels with casinos between the capital Mbabane and the second city, Manzini, filled up with burly Afrikaners behaving as if they'd never heard of apartheid.

I was half asleep in the back of Steve's VW bus, heading for Swaziland, when we ran into a police roadblock outside the tiny village of Mkuze in northern KwaZulu-Natal. The middle-aged sergeant major in charge barked terse instruction to two white and five Zulu constables. He pulled us over and ordered us out. It was late March and still the height of summer, the tarmac so hot it was molten, and as we waited for the police to finish searching the van

---

1 pickup truck, SUV or four-wheel drive

a meerkat[2] shot through the shimmering heat waves as if over hot coals.

Being the only whitey, every inch of my baggage attracted special attention. There was a sudden whoop, and the young constable emerged triumphant with four kaartjies of zol. I was locked in the back of their van while Steve and the band were sent on their way. My ride was hot and uncomfortable, up a mountain pass on a dirt road that exploded in plumes of dust under the wheels of the van.

We arrived at last at Ubombo, close to the border with both Swaziland and Mozambique, the site of the nearest jail and courtroom. During fingerprinting I was subjected to endless questions about how I could hang out with a bunch of blacks, degrade myself smoking dagga, and – even worse – wear earrings. That I had three in each ear mystified them more than anything. I was placed in the juvenile cell, where a small barred window overlooked the convict's courtyard, an area of about ten square metres surrounded by walls five metres high. There were six cells including my juvenile cell, each with about eight prisoners. A sturdy metal grid overhead sealed off the courtyard. At the back of the cell were three narrow windows each ten centimetres wide. There was no way out. Three young boys, aged about eight and twelve years, were moved to the main cells to ensure that the white prisoner remained separate from the blacks. The toilet bowl in my cell was smashed, and its remains were filled with shit and scraps of newspaper. The smell was unbearable, so I kept the windows open through the night. After the heat of the plains, it was striking how radically different was the frosty chill and whistling breeze of the Ubombo mountains. The walls had no graffiti but for a crude sketch of an ox and the letters "ixoxo" scratched below: a reminder that this was a children's cell. I lay on the thin felt mat and wrapped myself as best I could against the cold. From the cells around came the oppressed but sparkling laughter of the people of the great Zulu nation.

It was almost a week before I saw Steve again. In my cell I wasn't allowed pen or paper and even my shoelaces and belt were removed. But when I finally arrived home, I recorded my impressions, which were published verbatim in all their naïveté and passion in *Staffrider*, a literary journal with a strong anti-apartheid sentiment. It's a reminder of the enormous anger and outrage that filled my young

---

2 mongoose

112

heart then and guided my future musical journey.

Early on Sunday morning I woke to the sound of the main doors to the cells being opened. Rubbing my aching back, I looked into the courtyard, where a young white lieutenant and two black cops were shouting and whacking their batons against the cells' bars. The prisoners were lined up in the courtyard and then searched by the black policemen. Later I learnt that the search was a charade enacted for the benefit of the white lieutenant. The older of the black cops ran a thriving trade in basic comforts like tobacco, soap and extra food for the prisoners, and it would have been counterproductive to find their hidden cash.

The lieutenant then came to ask me if everything was okay. I pointed to the toilet bowl and explained that I needed to find one that worked. He escorted me to the charge office, pointed to the door marked "Gents/Here" and told me to hurry up. For years I'd thought these signs meant "gents here" until I discovered that "here" was Afrikaans for gents. I was then returned to my cell with a tin plate containing two slabs of stale brown bread with a hint of peanut butter and a tin cup of cold, dark tea. Once the cops left, the prisoners gathered around a huge, three-legged iron pot of mealiemeal, the stiff traditional porridge made from maize. There was clearly a pecking order, and the older prisoners directed the division of this dry, unappetising breakfast. The three little boys were served last, and squatted on their haunches around the tin plate on the floor, rolling small handfuls into tight balls that they tossed into their mouths. After eating, the inmates took turns peering in through my window, greeting me with great amusement.

Most of the inmates were rural Zulus in tattered, threadbare clothing, many with traditional scarification on their faces. My grasp of Zulu was poor to say the least, and only when Open Moses came to my window did I have someone to talk to.

"Hello brother, my name is Open Moses Brown." He was a "bruin ou"[3], he told me. His father was an African American who'd visited South Africa and made love to his mother, a Swazi, in 1945; this uncommon parentage meant that in South Africa he was classified differently from other blacks. His father had long since disappeared, and Open knew nothing of his history or whereabouts, but didn't seem to care. He'd just visited his mother in Swaziland. Caught

---

3 literally, brown guy, Afrikaans slang for coloured

returning to South Africa through the porous southern border without a passport, they suspected him of terrorism. By 1977, young people were going into exile in droves – Swaziland being a desirable destination – and guerrilla incursions back into South Africa were on the increase. Authorities wanted to stamp out this cross-border migration, and Open had been at the wrong place at the wrong time.

While we chatted, the inmates were taking turns washing under a tap in the corner of the courtyard. I watched one young boy, naked and shivering in the chill morning air, splashing his head and body and then rubbing the soles of his feet with a small smooth stone until they were spotless. He dried himself with a cloth the size of a hankie, wringing it out at intervals. His eyes looked wild and confused, and I was overcome with sadness and rage at this pathetic sight. Open told me that the boy had been caught crossing from Mozambique in search of food.

"Don't worry, brother, this is Africa," Open laughed, when I expressed outrage at the situation. "Look at the Zulu nation!" he exclaimed, gesturing towards the laughing, cavorting inmates. "Hey fuck man, these peoples are too much happy."

It was true. Everyone seemed exuberant, and I struggled to work out how it was possible under such awful circumstances.

Open excused himself. "We're going to have a small church," he explained.

They sat in a semi-circle around an old man with a bible who was in for theft. As they raised their voices in song, the courtyard walls amplified the sound until the resonance pulsed through my body. The Zulus are known for their gift of voice and singing is an integral part of traditional Zulu life. I lay back on my mat and let the waves of harmony wash over me.

Supper was served at three in the afternoon, and the lieutenant asked if I wanted a cigarette. I hadn't had one for over twenty-four hours and gratefully accepted. He took one from his pack and nipped off the filter before handing it to me. He explained that if the filter is burned and then squeezed between the fingers it forms a hard, sharp surface you can use to commit suicide: several had been carried out with this unlikely weapon. I pointed to the shards of porcelain from the broken toilet bowl and assured him I had a far more suitable weapon at hand. I meant it as a joke, but within minutes he'd ordered an inmate to come and clear up the mess. The other inmates shared out their usual pot of mealiemeal, instant gravy and coffee, and before long they were piling the empty dishes and rolling cigarettes with tobacco and newspaper.

Gumede, a butcher from Mandini, sauntered over to my window, told me his name and asked why I was inside.

"Caught in a roadblock at Mkuze with four kaartjies of zol," I told him.

"Ow, ow, ow, man!" he laughed. "Four kaartjies? This fokken' police is too stupid, man. Nsangu[4] is growing everywhere here. Me too, I smoke, even my father and my grandfather, they smoke. This fokken' police look for four kaartjies?" He went on laughing, occasionally shouting in Zulu to no-one in particular.

"And you?" I asked. "Why are you here?"

He recounted a long story about two cows he'd bought from a local farmer and slaughtered and skinned in the field where they were grazing, then he'd put the skins and carcasses in the back of his bakkie. On the way to Mandini, he came across a roadblock. The cops didn't believe his story about buying the cows from the farmer, and traced the branding on the skins to a nearby farm. It turned out to be the neighbouring farm of the farmer Gumede had dealt with, who denied ever having seen him. Being illiterate, Gumede had no proof of sale, and being black, his word meant nothing against that of the white farmer.

Several days later, Steve and the rest of the band arrived back in Durban. When my friend Mark Ford asked Steve where I was and heard I'd been arrested at a roadblock at Mkuze, he rallied the Rapson Road residents and raised enough to pay whatever bail would be needed to get me out of prison. Mark had a deep love of Zulu culture, never wore shoes, and never undertook a journey without his traditional Zulu fighting sticks. The following morning he was on the side of the highway with his thumb out. He reached the roadblock at Mkuze that evening. The police had a large campfire burning at the side of the road, which Mark approached barefoot and armed with his two sticks.

"Wharra fuck you want?" the young lieutenant asked Mark.

"I've come to fetch Roger," he replied.

A few hours later, I heard my cell door open and there in the dim light was Mark, beaming. He was tossed into the cell with me and

---

4 Zulu for marijuana

we spent the rest of the evening talking and laughing until we finally fell asleep. The next morning we were told that the magistrate had arrived. I was escorted into the courtroom and presented to the public prosecutor, who asked how I intended to plead. I said "guilty", and he explained that I would be released on bail but need to return to Ubombo for my trial two months later. Mark paid the bail and the prosecutor started preparing the papers for my release.

Open and Gumede had their trials later the same day; they reduced Open's charge to the lesser one of illegally crossing a border. While waiting for my papers, a squad of prisoners was walked past the charge office back to the cells. Open and Gumede were among them. When they saw me, each smiled and held up three fingers: three years. I never saw either of them again, but our conversations during those few days in Ubombo left a huge impression. I knew my country was a cruel place, and I'd witnessed much of it through hanging around with Jabula. But that image of the little boy, cold, naked and terrified, left an indelible mark.

Mark had an outrageous sense of humour, and we roared with laughter all the way back to Durban on the back of the truck we'd hitched a ride on. I got to know that kind of laughter well in the years to come; it was survivor laughter, relief and fear in equal parts. Months later, Mark accompanied me back to Ubombo to stand trial for possession of dagga. In spite of the shame of having her son in court on a criminal charge, my mother lent me her little car for the journey. We left before dawn, me in neatly pressed black trousers and a borrowed jacket and tie. The trial lasted a matter of minutes. I pleaded guilty, listened gravely to a lecture on the dangers of blacks and dagga, and then vowed to have nothing to do with either again. I received a suspended sentence and made the long journey back to Durban. I was twenty-three years old, without education or prospects, and now with a criminal record to boot.

While my mother was shocked and disappointed at the awful start I'd got off to in life, I didn't feel the same stigma at being caught on the wrong side of the law. The whole system was imposed by a government I despised, and in my opinion, the laws I broke were unjust and outdated. We were being regularly harassed by the police, and in a way, life had become a cat and mouse game with the law. But it was a dangerous game; a new viciousness had crept into police behaviour, and deaths in police custody were on the increase.

After my Ubombo trial, the police returned the bail money to

Mark who then paid back my friends who'd chipped in. Among them was a beautiful young artist and poet called Katy Hamilton. She'd been the girlfriend of a young filmmaker who lived at Rapson Road, but he was off to film school in London and they'd split up. Katy would look at me in a way that made me self-conscious and awkward. I wasn't confident with women and didn't see myself as interesting or attractive. I was a bit of a ruffian among this community of self-assured young artists and academics, and just starting on my musical journey. So it was a pleasant surprise one night when Katy crept quietly into my bed. With my heart beating like the jungle night, we embarked on what would become a tragic relationship. Sheila and I had drifted desultorily into different worlds, she reluctant to terminate the relationship, me already captivated by the lovely and talented Katy. I'm not sure if it was love, but whatever Katy and I fell into, it happened with speed and intensity. Some months later, Sheila announced that she was three months pregnant, and would be keeping the baby. I told Katy the distressing news but she was unperturbed.

The idea of being a father came as an enormous shock. I felt barely able to look after myself, let alone a child. I knew I couldn't go back to Sheila and make a happy little family. Whatever intimacy we'd shared over those last months were out of habit and an inability to face that it was at an end. I'd made a quantum leap into a new world.

At Rapson Road, everyone was involved in some kind of creative pursuit, and we regularly gathered to share ideas and collaborate with artists and musicians in other communal houses. Andy Mason brought out a magazine called *Praxis*, and everyone contributed in some way. The first issue featured a poem of Katy's as well as one of her drawings. Apart from my gigs with Steve and other friends, I also performed at political meetings that were held regularly at the university. In spite of the growing repression in the country, we all engaged in the most hedonistic behaviour, and our use of substances reached an all-time high.

One concert at the university's open-air theatre almost ended before it began, with Steve too drunk and stoned to set up his equipment. The theatre was in a verdant garden on the campus, the stage canopied by huge trees among thick foliage with access through narrow pathways. The main cable to Steve's amplifier became detached while we were setting up, and as he lurched around trying to connect the wires, it was clear he was in no state to perform.

117

Stumbling around barefoot with barely half an hour to go, he stepped on a live cable. He stood there pale and shaking for several seconds before finally leaping off it, shrieking. His younger brother Issy reconnected the cable, and by the time we were due to play Steve was sober from the shock. He played the whole concert without missing a note, but as we walked offstage he collapsed in a bush, moaning and vomiting. At another concert, Issy was on bass guitar when he suddenly keeled over mid-song from an excess of the deceptively powerful Scottish liqueur, Drambuie. No-one batted an eyelid as a muso from the audience stepped onstage, plucked the instrument from the unconscious bass player and continued where he'd left off.

The news of September 13 shocked us all out of our self-indulgent reverie. Steve Biko, who'd been in police custody for two and a half weeks, had died the previous day, after being driven naked in the back of a Land Rover for 1500 kilometres from Port Elizabeth to Pretoria. Biko had become an icon to us, and even though he preached the gospel of Black Consciousness, he'd achieved almost superhuman status. His death seemed unbelievable, and as word spread that he'd actually been beaten to death, we were left reeling by the level of political depravity South Africa had reached.

© Gerald Potgieter

Durban, Summer 1977

BIKO REFUSED TO EAT – KRUGER

The Minister of Justice, Police and Prisons, Mr Kruger, gave details yesterday afternoon showing that the detained former SASO and BPC leader, Steve Biko, had been on a hunger strike when he died on Monday.

Daily News, 14 September 1977

U.S. SHOCK AT STEVE BIKO'S DEATH

The United States has reacted with shock and revulsion to the death in detention of black consciousness leader Steve Biko, that may have a devastating effect on relations between South Africa and America.

Daily News, 14 September 1977

WEST GANGS UP FOR SANCTIONS: APARTHEID UNDER FIERCE ATTACK AT U.N.

South Africa stood perilously close to sanctions at the United Nations yesterday as Western countries announced that they were considering new and concerted action to end the Government's race policy.

Daily News, 27 September 1977

Steven Biko has been taken, and he is one of many.
My son, I hope you never feel the sickness now destroying
Your land that's still so fresh and new.
But the pain has been rearing,
Children prepared for battle, children now all singing
"The body may die but not the spirit,
It's now or never, we're going to make it."

Thabane, Roger Lucey, 1977

DESPITE BEING IN THE MIDST OF such dark political times, I now found myself in the company of likeminded people who were supportive and stimulating. I was writing songs at a furious rate and performing at every opportunity. My pending fatherhood was a gnawing complication at the back of my mind, but apart from that life had never been better, and dreams that once seemed impossible now appeared within range. I went up to Jo'burg for a week in August to open for a well-known folk singer, Ronnie Domp, at Dave Marks's new venue, the Market Café. Dave and my cousin Franny were now married, and he reluctantly agreed to put me on the bill. The gig in Jo'burg was a real breakthrough, and as I hitchhiked back to Durban in post-performance euphoria, I felt the road opening up ahead of me.

I was moving so fast. I can't remember how it came about, but one morning I woke up to find that Katy and I were engaged to marry. As her parents arrived from Jo'burg a few weeks later to meet their prospective son-in-law, I felt I was losing my grip. My world seemed to have become increasingly uncontrollable. For the first time in months, darkness and alienation returned, and I retreated into myself, unable to make sense of my situation. I cared deeply for Katy but the idea of marriage filled me with uncertainty and fear. While there was no possibility of reconciliation with Sheila, I'd promised to accept paternity and be present at the birth. As the day approached, Katy became adamant that I shouldn't attend. She said I'd be chaining myself to a life that would block my development as a musician, and that once I'd seen the child, the die would be cast. Confused and apprehensive, I slid rapidly from confident master of my destiny to tortured, drug-addled kid.

The issue of attending at the birth of my child drove a wedge between me and Katy, but when it came to the moment, I felt had no choice. On 5 September my son Tay arrived, and I was present in the operating theatre. It was a deeply moving experience, and Katy was right: as soon as I held the simpering infant in my arms, a bond was established.

When I returned home that evening, Katy's best friend, Didi, was waiting for me. Her eyes red from crying, she told me Katy was in hospital after overdosing on sleeping pills. This wasn't Katy's first attempt, she told me. The girl I saw in the hospital bed was unrecognisable: her sparkling eyes had gone dead, her skin pasty, her mouth crumpled and twisted. I had just witnessed the birth of a new life, and now here was another seeking to escape life. Katy's parents arrived the following day, and took her back to Jo'burg as soon as she was discharged. I learnt from Didi that they'd already rescued her several times. We'd only been together six months, but it left me deeply shaken.

I began spending regular time with my newborn son. Within three weeks of his birth he was weaned and started spending nights with me. Soon I was also utterly intoxicated by a young prodigy on the local music scene. Nina was a highly talented fifteen-year-old who sang beautiful, intelligent songs in a powerful voice. She was accomplished on guitar and piano and top of her class at school. Despite her youth, she had the wisdom and social graces of one much older, imparted from her elegant French mother. From her father, a Japanese diplomat, she had inherited dark slanting eyes, a mane of thick black hair and a beauty no-one could ignore. We started playing and performing together at the folk club and gigs around town, and our musical collaboration was powerful and unique, although our relationship was never intimate. Nina's mother had married an architect called Robin. I got to know him reasonably well through an initiative I was involved in to convert an old church into an arts

121

centre. He was the architect of the scheme, and was also supportive of Nina's creative liaison with me.

Then the time came to tell Nina's parents about my son. The calm, rational response we anticipated was anything but. All further contact between us was immediately forbidden. I went to try and reason with Robin, but he flew into a rage and ordered me out of his house. I attempted to contact Nina, but soon realised that this battle would get me nowhere. In my heart I knew he was only trying to protect his stepdaughter.

I felt bereft. This remarkable musical partnership I had established was severed, and my life in Durban was a mess. Everything I'd achieved had come with an equal dose of damage. There seemed only one solution: to get out of town.

As a grey summer mist tumbled relentlessly down the hillside, I stood shivering under a bridge with my thumb out. I was at the Howick turnoff, but the sign was barely legible twenty metres away. Ten thirty in the morning and it felt like dusk, yet I knew that as soon as the mist finally cleared it would be blazing hot. A truck pulled up in the swirling distance and I ran falteringly towards it, my backpack banging against my leg. As I approached, the driver lifted his middle finger through the window and pulled away. I hauled the rucksack onto my back again and plodded slowly back to the bridge.

More headlights loomed out of the mist and whipped past. I began to wonder if I was even visible here under the bridge, desperate for a lift.

A police van drove past, then screeched to a stop and reversed at high speed, forcing me to yank my pack further off the road.

"Where you going?"

"Jo'burg," my voice quivered, part cold, part fear.

"What's in your bag?"

"Just my stuff."

"Fuck you. Open up."

I undid the straps and strings and opened the top flap. The cop pulled out a couple of T-shirts, a plastic bag with toothbrush, toothpaste and shaving gear, and chucked them in the grass beside the road.

"Clean up this mess before I charge you with littering, you cunt." He was about my age, but the cruel twist to his lips made him look older.

As he swaggered to the van and drove off, I was tempted to shout after him, but I knew it wouldn't be wise. My heart was thumping from relief that he hadn't caused more trouble, or found the five hundred kaartjies at the bottom of my bag that I was taking to sell in Jo'burg. Things could have got much worse.

A few months earlier, Charl and I had been hitchhiking in the hills outside Durban, on the side of a narrow dirt road leading from the McIntosh Falls where we'd just attended a concert. Robin's little van that we'd borrowed sat sadly on the grass verge, a thin line of smoke rising from its engine. We were draped in kikoys – colourful east African sarongs – to project ourselves as Africans, not Europeans in waiting. That white South Africans were also Africans was a fresh concept. As third, fourth, sometimes even seventh generation South Africans, we'd lost our European roots and had nowhere else to go. It was an idea we were fumbling with in our songs and conversations, but something we felt with power and passion.

We perked up at the sight of headlights coming over the rise – a police van, as it turned out. Constable Kat Ferreira had a shaven head and a moustache like a Mexican bandit. In the passenger seat was a black constable with an assegai[1].

Kat ordered us both into the back of the van, rummaged for his shotgun and handed it to the black cop, then ordered me out again. Before I knew it I was on the ground spitting blood, as Ferreira kicked me repeatedly all over my torso. Finally he grabbed me by the hair and flung me back into the van. Then he grabbed Charl, lifted him by the hair and head-butted him on the nose. It sounded like a cricket bat smashing a pumpkin. Charl's white shirt was splattered red before he hit the ground. He was then shoved back into the van where he collapsed with a groan.

The black cop took my guitar, flute and bag of provisions to the front of the van. Kat pitched the van over the rough, potholed road as fast as he could without actually crashing, flinging us repeatedly against the sides. I clung to Charl in a bear hug to try and steady us both. By the time we reached the tar road, the van was awash with blood and we were in extreme shock.

We were locked up overnight in a Hillcrest police station cell. In the morning they drove us in the same blood-soaked van to Pinetown Magistrate's court.

---

1 traditional Zulu spear

The magistrate glanced at us only once, our kikoys now stiff with dried blood. We were granted bail, and I have no idea how we made our way home to wash the caked blood off our bruised and aching bodies. The next day we returned to the Hillcrest police station to collect my guitar and flute. I signed for them and left. When I opened the flute case back home, there, safely nestled under the mouthpiece, were the two microdots of LSD we'd planned to take at the McIntosh Falls.

At the trial some months later, our lawyer asked Kat why he beat us up. Kat looked at the magistrate as if checking whether such a question even warranted a reply. The magistrate nodded.

"They were wearing tablecloths, your honour." Then, as an afterthought, he added, "with nothing underneath."

At the beginning of 1978, Rick Turner was assassinated in his home in Durban. He was a University of Natal academic who'd been banned and confined to house arrest, and lived with his wife and children just a few streets from my parents' house. Although I'd never met him, he was a legend in lefty circles. On the night of January 8th he answered a knock on his front door and was gunned down by a faceless assassin. The state was tightening the screws on dissent, and this murder sent a message that they'd stop at nothing to "keep the peace".

© Lesley Lawson

Johannesburg, 1978

MAN HELD OVER "WRONG" BEACH

Police activity against coloured people using beaches in the False Bay area designated for whites only has been stepped up. A coloured man was arrested and jailed after he refused to leave Muizenberg beach or give his name to a police officer.

Rand Daily Mail, 29 December 1978

And the highway is just like a prison
From where I'm standing there's no place that near
And the one thing only that's certain
Is that the road is much longer than ever before.
                              The Road Is Much Longer, Roger Lucey, 1978

SINCE MY FIRST APPEARANCE AT Jo'burg's Market Café, I'd been back to Jo'burg several times, looking to break into its thriving music scene. But it was tough getting gigs, and I kept myself alive by selling dagga to many of the famous musicians I admired. By now I had a bunch of songs I thought Dave should listen to, but he was always too busy, and I sensed he was just humouring his wife's little cousin. But when I left Durban after the sad saga with Nina, I knew it was for good. It was the beginning of 1978, and like always, I headed for Dave and Franny, who put me up in a little room behind the house.

I still couldn't get Dave to listen to my songs, so I sought the advice of the elder statesman of South Africa's folk music movement, Keith Blundell. The Blundell family was famous in South Africa, and even had their own show in the newly established medium of TV. Keith had taken his kids out of school for a couple of years, and like a group of gypsies they travelled the country. They played every school hall, church hall, pub and theatre they could find in towns, cities and villages across the length and breadth of South Africa. His eldest daughter, Caroline, was already a regular on the Jo'burg circuit, and the only one who wasn't part of this incredible trek. The other three, Julie, Jonny and Teper, were all multi-talented, and along with their mother Pam, soon became household names across the country. It was a rainy day in Jo'burg as I sat in Keith's study and sang him a selection of my songs. When I finished he took a deep, diplomatic breath.

"Whew... well, it's not exactly the type of folk music I'm used to, but I think what you're doing is incredible. I don't know what to say to you except, don't stop doing what you're doing."

That was all I needed to hear. I rushed back to Dave and told him that Keith had loved my songs. I felt perfectly within my rights to exaggerate Keith's response, but it worked. Dave grudgingly listened as I thundered away, and agreed, finally, to let me headline for one night at the Market Café. Overjoyed, I set about preparing for my first real Jo'burg gig. All I remember about my performance is the lovely, confident young woman who came up and spoke to me afterwards. I was so entranced that my hormones obliterated all memory of what we spoke about.

Sue Cullinan was part of a wild clan who'd come to South Africa from Ireland at the turn of the century. Her great, great grandfather had found the Cullinan diamond, the biggest ever found in South Africa, which ended up in the British crown jewels. The story went that old Thomas Major Cullinan was thrown off a ship in the West Indies for drunken behaviour – their drink was a powerful homebrew called poitín, which was closer to poison, and could cause blindness, madness, melancholy or all three. When Thomas Major finally sobered up he talked himself onto a ship bound for India, but was slung off again when it reached Cape Town. Little did anyone guess that he'd stumble on the biggest diamond ever, or that the woman he picked up at the docks to warm his nights would become Lady Cullinan. Well, that's the fairy tale, but the facts are apparently less colourful. Indeed, it wasn't even Thomas Major who found the stone, but a local serf who received a bicycle in return.

Undeterred by her aura of fame and history, I fell quickly and hopelessly in love with this beautiful young intellectual, who hid her wild eyes behind gold-rimmed spectacles. Three weeks later I'd moved in with her. Peacock Cottage was near an old, disused gold mine where she lived with three other students. Crown Mines was among the oldest mining complexes in Jo'burg, and the cottage was surrounded by huge mine dumps covered with grass and scrub. At the bottom of the garden a grove of blue gums stretched to the distant railway line.

When Katy heard about this new person in my life, she came to visit. We wandered through the blue gums and over the mine dumps, talking about our lives, and finally accepting with some remorse that our relationship hadn't worked out. She was warm and friendly and seemed genuinely pleased at my newfound happiness. We parted with a hug, and I felt glad we'd managed to salvage an important friendship. A few weeks later Katy took a massive dose of sleeping pills and died in her parents' home. Sometime later I passed her father in the street; he didn't seem to recognise me, but when I saw his haunted face, I was glad he hadn't, and walked quietly away.

Sue was reading for an honours degree in political science at Wits, the University of the Witwatersrand. She'd completed her undergraduate degree in Cape Town where she'd also served as secretary of NUSAS, the National Union of South African Students. Her student comrades[1] in this radical organisation were the cream of the country's left wing. Fink Haysom was to become Nelson Mandela's legal advisor and a major player in the Burundian and Congolese peace efforts. Karel Tip and Charles Nupen would play major roles in the legal fraternity, both during the struggle and in the new democracy, among many others from this group who remain important figures today in our miraculous country. It was a crop of students whose legacy in the country's fight for democracy lives on.

Susan was not only gorgeous but smart and outspoken. Why the hell she chose me will forever be a mystery, and I lived to rue the day she did, but back then I wasn't complaining. Up the road from Peacock Cottage was the old mining village Langlaagte Deep, a part of Crown Mines, whose miners had long since moved on to more profitable diggings. Its vacated houses were slowly being taken over by academics, students, politicos and artists. This was Sue's social circle, and I was soon thrust into a world of new, radical ideas and bright, powerful people. I often felt insecure in this exacting company, and at times this insecurity would bubble over into squabbles and fights I'd pick with Sue. But Sue was extremely forgiving, and my shortcomings never seriously threatened the relationship. Compared with the other relationships I'd had in my short and turbulent life, what I felt for Sue was powerful and all pervasive, and I knew I was in for one of life's big experiences.

Peacock Cottage had a large vegetable garden which was tended on Sundays by a group of Crown Mines residents. It was part of the communal ideology of the time, and I eagerly pitched in. Among

---

1 popular term for activists opposing the State

them was Neil Aggett, a friendly, soft-spoken young doctor who was always eager to talk to me about my songs. By this time my songs were getting known around those circles, and Neil would pop into Peacock Cottage on his way to work at Baragwanath Hospital in the nearby black township of Soweto. He always listened intently and then gave a detailed and academic analysis of my new work. Sometimes I didn't understand a word, but was grateful for his input. I secretly suspected him of having an eye for Sue, but he was such a gentle soul, I never said anything.

My songs were becoming increasingly influenced by the spiralling tension in the country. The iron-fisted John Vorster was forced out of office after the Info Scandal[2] and the hawkish former Minister of Defence, PW Botha, became Prime Minister. On the surface, it seemed like things might be getting better as certain legislation was relaxed, but other ominous events foretold bleak times to come. All over the country, activists were getting rounded up and locked away without even being charged. I found myself increasingly busy playing at protest meetings and rallies. Not surprisingly, I was becoming known as a protest singer, and as the days and weeks wore on there was a lot to protest against.

Kessie Govender was a Durban playwright whose work literally took my breath away when I first saw one of his plays. *Working Class Hero* was the story of the trials and tribulations of a couple of Indian bricklayers in Durban. Like all Kessie's work, his powerful political message was wonderfully crafted with humour and pathos in the rough language of the streets. Amazingly, during each performance the brickies would build an entire wall across the stage, which was then dismantled brick by brick after each show in preparation for the next performance.

When the opportunity came to perform at Kessie's Stable Theatre in Durban, I jumped at the chance. The poster was hand printed by Jan Jordaan, now a senior lecturer in art at the Durban Institute of Technology. The theatre was a dark, dingy space in a scruffy building

---

2 Arguably South Africa's most notorious political scandal, this was a secret effort to use State resources to fight a propaganda war against the rising tide of dissent in the country. The plan included bribing international news agencies and purchasing the *Washington Star* as a pro-apartheid mouthpiece. The scandal was uncovered by the *Rand Daily Mail*, regarded by the State as a major influence on liberal thinking in the country.

near the railway station, but it oozed creativity.

Getting to know Kessie was a great joy, and I learnt a great deal from his robust humour and streetwise sensibility. Kessie never really "made it" in theatre, and when he wasn't hustling to get his work produced, he worked in the building trade to make ends meet. The last time I saw Kessie, some twenty-five years after we first met, he'd turned more towards painting as a creative outlet, and was exhibiting a series of works of the Hindu elephant god, Ganesh. As an arts journalist for a television station, I went to Durban to do a feature on him. Unaware that he hadn't been well, I was deeply saddened to hear of his death a few months later. Kessie was one of South Africa's great cultural heroes and his creative legacy lives on in the recently reconstructed Stable Theatre.

I often travelled to Durban for gigs and concerts, and always made the effort to connect with Jabula and smoke a few pipes together. He still worked for DJ on and off, and if he wasn't around to meet up, he was inevitably in jail for a petty crime. Each time I saw him he had more woeful and hilarious tales to tell, but also he looked more scarred and battered. He was slipping steadily and deeply into a dysfunctional cycle, set up by the myriad petty, sticky laws that filled the jails with people simply trying to get by in life.

21

Johannesburg, Summer 1979

FARMER SENTENCED TO JAIL
A Paulpietersburg farmer, Walter Prigge, 27, was sentenced to 12 months jail yesterday for killing a seven-month pregnant woman near his farm on June 1 last year. The court heard that he saw pregnant Mrs Bellinah Kunene carrying a 20 kg log towards the fence on the boundary of his farm. He shouted at her to stop but when she did not, he shot at her. He claimed he fired a warning shot and then fired at her buttocks.

Rand Daily Mail, 4 January 1979

SONGS THAT TERRIFY RECORD COMPANIES
Ever popular Mangles, the squashy little folk club in Braamfontein, is launching into its 1979 programme with old, new and vaguely familiar faces. One sort-of known face has sincere brown eyes framed by long, tousled blond hair. It is owned by Roger Lucey, a 24-year-old who belongs to a stable of singers and songwriters who travel the country and live cheap. His music is "pre-Azanian" and the record companies are terrified of it.

Rand Daily Mail, 4 January 1979

When you hear the dogs bark
You know they're coming near,
So you take your children into your arms
And you try to calm the fear.
You pray to God for mercy
And you hope that you pull through,
But as your walls come crashing down
There's nothing that you can do.

Crossroads, Roger Lucey, 1978

AT THE END OF 1978, SUSAN FINISHED her honours degree with distinction, and the pair of us took her little yellow bakkie down to Cape Town. Johnny Gevisser, who I'd remained friends with since my army days in Durban, was now studying at UCT, the University of Cape Town. He had a way with words and a charm that could get him in and out of trouble equally quickly, and somehow he'd managed to get himself the most idyllic cottage on the slopes of Hout Bay's beautiful fishing harbour, just over the mountain from the city. Here, in a little wooden shed behind Johnny's cottage, we based ourselves for a summer of love. It felt as if all the chaos of my life was finally behind me as my dreams started taking shape, my heart flooded with the love and happiness I'd found with Sue. Andy Mason was down from Durban, and Johnny's house was a buzz of people and music, laughter and loving. Johnny arranged sunset trips to the most spectacular parts of the peninsula, and sometimes it was difficult to remember that the rest of the country was on fire. But in the midst of all the fun and laughter, one incident brought reality back with a thump. Still politically involved since her time at UCT, Sue went to

Me, Patrick and the family chicken

First day of school

Mom and Dad in the tunnel of love

Me and grandpa at the motor race track

Cheeky little bugger

In the mielie field

The Zub Zub Marauders

Happy days with Amanda

The Frontline *magazine article*

On the road with Bill Knight and Dave Ledbetter

Me and Carlo at the battlefront, Huambo, Angola

Hungover at a Savimbi briefing in Jamba, Angola

Shooting the breeze with Peter Godwin somewhere in Angola

In a basement in Grozny with Chechen fighters

In full flight before the crash

In full flight, Nelson Music Room, Duke University, 2009

visit a couple of activists in a squatter camp known as Crossroads, and I tagged along. We arrived at a scene of devastation and horror. The place was swarming with armed police, while bulldozers roared back and forth, crushing corrugated iron shanties with single blows from their massive steel teeth. We ducked and dived around the back alleys, trying not to be seen. All around us people were in disarray, looking on helplessly or scrambling to salvage their meagre possessions. I'd read about these evictions, but the sight, smell and sound of this unspeakable brutality was overwhelming. I can't remember writing the song Crossroads – it was one of many that burst out of me at their own volition – but it brought the fury of the state crashing down on me.

On our way back to Jo'burg, we detoured through the Transkei, stopping in at the farm of one of Sue's friends outside Kokstad, where I'd done some gigs earlier. Mindy's parents owned a most beautiful corner of the countryside, and here, lying together one night in the back of the bakkie, we discussed our options for the future. We'd been talking about leaving the country and joining the ANC, but I was increasingly convinced that I needed to base myself in South Africa to sing my songs. I was also starting to see that joining an organisation could severely curtail an artist's freedom of speech. The more formal of Susan's politico friends already frowned on my undisciplined ways. I was also grappling with the idea that my songs were an important way to raise consciousness among the country's white youth, where it was most needed. We talked into the night without coming to any concrete decision, except that, saturated with love and idealism in the early hours of that crisp, starry East Griqualand morning, we decided to marry.

Sue's mother and stepfather were delighted with our decision. And why not? It was starting to look like a match made in heaven. Sue's one sadness was that her biological father wasn't around to see her grow into the beautiful, competent young woman she was becoming. Douglas Major Cullinan, like many Cullinans, had drunk himself into an early grave when Sue was just fifteen.

For me, everything was coming together; I couldn't have planned it better if I'd tried. I was playing several times a week and my reputation was spreading like a veld fire. Admittedly, many of my gigs were freebies for charities and political organisations, and Johnny Clegg had warned me that once you started you became a target for every organisation in town. But I was flattered and saw it as furthering my career. I was also doing concerts, and even got to play on the main stage of the newly established Market Theatre as support act to the hottest band in town at the time, the Radio Rats. Soon, I hoped, I'd be the star of the show. Sue's mother, Chloe, was editor of a leading women's journal, and introduced me to many of the journalistic fraternity.

In addition to the Market Café, Dave Marks was also running Mangles, a venue always booked with popular musos like John Oakley-Smith, Colin Shamley, Paul Clingman and others. Mangles was a hole in the ground in the middle of Braamfontein. Wits University straddled the edge of Braamfontein, and the neighbourhood was alive with student apartments, restaurants, bars and shops. Mangles was in the basement of a vegetarian restaurant one block from the university's main gate. I'd given my first performance at this wonderful little venue when I first arrived in Jo'burg; Dave had put me on as support act to Colin Shamley, a songwriter I'd revered since I saw him at the folk festival in Durban. Curiously, Colin's audience was mainly bikers, who weren't known for their progressive views. As always, I launched into my set with one of my most strident songs, which went down like a fart in a spacesuit. The bikers looked baffled, and I heard one shout, "What the fuck's he on about?"

I hastily reverted to my old stunt of playing cover versions and telling filthy jokes, and before long had them back onside. Once I'd been in Jo'burg a couple of months Dave gave me the regular Friday night slot at Mangles, and within weeks I was packing the place full. This only took about forty people, but I was on a roll, playing my own songs with the audience squeezing in to hear them. I was also getting calls to appear at political rallies on campus, and before long my Mangles gig grew so popular that we were turning away dozens of people every Friday. It was often so packed I had to force my way through the crowd to the stage with the audience passing my guitar forward over their heads.

Sue had a small inheritance, and one day she offered to sponsor a recording of my songs. Dave Marks's company, 3rd Ear Music, was producing many contemporary musicians at the time, but with the security police monitoring the so-called lefties, he was afraid my songs about forced removals and death in police custody would land his company in trouble. But he swears that I pestered him until he agreed just to shut me up.

When Sue dropped me off that Saturday morning, I'd never seen a recording studio before. It was big enough to hold an orchestra, and one corner held the most enormous drum kit I'd ever seen. A narrow flight of stairs led to a control room overlooking the studio, where Dave and Nino Rivera, the sound engineer, pushed knobs and buttons and sliding things on a mixing desk bigger than my bedroom. Dave had hired the best musicians in town, most of whom went on to become top international performers; I was by far the least accomplished of the bunch. Drummers Kendall Kay and Gikas Markantonatos are now based in the USA and George Wolfhaardt is one of Europe's leading bass players. Dave's younger half-brother Gikas was an awkward, pimply kid who was always sober and got repeatedly fired from rock bands for not being cool enough. Today he drums for the top Chicago blues bands. Other luminaries like Johnny Clegg and John Oakley-Smith made guest appearances. Kenny Henson had been an early hero of mine and had played with the legendary Abstract Truth and Freedom's Children. Kenny and Brian Finch were one of the most successful duos in the country, and it was a great scoop to have him as guitarist on the album. Kenny was one of those musicians who stayed in South Africa and tried to make a living from what he did best in the country of his birth. He made several brilliant albums, which were largely ignored by the industry and the media, and died penniless in 2007 from emphysema.

We were done in two days. I laid the guitar and vocals down with the drums while the other musicians overlaid their parts one by one. By Sunday evening the whole album was "in the can" and *The Road Is Much Longer* was ready for packaging. My one regret is that I caved in to Dave's cautionary approach in selecting the songs we recorded. I wanted the album to be a collection of my most powerful statements on the country at the time, but Dave persuaded me to temper the political tone with a couple of light ditties. By lightening the feel he felt we might avoid the attentions of the security police. A quarter century later Dave and I still argue about this decision. How fine the line is between angry young man and grumpy old fart.

Just before *The Road Is Much Longer* was released in February 1979, we had an enormous fight. He'd taken legal advice on whether a few of the more radical songs should be included on the album. One, Lungile Tabalaza, about a young man who died in police custody, accused the cops of killing him and covering up the murder. A couple of other songs also took no prisoners when it came to hammering the state. The lawyers said we'd be in deep trouble if we released these songs. I was all for releasing them anyway, but Dave was resolute. We finally ended up with a two minute silence where Lungile Tabalaza should have been, and edited a few verses from the other "offensive" songs.

We needn't have bothered. The album caused an almighty shit storm anyway. Dave had printed a few hundred unedited white label copies for promotion and overseas contacts, and somehow some of these ended up in record stores in Jo'burg. Even with all these hassles, the release of the *The Road Is Much Longer* caused a stir. Andy Mason did a series of drawings for the cover and the inside sleeve, the original of which now hangs in my entrance hall. The liberal press reviewed it glowingly, and, ironically, so did certain areas of the Afrikaans press. Dave gave it to the newly established Capital Radio, and a couple of their DJs loved it and pledged to play it. Later we discovered that the programme manager at the time, a hip, coke-sniffing but deeply conservative person, refused to allow it on air. I was once invited to a party where all the Capital Radio personalities were desperately labouring to be cooler than thou. Many were from Britain and had a hip, progressive aura. Among them was Martin Baillie, a very cool but tight-lipped DJ from Northern Ireland. He grilled me intensely about the purpose of my songs, and claimed I was preaching to the converted and setting a dangerous precedent through the accusations in my songs. His interrogation went on interminably until I finally escaped, aware for the first time that these "cool Joes" were mostly a bunch of conservative men in hip clothing. But there were exceptions. Chris Prior and Alan Pearce were different from the rest, and spent their careers swimming against the stream.

Tinus Esterhuysen, the head of radio programming at the SABC or South African Broadcasting Corporation, was enthusiastic about the album. He liked all the songs, he told Dave and Franny, but couldn't play them because they'd "corrupt the morals of the youth". We didn't really expect radio time on the SABC channels, which were mouthpieces of the state at the time, but Dave had hoped that by putting a few soft songs on the album we had a chance. While radio firmly but politely declined to have anything to do with the album, the print media went to town about this outspoken new singer. Some years later, Tinus Esterhuysen got some strong press himself. He'd been arrested for molesting young boys. Curiously, although he was eventually convicted, he never actually served a prison sentence, and still holds a senior position at a leading radio station, no doubt preserving the morals of the youth.

Despite the lack of radio play, *The Road Is Much Longer* quickly achieved notoriety. There was plenty of press coverage and ironically, even though the radio stations wouldn't play the songs, many of them asked to interview me.

We realised that the album had come to the attention of the security police when a plain-clothes cop walked into one of Jo'burg's biggest record stores, Hillbrow Records, and confiscated all their copies. Somehow, several of them were accidentally unedited copies. Meanwhile, Dave had sent a copy to his old mate, Manfred Mann, who asked me to audition for his Earth Band in London. Getting out of Jo'burg for a while seemed like a good idea, and maybe I could get my music heard further afield.

Sue and I got married in April. With the generous backing of her mother and stepfather, it became one of the social events of the year, hippie style. Sue's stepfather, Bernard, was a large, affable, heavy-drinking industrialist I should have hated. Instead we got on famously, and would often demolish multiple bottles of wine over a Sunday lunch. He hated what I stood for and I hated all he represented, but in spite of ourselves we liked each other. The formal part of the wedding ceremony took place in the garden of Sue's parents' elegant home. Sue's mother, Chloe, with impeccable taste, kitted me out in loose white clothes and white suede shoes. The ceremony was packed with the Jo'burg elite down one side, and the musos, artists, hippies and politicos on the other. My mother and father were there, and everyone remarked on my father's charm, master chameleon that he was. A folk band, Flibbertigibbet, who also played at Mangles, provided the music. Dave Williams and his wife Assie ran the group, and Assie had sung on *The Road Is Much Longer*. They launched into a traditional Irish wedding song as a proud Bernard led Sue towards the gazebo where I was waiting to formalise my life with this person who'd so enchanted me.

All I have left of that day is my marriage certificate and the photographs. These days I look at them and I am still taken by the rare beauty of my young wife. Sue later destroyed many of the photos in a fit of rage – like me, she'd inherited the Irish temperament from her father.

That night we went back to Peacock Cottage, where a marquee had been erected covering the entire back garden. The whole of Crown Mines was there that night, and the Radio Rats played on a stage in the corner. Chloe had arranged huge pots of food that were kept warm over a large fire, and the night was thick with laughter, wine, friendship and dagga. It was one of the most memorable nights of my life and it felt like nothing could go wrong. I was on the ladder to stardom and success. I'd won the love and affirmation of a beautiful and intelligent young woman, and we were soon to be on our way to England and the US to continue climbing the ladder. Everyone was in high spirits that night, and Sue and I weren't the only ones lucky in love – the dark corners of the garden and marquee were alive with flirting and kissing. I went to say goodbye to a friend and noticed Johnny Gevisser's VW van rocking in the driveway; as we stood there, the van's side door fell off its hinges onto the ground, revealing a naked Johnny among duvets and cushions with a gorgeous young woman. She'd arrived with someone else that evening, who was occupied elsewhere in the garden among the dagga smokers. That night she went home with Johnny.

The next day Sue and I drove down to the Wild Coast, where friends of hers had a beach cottage among an idyllic settlement of six or seven cottages on a deserted stretch of coast. The cottages were later demolished to build a hotel and casino, but back then it was heaven on earth. Sue and I were insatiable, and took off our clothes at every opportunity, on the beach, among the dunes, even in the fields and on the cliffs overlooking the ocean. A short while later, a red and black spot on my bum was found to be a tick bite, and the resultant fever laid me low for days; perhaps, with hindsight, not a bad thing.

22

Johannesburg, Winter 1979

TERROR RAID MAN ESCAPES FROM JAIL

One of the alleged terrorists who attacked the Moroka police station in May, killing a policeman and wounding five other people, has escaped from custody. The third member of the terror group has been on the run from police since the attack on May 3, which took the police station by surprise. All three were said to have been members of the banned African National Congress. ANC pamphlets were found at the scene.

Rand Daily Mail, 28 June 1979

LUCEY SHINES AT MUSIC FESTIVAL

Last night Roger Lucey signalled his arrival as a major performing artist. His transition from the small solo stage at Mangles club to the concert format was spectacular. Roger Lucey is one of the few local singer/songwriters to give serious attention to his social environment... could be the first to take that awareness and project it through the popular rock medium.

Rand Daily Mail, 28 June 1979

BEACON OF PROTEST

Surprise of the evening was the superb Roger Lucey and his band. His musical statements are the most relevant to come from a South African in years.

The Star, 28 June 1979

Some men take a hard line, and for that they get the rope,
Some men fall from windows, others slip on bars of soap.
Whether innocent or guilty, Lungile died just the same,
And in the halls of justice, the overseers just carry on with their game.

Lungile Tabalaza, Roger Lucey, 1978

BACK IN JO'BURG, *The Road Is Much Longer* continued to attract negative attention, which characterised its short but notorious life. The police continued to confiscate copies as they appeared in record shops, and before long shops refused to have it on their shelves. At one of my appearances at Mangles, the place suddenly filled up with tear gas. It poured into the tiny basement through the air conditioner, and we all spilled into the street, coughing and wiping our eyes. Someone said they'd seen a car full of suspicious men racing away. Someone clearly didn't like my songs, but I was on a roll. I felt invincible.

Just before we were due to fly to London, I was invited to play at a festival at the legendary His Majesty's Theatre in downtown Jo'burg. I was to be the support act for Paul Clingman and his band and a leading black group, Abafana Besishingishane. I hastily put together a band with Dave and Assie Williams who'd played at our wedding. Dave Marks's brother Gikas played drums and we rehearsed for about two weeks before the gig. I hadn't played with a band since Durban, but now it was *my* band and I was out in front.

The festival was a huge success and the reviews were flattering. I'd met with approval. In fact, it seemed like we'd stolen the show. In two short years since arriving in Jo'burg, pushing zol and peddling songs, I was up there with the best in town. And now, with my gorgeous wife, I was about to go international. The only thing that continued to torment me was the situation with my son, Tay. Sue's parents still didn't know of his existence, and whenever I raised it with her she persuaded me to delay telling them. The deception was heightened by the fact that on *The Road Is Much Longer*, Thabane is clearly a song from father to son. But once again we left it.

In July 1979 Sue and I flew to London. It was a completely different experience from my visit there a few years earlier. We stayed with friends of Sue's family, the Sussens, in a pleasant house in Putney. Aubrey Sussens, an icon among South African media and advertising, was now setting up shop in London. He'd left school at sixteen to fight in World War II in Italy and North Africa, and then became a sports reporter for *The Star* in Jo'burg. He was the first South African to win a Nieman Scholarship to study at Harvard, and later founded the PR company, Group Editors, which became immortalised in a South African soap opera based on the firm's shenanigans.

I'd met Aubrey soon after Sue and I got together, and I liked him instantly. He was large and ruddy, and when he drank he took on an almost cherubic demeanour. Aubrey had no sons, and took as much of a shine to me as I had to him. When Sue and I spent a weekend on his farm in Limpopo, I learnt that he'd built all the farm cottages himself, and was now building a road. I stripped to my shorts and dug that road alongside him. Burnt and broken by evening, I was glad to quaff the wine he laid out to ease the pain.

I also helped him slaughter an ox, an event that left us both shaken and ripe for vegetarianism. Aubrey believed that what you wanted to eat you should be willing to kill, and on Sunday morning we cornered the poor beast in the field near the labourers' cottages. There were about five of us including the farm labourers, and somehow the animal understood our malevolent intent. It bolted from one side of the field to the other, and finally stood heaving at the soggy end of the field, nostrils steaming. Aubrey approached cautiously, and slowly raised a .45 to its head. When he fired, instead of the beast dropping, it took off, blood and foam flying from its mouth and nose. Shocked, we pursued the unfortunate bovine. It took about five shots to drop the ox, by which time Aubrey was puffing and clutching at his pacemaker. By now we were completely traumatised, but the business wasn't quite done. The tradition among the people of this region is to build a fire as soon as the animal's dead, and to lightly roast and eat the liver while the skinning takes place. Aubrey and I had to force ourselves to eat that bloody organ, but as he maintained: if you want to eat it, you should be prepared to kill it.

I was inspired by all that Aubrey had built up with his own hands, and that weekend I resolved to build my own dream cottage one day in some faraway place. Little did I realise the significance this would have in my life.

Aubrey had moved to London with his wife Penny, his Rolls Royce and his black South African chauffeur, Phirus. One night we had a meal together at the legendary Indian restaurant, Khan's. Phirus had the night off and Aubrey drove us in Penny's Ford Fiesta. We ate and drank lavishly while I marvelled at the famous faces in the restaurant. After the meal we squeezed into the little car, Aubrey and Penny, their daughter Jane, and Sue and I. It was a balmy summer's evening and still light as we drove home after nine along the Thames. Aubrey was pleasantly pickled and had us in stitches with a tale about his youth. But it took him both hands and his entire body to tell a story, and as he turned to emphasise a point, he drove straight into a car that had stopped ahead. It was a minor bang, but it happened right outside a pub where everyone had spilled out to enjoy the late evening light. The entire clientele burst into spontaneous applause as Aubrey sat shocked behind the wheel. Regaining his composure, he slowly got out of the car and, like a member of the Royal family, waved and bowed to his well-wishers. The applause increased and Aubrey again acknowledged his audience before the two drivers laughingly exchanged details and went off home.

A few years later when our marriage started to unravel, Aubrey took me out for a lunch of prawns and too much wine at Norman's Grill, a well-known eatery and drinking hole on the seedy side of Jo'burg. We spoke and ate, laughed and drank, and eventually he asked me about our marital problems. He was warm and wonderful and never prescriptive or paternalistic. He asked if there was anything he could do to help, but at such times, of course, there never is. There were many who disliked his uncompromising ways, but I didn't have to work with the man, and I just loved him. I never saw him again – broken marriages do that to relationships – but when I heard years later that he'd died up at his farm, I felt not just deep sadness but also gratitude that I'd known and been inspired by such a giant.

In the Sussens' house in Putney, I spent hours in the basement learning and rehearsing songs for my audition with Manfred Mann. They were mainly covers of popular songs, one being Bruce

Springsteen's Blinded by the Light. I'd never met Manfred, and was tingling with anticipation at meeting him and the Earth Band. I imagined a group of supercool hippie musicians grooving around England and Europe spreading good vibes. When I finally walked into Manfred's studio, that image was smashed as surely as the bulldozers at Crossroads smashed those shanties. The guitarist didn't even look up. He sat on a chair, his guitar sitting on his enormous belly, a large bottle of cider at his feet. The bass player grunted in my direction and carried on talking as if I wasn't there. I sat around trying to salvage my shattered expectations until Manfred finally appeared.

"'Ere's ya money, ya cunt," he said to the guitarist, dropping a cheque on the table beside him.

He then introduced himself and settled behind his bank of keyboards.

"Right, let's get on with it then. Blinded by the Light, one, two, three, four..." and off they launched. I was completely disorientated as I reached for the microphone and started singing along. The key didn't suit my voice, so I asked to try it in a lower key. The guitarist mumbled, bitched and played through the chords, but being unfamiliar with the key, the song unravelled a bit. It was one of the most awful musical experiences of my life. I felt like walking out. We finished the song and launched into another, and when we stopped a while later, Manfred ushered me into his office.

"You know, Roger, music for me is like standing at the edge of cliff. Every day I wonder if I'm going to survive or go over the edge. Some days I'm hanging on by my fingernails."

It was like being interviewed for some army regiment rather than a rock band. After a while, he seemed to warm to me and we had a pleasant chat. But he was worried that as a solo artist I wouldn't fit into the group, and that they'd have to alter the key of their songs to suit my voice. What I didn't say was that I wasn't sure I'd cope with his sour, bad-mannered musos.

He asked me to think about it, but I already knew I wouldn't be singing for the Earth Band. For a start, I'd never encountered such a mercenary approach to music, especially from people called the Earth Band. No doubt what seemed mercenary to me was pure professionalism for them, but the whole atmosphere was harsh, without warmth and friendliness. We met a few times after that, but I had little desire to become a singer in a band that did the German club circuit, and pretty soon the whole thing fizzled out. Still, I have the highest respect for Manfred; few musicians have the fortitude to keep going for decades the way he has. It may have turned him into a grumpy old fart, but he's still an incredible musician.

After a few weeks in London, Sue and I rented a Hampstead apartment from a South African friend who was going on holiday. We started meeting up with all sorts of South African exiles and activists. Through these contacts and interactions I learnt the deep sadness that came with exile. Many, like Gavin Cawthra who ran the anti-conscription organisation COSAWR, were wonderful and friendly, and keen to connect with people from home. Gavin and I spent a couple of great evenings drinking warm English beer and exercising our Durban accents. But others were tight and suspicious, and dogmatic about how the struggle had to be waged; these types had no time for humour and fun, and put me off joining the organisation.

I also met quite a few musicians who'd settled in London and were doing okay; Dave Marks had put me in touch with them. What astounded me was how many of them frowned on my assertion that for South Africans, music and politics were inextricably linked. And these were black musicians from the townships. As one put it, "music and politics don't mix, man. You gotta leave politics to the politicians." No amount of discussion would change his mind; he was having a great time in London, and didn't need politics upsetting his apple cart. In 2003 I saw a documentary in which he talked about the pain of his exile and his difficulty waging the struggle from abroad. A lot of personal histories have been rewritten, I suppose. Just as you couldn't find a Nazi in Germany after World War II, it's hard to find a white South African who wasn't against apartheid.

I called on Warner Brothers, as they'd been involved in the distribution of *The Road Is Much Longer* in South Africa, and there was a chance they'd distribute it in England. Their A&R man[1] looked like a gangster with a heavy gold chain and medallion round his neck, and was having trouble with his nose.

"Jo'burg (sniff)? I once shagged a girl from there; huge tits. Lots of pussy in Jo'burg, yeah? Now (sniff) wot's this album of yours? 'Ow many copies you sold in the 'ome territory so far?" He talked incessantly, not giving me a chance to answer.

Finally I was able to explain the difficulties the album was having back home.

---

1 artists and repertoire man: person responsible for signing, developing and recording musicians for a record label

"Yeah, but you should be gettin' radio play, know wha' I mean? 'Ow can you sell the fookin' thing without radio play, you wiv me?"

It was clear South Africa meant nothing to him beyond its pussy ranking, although its increasingly brutal war was making the BBC and ITN most evenings.

"I don't watch the news, mate. Fook tha' for a lark. Too depressin', you wiv me?"

So much for a British distribution deal.

There was also the cultural boycott. This meant I needed clearance from the British Musicians Union before I could play at a British venue. In protest against apartheid, the BMU decided in 1961 that its members would not perform in South Africa. The boycott also applied to South African musicians abroad. I couldn't even do a cameo performance at the local folk club without my union ticket. By the mid-1960s the Irish Anti-Apartheid Movement, the British Screenwriters Guild and the American Committee on Africa had all joined forces in a high-profile effort to isolate South Africa. Soon the movement was in full swing throughout Europe, England and America, with the full support of South Africa's progressive arts community – we'd help by staging protests against artists who broke the boycott.

Somehow, as a vocally anti-apartheid musician, I'd naïvely expected a warm reception from my musical "brothers in arms" in the UK. No such luck. The only real way around it was to go into political exile and apply for refugee status. Many muso's has done this, some of whom could barely string two chords together. A white punk band from Durban had gone to Holland, changed their name to the AK47s and taken refugee status; in no time they had Dutch papers and were on the dole.

All the black musos I'd met had their BMU tickets, even those who insisted that "music and politics don't mix". But when I enquired about my prospects, it was made clear to me that, as a white South African, they were extremely slim. I wasn't ready to give up my rights to my infuriating but beloved homeland, but despite this disappointing news, Sue and I continued to have a good time in London.

Mike Maxwell rode a Triumph Bonneville road bike and had the jacket and boots to match. He and Fink Haysom had been mates through school and university, and Mike was always the one to sort out trouble when boys from other neighbourhoods came looking for a fight. When we met up in London, Mike was now in an old, condemned three-storey house, a London squat started by a Durban friend of his. Far from homophobic South Africa, his friend had finally come out as gay. All the other residents were gay men too, but Mike was secure enough in his manhood not to let that bother him. One night their squat was attacked by a group of gay-bashing skinheads hurling rocks and dustbins through the windows. After a few minutes of this abuse, Mike got up, took off his jacket and opened the front door. The skinheads halted in surprise before the beefy monster standing in the doorway. Mike then walked calmly down the steps, picked up the spade lying in the front garden, and with a sudden roar, charged through the gate at them. They scattered, but Mike's sights were set on the biggest of the bunch, whom he cornered at the end of the street and delivered a thorough chastisement with the flat edge of the spade. The squat wasn't pestered again.

In place of military service, Mike had served in the police force, ending up in the same police station as Kat Ferreira, the cop who'd given me such a beating. One night over tandoori chicken in a Hampstead restaurant, along with Paul Clingman and his wife, Mike described how he'd finished his tour of duty with the police force. Kat had been taunting Mike for months for being an Engelsman[2] and a soutpiel[3], and on his last night of duty at Hillcrest police station, Mike had decided to take action.

Mike's voice rose as he got into the drama of the story, and the two chaps at the next table almost had to shout to each other to be heard. But Mike was in full swing, dominating the small restaurant like Peter O'Toole.

"So Kat looks at me and starts getting up slowly from the stool. 'Jou fokken Engelse naai poes,' he says to me. That's when I grabbed him by the shirt and planted him. I thumped him five times before he hit the ground, then I picked him up by his shirt and thumped him another five times."

As Mike paused for breath and let the story take effect, the raised voices of the conversation from the next table took prominence in the small restaurant.

"I'd like to see that!" enthused our neighbour to his friend.

"Oh you would, would you!?" Mike boomed, turning on the startled pair. "Well, I'll tell you what else I did..." And in vivid detail, he did.

---

2 Afrikaans for Englishman
3 Afrikaans for salty penis, a reference to straddling the ocean with one foot in
   South Africa and the other in England

In the surprised silence that descended over the restaurant, it slowly dawned on Mike that he'd rather misunderstood the situation. In the ensuing apologies and explanations, it turned out that one of the men ran a school teaching English as a foreign language. Before the night was over, they'd hired Mike as a teacher. And he didn't even have to threaten them.

Around this time, I got a message from Dave Marks that one of the bigwigs at Warner Brothers in New York wanted to see me. His name was David Horowitz, Dave said; he'd heard *The Road Is Much Longer* and wanted to talk to me. So Sue and I got US visas and boarded a plane for New York.

We didn't know a soul there, but a friend of Sue had a large house in Boston and had invited her to stay. New York was a little intimidating for a pair of wet-behind-the-ears South Africans, so we caught the "night owl" to Boston from Pennsylvania station, leaving at three in the morning and stopping at almost every station on the way. Late night weirdos and predators slunk around the huge marble halls of Penn station, and as we sat there like desperados, a mild looking man with glasses and a briefcase approached.

"If I were you, I wouldn't stray far from that guitar case," he smiled.

"Why's that?" I asked.

He sat down beside us and started pointing out various people lurking beside the great marble pillars, casually scanning the scene from behind yesterday's *New York Post*. Sue and I had the sense of being in a giant cage with wild predators all around, waiting to pounce. Our guardian angel was awaiting a friend and introduced himself as Mark Shapiro. Surprisingly for an American, he was very interested in South Africa, and knew a lot about what was going on there. He left us his phone number and offered to help us find accommodation when we returned to New York. I was somewhat suspicious of this show of hospitality, but it was nonetheless a pleasant meeting that saw us safely onto the night owl to Boston.

Sue's friend in Boston was a good mate from university, and had married a young doctor from Cape Town. Helen and Raun were wonderfully hospitable, and, like so many South Africans in self-imposed exile, liked to talk about home. When he finished his medical degree, Raun had had to choose between leaving the country or doing time in the military; either way he had to lose a part of himself. The reality of our beloved, beleaguered country was never far away. Yet I

147

was shocked at the level of unbridled racism that existed right here in beautiful Boston. Race riots broke out just as we arrived. A black kid had been shot while watching a sports event, but it wasn't clear where the bullet had come from. Within hours, rumour, conjecture and fury sparked a gang war between youths that threatened to disrupt the city. It was black against Irish, Irish against Italian, Polish against black. The bellicose graffiti on the streets, buses and subways told of a youth divided along racial lines and ready to kill to uphold their ethnicity. To find such deep-rooted prejudice in the Land of the Free and Home of the Brave offered a sobering reality check.

I wasted no time trying to get hold of David Horowitz at Warner. From his secretary's secretary, I realised he was a big fish, and was rigorously interrogated about my business with him. I approached the whole negotiation quietly and modestly, which, I later realised, wasn't the way to do things in New York. Eventually I got an appointment with Nesuhi Ertegun, an executive at WEA Records, a Warner Brothers subsidiary. Nesuhi was the brother of Ahmet Ertegun, known as the man responsible for the Motown explosion. He'd "discovered" Diana Ross, Aretha Franklin and many other superstars. Being of Turkish descent, Ertegun had gained the trust and respect of the black musical fraternity where many white Americans had failed.

Boston was a lot of fun and we went to some really great concerts, the most astounding being Tom Waits at the Boston Square Theatre. Now, having secured an appointment with one of the most powerful men in the record business, I imagined myself up there at the Boston Square Theatre. My excitement was building; I struggled to sleep at night and was becoming too well acquainted with that old rogue Jack Daniels. Back in New York, Sue and I headed to Greenwich Village where another friend of hers offered us a few nights in his loft apartment.

My palms were sweating on the tube to midtown Manhattan to see Nesuhi Ertegun. His office was high in a block beside Central Park, and way down below the figures in the park looked tiny. Nesuhi was short and fat, puffing on a cigar the size of a salami.

"So where ya come from?" His accent had a strong Turkish lilt.

"From South Africa; Jo'burg actually."

"Yeah, I know South Africa. Jomo Kenyatta. Ya know Jomo Kenyatta?"

"He's in Kenya, actually," I offered diplomatically. "Nelson Mandela comes from South Africa, but he's in prison right now."

"Prison? No shit? Well, I guess ya gotta keep ya nose clean. So what can I do for ya?"

I started telling him about *The Road Is Much Longer*, but he cut me short.

"Let me tell ya somtin' 'bout de music beezneez. Ya see dis?" He pointed to a thick pile of records on his desk. "Dis I get send in one week. 'Ow many units ya move back in South Africa?" The cigar salami had gone out and he puffed furiously to revive it.

"Well, actually I've been having a bit of trouble; you see, the police have been confiscating…"

"Jeesis Cries, why ya get da cops involved? What de hell you singin' about?"

"No, no, it's not like that." I was starting to feel cornered. "Could you have a listen to the album and tell me what you think?"

"Listen to me, lemme tell ya one ting. I don't got time to listen to music. I look at figures. Ya got de figures, I look at ya album."

I was finished. I couldn't think of any more to say and my ears flushed. The image of playing the Boston Garden had died just like Ertegun's cigar, which he stubbed in disgust in his ashtray.

Later that night Sue and I met up with Paul and Elaine Clingman. Paul was also in New York seeking a record company for his fine songs. I told them about my deflating afternoon. Paul felt a little comforted, as his endless phone calls still hadn't got anyone to talk to him. The American record business didn't give a damn about South African music unless there was a lot of money to be made. Our big plans had taken a knock, and Sue and I weren't quite sure how to proceed in this fast and unforgiving metropolis.

We needed a place to stay, but the apartments advertised in the newspapers were way out of our price range. Remembering Mark Shapiro, the guy we'd met at Penn station, we decided to give him a call. To our amazement he was genuinely friendly, and suggested we meet near Columbia University. It was an area of upmarket brownstone houses just a block from the Hudson River. Mark told us we could stay in the spare room of the apartment he shared with two Columbia students. The apartment was on Riverside Drive beside the Hudson River, one of the better addresses in New York. It was owned by the wealthy father of one of Mark's flatmates, for whom money was no problem, so they let us stay free of charge.

The room was short of furniture, but Mark was a skilled dumpster diver, and showed us how. There's appalling wastage in the wealthier parts of Manhattan, which dumpster divers thrive on. If a TV set goes on the blink they'll throw it out and get a new one, even if the problem's just a blown fuse or a faulty plug. Just one afternoon wandering the streets turned the room into a comfy, well-equipped space. Mark was a rare breed in this capital of world finance. A committed communist, he showed us many ways to cheat the system, from riding free on the subways to making free calls on public phones. More importantly, he'd sourced several places one could get a free meal, from the Salvation Army to the Hare Krishnas.

Suddenly New York was a lot less intimidating, and Sue and I started enjoying our bite of the Big Apple. During a brief conversation with Dave Marks from a free call box, I told him about my conversation with Nesuhi Ertegun. I also gave him the phone number at the apartment in case anyone needed to get hold of us. A few mornings later Mark woke me saying someone was on the phone for me. I quickly shook the previous evening's Jack Daniels from my head and took the phone.

"Hi Roger, David Horowitz from Warner Brothers. I'm so sorry, there seemed to be some confusion about our meeting." At first I thought Paul Clingman was having me on, so I answered slowly and cautiously.

"I have a gap this afternoon, could you make it?" he asked.

It began to sink in that this was indeed the man I'd failed to reach through his phalanx of secretaries.

If Ertegun's office was impressive, Horowitz's was outrageous. It covered the entire top floor of the building. Central Park stretched out below on one side and downtown Manhattan on the other, with the World Trade Center, the Chrysler Building and the Statue of Liberty in the distance. He sat me down, ordered coffee and asked about South Africa, my life and my music. Attentive and informed, he completely understood the situation I was in back home. He suggested we develop our relationship and that I record new material in Jo'burg that would introduce me to an American audience. He pointed out that Americans knew nothing about South Africa and wouldn't understand the songs on *The Road Is Much Longer*.

After about an hour he looked at his watch. "Mr Ertegun will see you now. I've briefed him about your situation and hope all goes well." We shook hands. Suddenly all my dreams had burst back out in Technicolor.

Ertegun was furious. "'Ow could ya go see Mr Horowitz be'ind my back?" he shouted. "In this building, Horowitz is God! What are ya thinkin'?"

I explained that Horowitz had asked to see me. That calmed him down a bit, but he was clearly miffed at being told to see me again, especially after having dismissed me with such finality. The plan now was that I'd go back to South Africa and record another album, this time on the WEA label. The local record company would give me the necessary support and backing to build my music career.

Meanwhile, it was party time in New York. Sue and I decided to spend a little longer in the Big Apple and enjoy a brief respite from the constant strife, violence and insecurity of South Africa. My newfound status with the record company suddenly got us free passes to concerts and gigs around the city. For a young couple with little money, Sue and I were having a ball. After several weeks in Mark's apartment on Riverside Drive, we stumbled on another lucky break. Sue was friendly with a human rights lawyer from Jo'burg, Shun Chetty, who'd gone into exile. At short notice, he took a job as a United Nations commissioner for refugees, and had to leave New York. He offered us his apartment for which he'd paid three months in advance, and refused any payment from us.

Once again, we'd landed with our bums in the butter. We spent the next couple of months in New York at shows, listening to music and meeting a dazzling array of artists, musicians, playwrights, actors and others who seemed to converge in that great city. My only regret was that I wasn't allowed to play officially, and even the smallest venue in Manhattan required the correct paperwork before you could even take your guitar out of its case. In frustration, I decided to do a bit of busking in Washington Square Park, a popular busking spot; at least I'd be exercising my voice. The park is a popular spot for buskers and I soon found myself a good corner and started belting out my very South African songs. An enormous black man in a sharp suit stopped and listened for a while, settling on a park bench and continuing to listen intently to my slightly rusty repertoire. When I stopped, he approached me.

"Shit man, I bin listening to you an' I'm askin' myself 'where dis cat come from?' Where you from, man?"

"I'm from South Africa, Johannesburg."

"Johannesburg, man I heard of Johannesburg. Near Nairobi, isn't it?"

"Quite near, just a few thousand miles south."

"Shit man, I was right! I'm sitting looking at you an' thinking 'This dude looks like an African' an' hell you are. Let me shake your hand, brother."

He shook my hand warmly and thoroughly and went on his way. If only it was that easy. Back home, the questions of identity, belonging, and where we fitted into the future of our country burned fiercely in the minds of many young white lefties. And many of them were living in places like New York, hoping that the time would soon come when they could return to South Africa and confront these difficult questions.

Paul van Wyk was one such young exile, and we immediately found common ground and formed a good friendship. He was an ordinary boy from Durban who'd left rather than fight someone else's war. He was doing odd jobs around the city and working for COSAWR, fighting conscription in South Africa. He was terribly homesick, and like so many exiles, pumped me for information about the situation back home. This homesickness, fuelled by alcohol and marijuana, always got the tears flowing, and we spent many hours laughing and crying, trying to make sense of our troubled country. Looking at the pain of these young people, I was deeply relieved I was able to return home, despite its violent and uncertain future. Not long after I left the US, Paul got a job as a taxi driver. Late one night, the cops found his body slumped behind the wheel of his cab, riddled with bullets. It was suspected that this was the work of South African undercover agents, but no evidence was ever found. Paul became another silent statistic.

I noticed in London and New York that the exiled politicos were much more meticulous about the company they kept than the politicos back home. In South Africa, if you operated outside of the law you were all lumped together, whether you were an activist or a dagga merchant. Crown Mines was the perfect example of politicos and academics living harmoniously beside drug dealers and other reprobates. It was as if the crazy times we were living through allowed a certain camaraderie that wouldn't have existed in normal times. But times in New York and London *were* normal, and the fact that my songs were strongly political didn't in any way endear me to many of the po-faced politicos we met. By that time, I knew with certainty that I'd never join a political organisation; their rigidity and humourlessness turned me right off. When all was said and done, I was little more than a dagga-smoking muso.

We'd become friendly with a *Rand Daily Mail* correspondent, Richard Walker, who was based in the UN Building. He was the archetypal hack and always poured me a shot of whisky in a paper cup from a bottle he kept in his bottom drawer. Occasionally he'd arrange for us to attend functions sponsored by the UN, one of which was a concert by one of South Africa's jazz icons. It was exciting to hear a local boy who'd made good in the competitive American market, and his show was great, but I was disappointed at how little he referred to South Africa's struggle. He did one song about the migrant labourers and their plight, and I jumped to my feet, fist in the air, and shouted "amandla[4]". He looked laconically into the audience, and said, "Yeah, whatever," and then, as an afterthought, "I see we have some folks from South Africa in the house tonight." Richard Walker told me that he'd become very much the New York jazzman, and had realised that talking about South Africa and its problems wouldn't do his career much good. Later, when I heard him on radio claiming how tirelessly he'd worked to conscientise American audiences, I thought of that concert.

Our visas were running out. New York had been wonderful, but it was time to get back to South Africa. Meantime, Mark Shapiro, who we'd met at Penn station on our first night, had become a good friend. With his marketing background, he'd started advising me about my music career. Despite his commitment to communism, he understood how things worked in New York and was keen to help. Before we left, we suggested Mark come to South Africa with us as my manager.

He gave it a few minutes thought. "Why the hell not?"

And so, armed with a New York manager, we headed back to South Africa for the next phase of my blossoming career.

---

4 amandla ngewethu: power to the people, the African liberation slogan

153

23

Johannesburg, Summer 1980

MUGABE AIMS TO WOO THE WHITES

Mr Robert Mugabe will seek a coalition with the white political bloc if his Zanu (PF) party gains a majority of black seats in next month's elections.

Rand Daily Mail, 23 January 1980

FIVE "DEFIANT" GUERRILLAS DIE

Rhodesian security forces have killed five guerrillas who were defying the orders of the Governor, Lord Soames, to stay inside assembly places, sources said in Salisbury last night.

Rand Daily Mail, 23 January 1980

SOAMES ACCUSES MUGABE OF TERRORISM

The British Governor, Lord Soames, last night accused the ZANLA forces of Mr Robert Mugabe of "intensifying intimidation to the point of terrorism".

Rand Daily Mail, 5 February 1980

NEW DRIVE, NEW LOOK, NEW MUSIC

Roger Lucey, the aggressive rock singer and composer of political lyrics, arrived back in Johannesburg from New York last week with loads of new material and plans for an all-out drive to reach a bigger public.

Rand Daily Mail, 5 February 1980

ON ARRIVAL IN SOUTH AFRICA I picked up flak for having cut my long, curly locks and shaved my beard while in New York. I'd never realised a haircut could have such treasonous overtones. Some saw it as a sign that I'd sold out to the corporate world and the need to create an image, rather than just being myself. I'd grown tired of the daily grind of maintaining a huge head of hair, but that seemed beside the point. Bringing Mark to Jo'burg as my manager drew further derision from sceptics and purists. After all, why not find a manager in South Africa? But among the handful of South Africans who called themselves managers, none saw any business prospects in a young white singer who insisted on attacking the state rather than "playing the game". Despite the sniping and bickering of purists, it was time to get on with my music and continue up the ladder to success. The first thing I did was sign a record contract with the South African subsidiary of WEA Records. But, aware that my real strength was the live concerts, I went straight to the Market Theatre and spoke to Mannie Manim about doing a week of concerts. Always the hard-arsed theatre manager and administrator, Mannie drove the toughest bargains in the business. Today he's Chairman of the National Arts Festival's committee, having turned Cape Town's Baxter Theatre from a white elephant into a thriving venue. Many quake in their boots when Mannie's name is mentioned, but to me back then, he was a saint. He bent the rules and made special deals so I could afford that wonderful theatre, and we booked the Market to launch my new songs in the last week of March, 1980.

Out on the streets, the battle was heating up against the increasingly intransigent state. Archbishop Tutu had launched the Release Nelson Mandela Campaign and, across the border, Zimbabwe was preparing for independence after the Lancaster House talks had finally brokered a lasting peace deal. For the apartheid government, this was further proof of the Total Onslaught we'd been warned about: the dreaded communists and neighbouring black states were massing on our borders. The police and army were given secret mandates to stop them by any means at their disposal, whether it be abduction, torture or murder.

Sue and I moved into a lovely cottage owned by Sue's mother, Chloe, in the leafy eastern suburbs. Mark lived with us, but I started to notice that he was struggling to come to terms with the daily reality of life in South Africa. The ever-present evidence of ridiculous laws to which we were long accustomed shocked Mark, and constantly reminded him of how far he was from New York. He became depressed and spent more and more time in bed. Eventually we took him to the airport, where he said a sad goodbye and headed back to the world he knew and understood.

Most of my songs still strongly reflected the South African situation. But after discussions with the record company, we tried to choose more "accessible" ones for the new album, though I insisted on a strong social element. We haggled a lot. Meantime, I was getting a band together for the Market Theatre concerts. With the help of Dave Marks, we hired the best musicians in town: Jethro Butow on guitar, Les Goode on bass and Steve Spangenberg on drums. I also got an old mate, Gerald Prosalendis, to play some very fiery keyboards.

Part of the deal with Mannie, to keep costs down, was that the theatre supply one technician and I do the lighting myself with his help. On the day of the first concert, I spent most of my time up in the lighting grid, hanging and focusing lights and giving the technician the lighting cues. It was exhausting, and I finished just twenty minutes before the show was due to start. With just enough time for a quick shower before the theatre filled up, Dave told me that the supporting band still hadn't arrived. They were a new band called Era, recently arrived from the Eastern Cape. As a friendly gesture, I'd agreed to let them on board as the support act when their promoter approached Dave about it.

With twenty minutes to go before the curtain went up, we jumped into my old VW and raced to the promoter's office. The door was locked but we could hear voices, so, with a swift kick, I disarmed the lock and we went inside. The group was sitting around smoking zol and drinking beer. The singer, a creep called Stompie Mavi, launched into a heartfelt story about how the promoter had locked them up and forgotten to come and fetch them for the concert. We piled four of them into the car and raced back to the theatre; then I dashed back to collect the rest of the band. They finally started about ten minutes late.

The next day, one of the group confided that the plan had been to force me to play first, so they could headline the concert. A strange show of gratitude. When confronted, the promoter became abusive and accused me of being racist. Years later he was shot by a fellow promoter who caught him trying to escape from a concert with the night's takings. This wasn't the last time I'd see desperate and unscrupulous actions by musicians trying to inch their way up the ladder.

In spite of this slight unpleasantness, our opening night was a cracker. Reviews were generally good, although one critic hammered me for my new "image". He was a loathsome little man who held sway over the music fraternity like a diminutive emperor, and had a reputation for accepting free lunches in return for publicity. We'd evidently forgotten to buy him lunch. He'd given me good reviews before I went overseas, but now he took exception to my flashy clothes and neat hair while singing about the country's problems; he didn't even mention the music, although there was no doubt that the band was tight and my new songs powerful.

It was a difficult time creatively. I needed to market my music to a broader audience, but many in my old support base thought I was "selling out". I was straddling a high wall between two worlds and being pulled from both sides, getting my balls crushed in the process. Still, by the end of the week, the shows had done extremely well, and I *was* reaching a broader, more varied audience. Dave recorded the shows on an old Revox two-track tape recorder for his archive. The recording was primitive, but the tapes sounded so good we started thinking of using them for the next album.

That was how *Half a Live* came about. Half the album was the live recording of the Market shows, and the other half we recorded in a small studio in the heart of Hillbrow. By midyear the album was released, and we started with the marketing plan. The first disappointment was that the radio stations still refused to play the new album, despite the soft approach we'd taken on the political angle and the fact that I was signed to a major record label. The record company was surprised; they'd got tacit confirmation from various radio people that the album would get airplay and support. But once again it was warmly received by the print media, and I forged ahead planning gigs and concerts around the country.

In the midst of all this activity, Sue came home one evening with big, big news. She was pregnant.

I was still doing solo gigs, which brought in a small but steady income. I was therefore really surprised when Mangles refused to have me play there again. After all, Mangles was where my career had been launched, where I'd found my voice and become known on the Jo'burg scene. It was also a guaranteed full house if I appeared. The manager offered no explanation but made clear I wasn't welcome.

He wasn't the only one. I'd meet with venue managers to arrange gigs, and they'd call back a few days later and mumble some excuse about a double booking or a change in their schedule. It didn't happen with every gig, and I didn't mention it to anyone, not even Sue. These rejections were embarrassing after being in such high demand, and I hoped it was just a short run of bad luck.

There were still a couple of venues in Durban where I'd go and play for a week at a time, and during one such trip my old Portuguese mate from school, Neill Solomon, called. Neill was doing really well with his band, The Uptown Rhythm Dogs, with Dan Chiorboli on percussion and Tony "Lizard" Hunter on sax. He'd just had a visit from Graham Jordan, a guy we'd been at school with, who was now a security policeman. He told Neill I was under surveillance for "suspected communist activities" and was heading for big trouble. He wanted Neill to report on me and my musical activity. Neill didn't take kindly to this.

Around the same time, Dave Marks was approached by a plain-clothes security policeman while setting up for a concert at a shopping mall. The cop had a copy of *The Road Is Much Longer* in his hand, and asked Dave what the hell he thought he was up to. He warned Dave that associating with me would bring trouble. Dave got further visits, though he remained vague about these encounters. But it was clear the cops were onto me. I just didn't know to what extent. The head of WEA Records, Derek Hannan and their new head of marketing and sales, Benjy Mudie, issued a press statement saying that in spite of being controversial, they believed in what I was doing and would support me through whatever trouble might arise.

Meanwhile, I was trying to form a permanent band, which proved a difficult task. Many young white musos weren't at all conscious of what was going on in the rest of the country. One hot young guitarist came to see me, very interested in joining the band. After a lengthy discussion over a few pipes of zol, he got a worried look. "Just one thing I don't understand," he said in a sincere voice. "Are you on the side of the kaffirs?" Twenty years later, I overheard him at a music festival saying he'd been fired from a job in his youth because of his support for the ANC.

Conditions in the country were deteriorating. ANC guerrilla activity was on the increase, and so was internal strife. A schools boycott in the Western Cape brought deadly clashes with the police, and thousands of students, teachers and activists were arrested. One ray of hope was the successful election in Zimbabwe. For many of us in South Africa, it was a beacon of hope that democratic change could happen, and that maybe, just maybe, our turn was next.

The Rhodesian bush war was never far away. The South African police fought beside the Rhodesian army until August 1975. Like the conflict in South Africa, it was a war against the majority of the population. I had cousins in Salisbury and as kids we'd spent the odd holiday together, either in Rhodesia or South Africa. In my early teens I'd been to Salisbury, a beautiful city on a high plain in the middle of the country, with sprawling suburbs covered in jacaranda trees and clumps of bungalow-style houses beside huge areas of open woodland. Acres of tall grass dotted with msasa trees were punctuated by small streams and gullies. Even in the late 1960s we were aware of a low intensity war being waged not far from where we played. My cousin Paul had tried to describe how the Rhodesian situation differed from South Africa's. There was no apartheid in Rhodesia, and black and white policemen fought side by side against the "terrorists", he told me. He was about to leave school and join the police force. When I next saw Paul almost ten years later, it was startling to see how our lives had diverged. Like all young Rhodesians, he'd been battered by propaganda and then conscripted to fight an un-winnable war. He'd ended up in a special unit of the Rhodesian police force, fighting "urban terror". Badly injured by shrapnel in a grenade explosion, he'd come to Durban on recovery leave. It was great to see him, but it was clear we lived in different worlds. He may not have died for his country, he told me, but he'd "made damn sure a lot of terrs[1] died for theirs".

That statement drove a deep wedge between us, though I loved

---

1 terrorists

him dearly. By that time I was vehemently opposed to the regime of Prime Minister Ian Smith. In 1965, instead of taking the path of independence from Britain, as many African countries had, Smith had declared UDI, the Unilateral Declaration of Independence. The declaration remained unrecognised by any other nation except the South African government and Portugal, who still controlled neighbouring Mozambique. This marked a new phase in the insurgency led by the black nationalists Robert Mugabe and Joshua Nkomo. It also marked the beginning of a decade and a half of bloodshed and trauma, from which many are still struggling to recover. Years later, Paul came to see those years in a different light, with a new circumspection and cynicism. Thousands of shell-shocked ex-Rhodesians now live in South Africa, many still talking about how the "houties[2] fucked up the country", oblivious of the damage done since Cecil John Rhodes marched in and claimed it for the Queen of England.

My cousin Miranda was working for a TV news agency, and in April she called to ask if I could do a quick job for her. She needed someone to urgently carry a roll of cable to Zimbabwe. They were covering the independence celebrations to be held that night at the Rufaro Stadium, and someone had left the vital cable behind in Jo'burg. Within an hour I had the cable and was waiting to board a plane for Salisbury. It was rumoured Bob Marley and the Wailers would be playing at the celebrations, and although no official announcement had taken place, my head spun at the prospect of attending such a monumental event. I arrived at the stadium with my media pass hanging like the freedom of the city around my neck, and headed backstage with my hefty roll of cable. As I approached, I was overcome by the thick smell of dagga.

Clouds of smoke were coming from a cordoned off area behind the stage. There, among a cluster of massive dreadlocks and women in bright dresses, was Bob Marley, pulling on a huge clay pipe. I would have loved to have a smoke with them, but just watched and smiled and pinched myself, feeling utterly blessed to be there at that moment in history.

Most incredible to me was Mugabe's call to the population to reconcile. He held out an olive branch to the whites to join with the black masses in building a new country. But the ideal was short-lived.

---

2 short for houtkoppe, Afrikaans for wooden heads

There were those who did reconcile, but many white farmers carried on as before, not even acknowledging how easily they had escaped retribution from the victors in the war. A further complication was that the armies of Robert Mugabe and Joshua Nkomo – ZANLA and ZIPRA – started fighting among themselves. ZANLA was made up mainly of the Shona population from the north, while ZIPRA was mainly Matabeles from the south. In 1983, Mugabe sent his North Korean trained fifth brigade into the south, where they killed two thousand in six weeks to quell the Matabele dissent. It was the beginning of a slow slide into nepotism, corruption and torture. How many like me must look now at that once great hope, Robert Gabriel Mugabe, and feel the deep disappointment of seeing greatness crumble into tyranny. It's often suggested that things were better under the old regime. For the whites it certainly was, but for the majority it's hard to know. Whatever the answer, domination of any people over another is always unacceptable.

Life at the time was filled with ironies. Clem Tholet, married to Prime Minister Ian Smith's daughter, was a massive bull of a man whose songs rallied white Rhodesians around campfires during what they called their "war against the terrorists". I found it bizarre that both my songs and Clem's were published by the same company. Whenever I took Dave to task about publishing "fascist" rantings, he pointed out that Clem wrote beautiful songs. His most notorious anthem was a Green Berets-esque sing-along called Rhodesians Never Die. One morning, I was smoking a cigarette outside Dave's office when a large four-wheel drive with Zimbabwean plates pulled up. I instantly recognised Clem, his robust, ruddy face set in stone as he slammed the car door and walked up with a rigid military stride. He'd obviously heard of me, and it looked like he was about to take a swing at me. Instead, he thrust his beefy hand into mine, still scowling.

"Clem Tholet, a fucking pleasure to meet you." I tried to regain my composure. "That song of yours, Lungile Tabalaza, it's the most powerful fucking thing I've heard."

This song was my most strident attack on the South African police force, accusing them of murder. I thanked Clem, and we got talking. I soon realised that the man I'd painted into a "white right" corner was in fact a warm, compassionate person with a wicked sense of humour. My black-and-white view of the world took another huge knock. There were always issues we disagreed on, but we agreed to disagree agreeably. I last saw Clem in 2004 at his home in Cape Town. He'd developed a degenerative disease, which pulled his hands into hard, claw-like shapes so that his fingers were unusable. Several fingers had been amputated, and his beloved guitar sat dejectedly in the corner. I brought him a copy of my new album and he listened intently as we drank beer. He was barely able to move, and his wife, Jean, lovingly filled his glass and brought him a snack. As the music played, his eyes sparkled with humour and mischief.

"Fucking brilliant," he said. "Don't ever stop playing."

At his funeral a few weeks later, I fought back tears as his beautiful song, Peace Dream, filled the ugly Methodist church.

But back in 1980, dreams of peace were a long way off, and my own dreams were starting to unravel. Yet I couldn't put my finger on what was wrong. The cracks began to show, and I was growing frustrated and moody. On the way back from a party in Yeoville one night, Sue and I had an almighty row. I don't recollect what it was about, but suddenly the world exploded and we were lashing out, screaming and swearing. By the time we got home the madness had lifted slightly, but when I saw the bruises and welts I'd inflicted on my beautiful young wife, I felt like dying. Sue quickly gathered up her things and left for her mother's house. I sat there like a country singer, drinking whisky and cursing myself. I'd crossed a sacred line. It would take me a decade to come to terms with it, but I could never uncross it. I felt I'd become like my father, which alone was a source of deep shame. While we managed to patch things up fairly soon, it was never the same, and I cursed those Irish genes that could fill my head with such steam and anger.

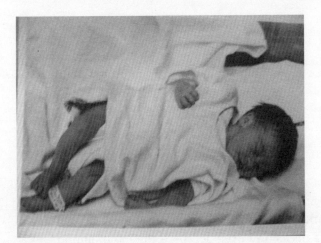

Johannesburg, Spring 1980

WHAT THE REAGAN WIN MEANS FOR S.A.

The impact of the landslide victory of Mr Ronald Reagan over Mr Jimmy Carter and the defeat of many of South Africa's most powerful United States critics in the Senate is set to resound to Pretoria's advantage. The threat of sanctions is likely to recede and a much more conciliatory US attitude on the arms embargo and the supply of nuclear fuel is being predicted.

Rand Daily Mail, 6 November 1980

U.S. ACTOR IN COURT FOR DAGGA

American actor and TV star, David Carradine, appeared in the Johannesburg Regional court yesterday charged with possessing 141g of dagga. Mr Carradine, 42, staying in a Johannesburg hotel, is in South Africa to film Rally *– a motor racing comedy.*

Rand Daily Mail, 6 November 1980

I CONTINUED DOING SOLO GIGS AND ANY other work I could lay my hands on. On one occasion I even accepted the job of announcer at the Market Theatre for a concert by David Carradine, an American actor who was making a film in South Africa. In the dressing room before the show, he started showing me his prowess as a martial arts expert. He almost knocked my head off demonstrating a routine he'd performed in a karate movie, and aside from my head, he also knocked a jug of water all over the dressing room. He calmed down a bit after I made him a huge joint, which he smoked all on his own with his cowboy boots planted on the make-up table. He then floated onto the stage and stumbled from song to song, while the audience slavishly applauded.

I was surprised to find his performance amateurish and lacking in substance. But if he was good enough, then so was I. It was enough to convince me that it was time to form a new band and hit the big stage again.

I called the band the Zub Zub Marauders, zub zub being township slang for okay, alright or cool – and I'd finally found the musicians to make it happen. My old friend Titch came up from Durban to play drums and Jonny Blundell agreed to join on electric guitar. We had a few false starts with bass players, one being Jeremy Crutchley, who was to become one of South Africa's greatest actors. Jeremy was a good bass player, but just couldn't keep his mind on the music when surrounded by gorgeous women in the audience. He'd lose his way and play bum notes while checking out prospects from the stage, and finally we had to say goodbye to him.

Jonny and I heard of a young woman, Ilne Hofmeyr, playing bass in a pub duo down on Rockey Street. As soon as we heard her, we knew she was the one. It wasn't so much her playing as her charisma that we found alluring. She was so tiny she looked almost ridiculous as she worked the elongated neck of her Fender Precision bass. Her enormous blue eyes sparkled with mischief as she bounced around the smoky stage. She wasn't the greatest bass player in town, but she was far and away the greatest looking one, and the following morning she started rehearsing with us. Sue was patently uncomfortable with this new band member, a situation not helped by the fact that she was by now an uncomfortable eight months pregnant. Aware of Sue's insecurity, I tried to allay her fears, and spent my free time at home, cooking, washing and doing chores most South African men wouldn't be caught dead doing. I also attended prenatal classes with Sue at the active birth unit of Jo'burg General Hospital, where fathers were encouraged to actively participate in the birthing process. In spite of my violent lapse, months earlier, I saw myself as a progressive father-to-be, and was ecstatic at the imminent arrival of our baby.

When Sue's first contractions rippled through her tight, shining belly, I was ready and prepared. We raced off to the hospital in the little white Volksie, pausing for Sue to puke out the window. The midwife did a brief examination, told us to calm down and sent us to the waiting room. I spent the next several hours deep breathing and shallow breathing with Sue, then racing to the midwife's office to be told to calm down and carry on. At every whimper from Sue I thought the baby was on the way, but finally after several hours, I was told to scrub up and get my sterile gear on.

In the theatre, I stood at Sue's head as the midwife peered between her legs, Sue pushed and shoved, cajoled and screamed, and moaned and puffed and panted until a little head of thick black hair appeared. Actually, it was a frightening sight: the hair was slicked down and covered in vernix, looking like a deformity on top of the crumpled, purple little face. She gave a small breathy cry and was immediately placed on Sue's breast. As I looked at this tiny, icky, gooey little girl, her face began to uncrumple, and she lay quietly while her exhausted mother laughed and cried as if they were all one sentiment. After a while the baby was bundled in a thick swathe of soft blankets and handed to me. Her little face kept changing shape as she recovered from the traumatic experience of being pushed through a space clearly way too small. She lay quietly in my arms and then, with a small sigh, opened her eyes. They were large and dark, and I knew immediately that these were the black eyes of our Irish Romany ancestors.

Being part of her birth was a monumental experience, and in the weeks that followed, we drifted in an idyllic nuclear bubble, with the beautiful little Amanda at the centre of our lives. But childrearing is difficult, and pretty soon the strain started to show on our fragile marriage. The Zub Zub Marauders were getting lots of gigs, and late nights and rock 'n' roll didn't sit comfortably with homemaking and baby care. Sue wasn't the Earth Mother type, and grew resentful that I was out getting glory while she was stuck at home holding the baby. But the band was on a roll, and whatever had previously put obstacles in my way seemed to have disappeared.

One venue we played regularly was Le Chaim, another hole in the ground, this one in deepest Hillbrow. It was the basement of a Jewish residential hotel and was run by the hotel owner's son, a lovely man called Dave Goldsmith. He was committed to promoting local music, and many of South Africa's best groups and artists kicked off their careers at Le Chaim. Dave Marks, meantime, had started a venue nearby called the Chelsea, along with the Austrian ex-Olympic swimmer Herbert Scheubmayr, who went on to create the legendary Jo'burg club, Jamesons. What with these venues and a variety of bars along Rocky Street, we were kept fairly busy. At home, I was obsessed with my baby daughter, and very much a new-age father as I fed and burped and bathed and changed nappies and got up at all hours of the night. But the distance between Sue and me was increasing, and instead of dealing with it at the time we just let the increasing chaos of our lives overtake us. As we grew more alienated from each other, I found myself fighting off an intensifying warmth for Ilne.

To outsiders and even to Jonny and Titch, it must have looked like the typical rock 'n' roll scenario, but for me it was a period of pain and torture that brought incalculable damage to all our lives. By early 1981 we were one of the most popular acts in Jo'burg, and preparing a Cape Town tour. Cape Town in February is one of the most beautiful places on earth, and just as Sue and I had fallen in love in this special place, it now worked its magic for me and Ilne. Soon we were embroiled in a deep and passionate relationship. Jonny and Titch were vocal in their disapproval, but the damage was done and I didn't have the fortitude to end it. The gigs became almost secondary as we accelerated into the madness of our infatuation, and by the time we got back to Jo'burg there seemed no way of avoiding the turmoil ahead.

It came sooner than expected. Arriving unexpectedly at Jonny and Ilne's house, Sue found us in the bedroom instead of the rehearsal room. The fallout was massive and immediate. Sue told her mother, who called mine. My mother accused me of behaving just like my father, while Sue packed a bag and left for her mother's house with Amanda. Reeling, I was left with the realisation that in a few passionate weeks, I had wrecked my marriage.

So toppled the first card in a deck that was soon strewn like litter across my life.

The phone booth outside Kentucky Fried Chicken stinks of piss. I stretch the cord to stand outside and escape the stench. But it's too noisy out here on the corner of Rockey Street and De la Rey, so I go back inside as the phone rings in my shaky, sweating hand. Her voice is hard and uncompromising as I try to coax her into conversation. A man with a ruddy red nose and tragic eyes waits outside the phone booth, and I turn away to escape his impatient gaze. Yeoville is full of desperados, and with my dirty jeans and stained green jacket, I look like just another one. Which I am. There's nothing left to say. She's silent on the other end of the clammy receiver, and its beep-beep-beeping is telling me to pay up or fuck off. I put my hand to my chest, not sure if this pain is physical or emotional. It's physical, like an injury, a wound. I'm struggling to breathe. My stomach is knotted, my mouth dry and bitter. I cross the busy street to the block of flats on the opposite corner. The staircase is like a prison cell, cold and ugly, shithouse graffiti scratched on the walls: *Hannes is a poes*; *I naaied Sandy van der Westhuizen*.

Ivor Powell is an artist who's let me stay in his spare room. I have no money for rent but I've offered to clean the flat and fix the broken light fittings. The pot plant is full of cat shit and as I gather it up, I'm suddenly overwhelmed by the smell, but don't make it to the bathroom in time. Now I have to clean my own disgusting vomit as well as the grimy bathroom floor. I sink onto the narrow bed, my eyes damp from retching, but the tears now coming from deep inside me. I sob and weep and pull at my hair. It's not even four years since we returned from New York, and somehow I've managed to turn my dream into a little corner of hell.

It's not possible to reflect the events of that time accurately; I have vast holes in my memory brought on by my increasing use of Wellcanol. I was introduced to this killer opiate by an anaesthesiologist among my friends, who to this day still wrestles with the allure of narcotics.

Wellcanol is a bright pink tablet used as a painkiller for terminal cancer patients. Resourceful Jo'burg junkies discovered that by mixing "pinks" with water and sucking it into a syringe through a cigarette filter to eliminate impurities, you could inject it straight into a vein. The effect is so dramatic that many junkies keel over and choke to death on their own vomit. The initial rush feels like intense but pleasurable pins and needles all over. Then it hits the stomach, and if you've shot too much, whatever is in your stomach becomes a projectile. But Wellcanol's painkiller properties, for both physical and emotional pain, are extremely efficient, and what started as the odd hit soon became my daily routine.

Sue moved back to Crown Mines while I moved in with the rest of the band into a dark, cold place in Doris Street on the edge of Hillbrow. My room was a typical junkie's den with a foam mattress on the floor and a single bare light bulb dangling from the ceiling. I had no furniture, and piled my clothes on shelves fashioned from packing crates and bricks. But the pinks also took care of discomfort, along with the pain and memories. Sadly, things hadn't worked out with Titch. It was as if his time in the terrible Greefswald detention camp had left permanent wounds on this gentle soul, and he couldn't keep focused on the difficult task of professional performance. The Cape Town tour wasn't a happy time for Titch, and when we returned to Jo'burg he left the band, took his wife and two daughters and went back to Durban.

Musically, it was a strange time. The punk scene was becoming big in South Africa, and I always found it weird that these wealthy, upper middle class kids were singing about British working class problems. We were friendly with some of the punk bands, but I always took issue with their refusal to address the issues in their own backyard. It may have been an important social movement in Britain, but I still believe that in South Africa it was just another distraction for white youth from the country's real problems.

Jonny had met a sensational seventeen-year-old drummer from the coloured township of Bosmont called Ian Herman, and within weeks Ian was in our band, living with us in Doris Street. But Ian's virtuosity on the drums started showing up Ilne's shortcomings as a bass player. Still, we forged ahead and tried to play as often as possible. But an old problem was starting to resurface. Slowly, almost imperceptibly, gigs started drying up and getting cancelled. Several venues where we'd packed in audiences started saying they were too fully booked to fit us in. An old friend, Tony Campbell, who had started 3rd Ear Music with Dave Marks, was doing the bookings at Le Chaim, and regularly put us on, but in many other places we'd suddenly fallen from grace. At an open-air festival in Soweto, we were about to walk onstage when the promoter ran up and told us that there was a problem and we couldn't go on. He refused to look me in the eye or give reasons, but he was clearly shaken. It became more of a battle every week to get enough gigs to survive, and we even thought of turning ourselves into a cover band to earn money. My dependence on pinks had become a daily routine, and much of what I earned went to maintaining the habit.

The events of the previous few months were as traumatic for Ilne as for me, Sue and everyone else caught in the crossfire. Ilne moved into a communal house a few blocks from Doris Street, and we still saw each other outside of band rehearsals and the ever-diminishing gigs. But I couldn't have been much fun to be around. The illicit excitement of our relationship had given way to guilt and anguish, and I suspect she'd already decided to move on from the relationship, but she wasn't about to walk away from the band. I wandered around, punch drunk and oblivious, unable to pick up the signals as everything became a muddy, messy quagmire.

One night during a particularly energetic set in a club, waves of darkness slowly descended on me as I stood singing. I woke up in the dressing room, surrounded by anxious friends. Until that point I'd been able to carry on my daily activities fairly normally, but now the drug began to disrupt my pretence of normality. What had been a secret habit became known to the rest of the band. Everything was falling apart. I tried desperately to stop shooting up, but the harder I tried, the more I realised I was hooked. One consolation was that I was able to spend more time with Amanda, even though I'd become useless as a breadwinner. Sue had started working for a radio station, and Amanda needed looking after.

Then came another excruciating twist in the road. Jonny and Ian had been working on new, more intricate arrangements and felt Ilne wasn't up to the task. They told me it was time to get a new bass player. I agreed, but couldn't bring myself to tell her. Like a traitor, I went out for a drink while Ian and Jonny gave her the bad news. A further blow came when the guys at WEA Records suddenly refused to have anything to do with me. They stopped taking my calls and wouldn't see me when I went around to the WEA office.

One freezing morning in Doris Street, Tony Campbell's girlfriend wandered into my room and found me out cold with the needle still in my vein. Beverley Oskowitz was a nurse and a beautiful, gentle woman who immediately set about helping to get me off the pinks. She got me various supplements as well as a medication similar in effect to methadone, which is used to help junkies rehabilitate. But it took a while before I was able to escape the seduction of the drug and its remarkable efficiency in blocking pain. I only realised its power over me once I tried to stop. Nonetheless, knowing that people like Beverley were in the world made a huge difference to my resolve to break the habit.

Before long, I'd run out of money, had no work and no legal way of earning anything. I had only a mattress on the floor, some bricks and boards as shelves, a few meagre possessions and an old sheet tacked up as a curtain. The only things I owned of any value were my two guitars and a soprano saxophone.

And so it was that I opened the door to Eckie, a musician I'd known since boarding school days at St Charles. He used to play at the Arab coffee bar, and I'd bunk out to listen to him on a Sunday night. He was part of a group of young radicals, along with Tim Dunne, Jeremy Hurley and others, and he looked the part with his John Lennon spectacles and long hair. He'd played together with Jonny Blundell, and had heard from him that I needed to sell some instruments to raise money. So he came around to Doris Street and sat scratching his chin, looking lugubriously at my Gibson 335 and my Yamaha soprano sax.

"Not much market for second-hand instruments these days, you know." Beneath his cool exterior lurked the heart of a cunning street trader. "You won't be able to move them at the music shops. And it's not like I need these things. But I tell you what, I'll give you three hundred for the guitar and five for the sax."

I'd recently spent three hundred rand getting a flight case made for the guitar, but I was so wasted by the pinks that I agreed and took the money. Later I mentioned the sale to a friend who worked at a music shop.

"Are you fucking crazy? The horn alone's worth twelve hundred."

I saw Eckie on TV many times after that, playing his bargain saxophone. After South Africa's transformation to democracy, he became a senior music producer at the SABC.

It's July 1971 and I'm gated at St Charles for yet another weekend, although all Brother Brendan has on me is the sweet smell of tobacco on my clothes. One consolation is that Eckie is playing on Saturday night at the Arab coffee bar in Friars Lane at the bottom of town. Our dormitory is like an army barracks: thirty-six beds and only Brian Boyd and I in residence for this long, lonely weekend. Boyd doesn't leave his bed once. Tim Dunne is a resident student teacher who takes over Brother Brendan's duties on weekends. Fuck knows what Brother Brendan does with his free time. But Tim is cool, a political activist and, like Eckie, a member of the student council at the university adjacent to our college. Tim probably knows I'll slip out through the shower window and down the back stairs.

I can hear Eckie from the far end of Friars Lane, a narrow cobbled street crowded with gloomy British Colonial architecture. These buildings seem so incongruous in this dusty little South African town, but the basement with its deep recesses and low arches is the perfect setting to hear Eckie play. Like a growing number of South Africa musicians, Eckie's songs shout against injustice and fire our youthful revolutionary zeal. During the break I join Eckie and a clutch of university students in the alley where we take turns pulling on the small clay chillum Eckie has carefully packed. We hold in the great clouds of smoke and then release them into the still, warm night, coughing and keeping a keen eye for passing cops. None of these guys really talk to me; I'm just a laaitie[1] hanging round the fringes.

The walk back to St Charles takes me past the racecourse and through an open field below the cricket oval. From there I see Tim's light still on, so I creep quietly up the back stairs and ease through the shower window. Suddenly the light blazes on and there's Brother Brendan, thumbs tucked into the pockets of his robe, his mean little mongoose eyes burning with fury.

I find out the next day that Tim's been picked up by the security police. I get six of the best and am gated for the rest of the year. The police round up all the other student activists, leaving a fog of fear and anxiety on campus.

Three weeks later I pick up a copy of the *Sunday Tribune* lying on the table outside Brother Brendan's office as I wait for yet another caning. On the second page I read "POLICE SPY EXPOSED. The Secretary of the Students Representative Council yesterday revealed

---

1 lightweight

171

to the Tribune that her friend and colleague, Mr Eckie Eckhart..."

Eckie owned up to the students' accusations and begged forgiveness from those he'd betrayed. He'd grown up in a conservative Afrikaans family and felt torn between the South Africa his family occupied and the one he'd discovered through the lefties at university in Pietermaritzburg. Over time Eckie's muso friends forgave him and he regained prominence in entertainment circles. Jonny Blundell appealed to me on several occasions to put the past behind me, insisting that Eckie was now a different person. I still had a lot to learn about forgiveness, but as Eckie relieved me of my instruments, I still wasn't convinced. The memory of his treachery to those heroic young activists in Pietermaritzburg still lingered.

With a sense of remorse and humiliation, I moved back to Crown Mines. A friend, Moira de Groot, let me stay in the maid's room behind her house – a corrugated iron shanty with a cold concrete floor – but a roof over my head at least, and closer to Sue and Amanda. We'd been seeing a family therapist, and despite the seemingly irreparable state of our marriage, I still felt a ray of hope that we could recover and start again. Despite the deep feelings I'd developed for Ilne, I wanted nothing more than to be reconciled with my wife and daughter. Sue had taken the betrayal badly, which occasionally brought out the worst of her wild Irish genes. I'd regularly walk down the quiet road on the outskirts of Crown Mines to Sue's house to pick up or drop off Amanda. During one of these walks I saw one of our neighbours at the end of the road, the young lawyer David Dison, who was friendly with both Sue and me. Suddenly, Sue's car raced around the corner straight towards me. The determined, manic look on her face suggested a devilish mission, and I leapt into a ditch, her car missing me by inches. She drove on and I dusted myself off. Our lawyer friend had disappeared. When I asked him later if he'd seen the malevolent little episode, he replied, "No way, china!" He'd quickly turned his back and ducked around the corner. "I wasn't going to be a witness to *that* murder."

Jo'burg winters can be bitter, and Moira didn't mind me spending evenings in front of her fire in the living room. She was out the night Sue banged on the front door to be let in. Through the window I saw she was carrying a large bag, and I sensed she was up to something wicked. I asked her to leave me alone, but she persuaded me to let her in. She sat talking for a while, then started surreptitiously feeling around inside her bag. On impulse I jumped up and grabbed the bag. In her hand inside the bag was a hammer, and her eyes flashed with revenge. I quickly took it away and bundled her out the door, locking it behind her. I couldn't blame her for her anger, but these displays made it damned difficult for me to show contrition.

To be fair, it wasn't only Sue who was volatile. We once had a heated conversation outside her house, she in her car and me talking through the window. As always, it turned nasty. Bickering turned to shouting, and I kicked the car door in a fit of rage. In my fury I hit the chassis instead of the side panel, breaking my foot in a dozen places. Sue drove off leaving me hopping and swearing in the quiet, potholed street.

One morning I woke up and surveyed the battleground around me. The band was all but dead, it was over with Ilne, I'd sold all my instruments just to stay alive, and I still couldn't stop shooting that bright pink poison into my veins. I'd managed to hold onto my old acoustic guitar, but it was cracked and broken, as if it had been through a war.

It was time to do something about the disaster of my life. But first I had to get off the pinks. So I packed my broken guitar, my small cardboard suitcase and my battered pride, and hitchhiked home to my mother.

© David Goldsmith

25

Johannesburg, Summer 1982

TWIN BROTHERS DIE IN LANDMINE BLAST
Twin brothers were among the three national servicemen killed in the second landmine blast to have claimed lives in the Operational Area this week. Pieter and Ockert Kruger, the youngest sons in a family of five children, would have celebrated their nineteenth birthdays next month.

Rand Daily Mail, 22 January 1982

TINY JANIS CHARMS CITY BY BEAUTY OF HER BALLADS
Toast of the Golden City... The imaginative ballads of tiny songstress Janis Ian have proved so popular with Johannesburg audiences that seven extra shows have been added to her Johannesburg tour.

Rand Daily Mail, 22 January 1982

IT WAS MONUMENTALLY HUMILIATING having to own up to my utter defeat at the hands of my own bad judgment, especially to my mother, who'd told me all along to get a proper job and settle down. All her friends – with the exception of an eccentric but affable Irish woman called Pat Bailey – knew I was a ne'er-do-well, and I'd fulfilled their expectations. Pat Bailey, on the other hand, had treated me with dignity and respect since my early teens, and in many ways she was something of a mentor to me. Pat was sister to the author, Edna O' Brien, and had an understanding of people with creative aspirations. She was the one person I could talk to about the shocking state I was in. My mother, surprisingly, was quietly understanding, and even helped administer the various injections that aided my recovery.

All the stories about withdrawal are true. It's an excruciating process that involves regular and undignified explosions from both ends, and sweaty, sleepless nights. The discomfort and lack of dignity, however, are nothing compared to the depths of despair and depression that come with cold turkey. For me, getting through that terrible blackness was far, far worse than the physical distress of withdrawal. After about three weeks I started feeling better, and readied myself to go back to Jo'burg to try and put my marriage back together. Three weeks of home comfort had helped me to negotiate that tricky detour in my life, and all I had to do was endure the odd lecture from my mother telling me what an irresponsible fool I'd been. In the months ahead I'd have the occasional slip into Wellcanol's dreamy tranquillity, but eventually I was able to turn my back on it forever. But addiction never quite goes away, and other substances still came to haunt me and undermine my sanity.

Sue agreed to let me move back in with her at Crown Mines, but I needed to start earning money. Dave Marks was still running the

Chelsea, and needed someone to run the door. I was happy to do anything to earn a few bucks, and a few nights later I was sitting at my little table taking money, issuing tickets and stamping the backs of punters hands. As one young couple walked down the stairs, I heard a muffled whisper.

"Shit, that's Roger Lucey! How the hell did he end up on the scrap heap so quickly?"

The following night I couldn't drag myself back to the Chelsea. Instead, I went out and bought a couple of pinks to ease the humiliation. I called Dave and told him I wasn't well, but it didn't matter much to him because Stan James was always around and he needed work. Stan was a tall, skinny, good-looking kid who wrote some of the best songs in the country. He lived around the corner from Mangles, over the road from Wits University. In the flat next door lived James Phillips, who'd been the singer and guitarist of the band Corporal Punishment. James had gone back to university to study music, and this is where he and Stan had hooked up.

Stan became one of my closest friends, and I was constantly amazed at the stories he told of his talented but whacky family. Stan's father had grown up in a Jewish orphanage in Jo'burg, and gone to England as a young teenager where he started boxing in the booths of East London. They were bare knuckle fights to the finish, and the young Alf James soon became a legend. He went on to become a British champion, Commonwealth champion and South African champion, but often ended up on the wrong side of the law in prison, both in England and South Africa.

Stan's older half-brother, Davey, was a singer and songwriter who produced *Ballads of a Working Man* in the 1960s, one of the first albums of original songs in the country. Listening to Davey's incredibly pure singing voice, you'd never know he had a stammer that made it impossible to conduct a conversation. Tragically, Davey was a deeply tortured soul who ended up in the psychosis ward of the Sterkfontein Psychiatric Hospital. One day he escaped and headed for Jo'burg with a bunch of warders in hot pursuit. Near the railway station he leapt over a wall in a desperate bid to shake off his captors. On the other side, unfortunately, was a railway line dozens of metres below. On the way down, Davey hit a high voltage cable and lost an arm and an eye before he hit the ground. He was taken back to the hospital. Stan and his brother, Alf Jr, went to enormous lengths to get Davey out of the institution and back into the world outside.

They started having him for weekends, and soon moved him in with them fulltime. But he never managed that difficult transition, and lived out his days in the Sterkfontein Psychiatric Hospital, where he finally died. *Ballads of a Working Man* is a great contribution to South African music, well worth the effort required to track it down and listen to it.

Dave Goldsmith, meanwhile, was looking for a barman at Le Chaim, and I asked him to give me a try. I'd recovered from my previous humiliation at the door of the Chelsea, and was so broke I'd have done anything for a buck. I was also on a very short leash with Sue, and I needed to pay my way to start showing I was serious about reconstructing our marriage. I started at Le Chaim right away, and quickly got into the rhythm of keeping the thirsty customers well plied with drinks. Every so often I'd grab my guitar and do a couple of songs while the band took a break. Things seemed to be looking up, as I slowly drifted away from the seductive allure of the pinks.

Tony Campbell did the booking and the sound for the bands, and was a great friend at this trying time. A stalwart of the folk music scene during the seventies, he'd helped Dave Marks establish the sublimely subversive Free Peoples Concerts. Dave started the concerts to get around the socially and creatively restrictive laws that governed who could listen to what music when. Keeping the concerts free of charge exploited a loophole in the law, allowing black and white musicians and audiences, albeit just for the day, to get together in a show of peace and solidarity. Tony was a solid and consistent friend throughout those bewildering times, yet he passed away almost unnoticed from cancer, far from his friends in a hospital in Canada.

At home, Sue dreamt up new and ingenious ways to make me atone for my poor judgment, but I was determined to sit out my period of contrition in the hope of returning to a semblance of happiness together. We shared the house with a wonderful activist doctor, Liz Thomson[2]. Poor Liz was driven mad by our constant marital upheavals and finally made plans to find a more peaceful home. Before she left, a young woman from the impoverished homeland of Venda arrived at our door one day, asking to stay in the little servant's quarters behind the house. She had a baby on her back, could barely speak English and winter was on the way. So Sophie Mudau moved in and started doing occasional work around the house. Her little boy,

---

2 in 2010 Dr Liz Thomson was elected Director General of the South African branch of Médecins Sans Frontièrs

Joshua, entertained Amanda endlessly around the house and garden.

Along with other parents in Crown Mines, we created our own little crèche in a disused building that had once been the mine recreation club and scout hall. Since I didn't work during the day, I became one of the "mothers" who looked after the kids on a roster system. Like the rest of Crown Mines, our crèche was a tiny island of normality in a country where everything was divided, fenced and forced into domains based on skin colour.

Fortunately, the kindly man who ran the rowing boat rentals at Zoo Lake didn't mind that the kids I'd brought for a mid-winter row were all shades from pink to black. Zoo Lake was a smelly bit of water surrounded by pleasant lawns and shady trees. In the winter the trees are bare and the grass crisp and brown, but on freezing Highveld days we tried to catch every ray of sunshine that gleamed bleakly through the photochemical haze. Scraggly ducks surrounded the boat as we tossed handfuls of breadcrumbs into the soupy water. I noticed a group of women picnicking on the bank, and recognised two of them from Crown Mines. As I gave them a wave, one of the kids stood up in our little boat and stumbled across to the other side, causing it to lurch dangerously to one side, just as Amanda leaned out to toss breadcrumbs. She popped over the side and disappeared beneath the primordial waters. In a second I was over the side, without thinking to take off my heavy jacket. Thrashing around under the freezing water, I thankfully found my sinking daughter without trouble. But my spirited dive, I discovered, had sent the boat swiftly to the opposite side of the lake.

Half a dozen shocked little faces peered from the tiny vessel as I shouted at them to stay seated and not move. My boots and jacket were now perilously waterlogged, and I struggled to get Amanda and myself back to the boat. I rowed rapidly back to the bank, piled the kids into the Volksie and raced back to Crown Mines. After dropping the other kids, I ran a hot bath, stripped off Amanda's soaked, smelly clothes and immersed the shivering child in the bathtub. Only when I tried to wash her hair did her tears finally flow. I patiently explain to her that her hair was now full of all sorts of horrible stuff, including duck shit.

With streaming eyes she protested, "But I like duck pooh, daddy!"

Our recent experience with ducklings had surely sparked this unexpected response. A few weeks earlier I'd noticed a cage of fluffy yellow ducklings in a pet shop window, so cute that I bought one and proudly took it home to my daughter. She was so enthralled with the chirping bundle of feathers that within minutes she'd hugged it to death. Mortified, I distracted her with some deft manoeuvring long enough to remove the diminutive corpse, hurry back to the pet shop and return with a live replacement. I was relieved that the switch had worked and my poor child wouldn't have to live with the blood of that departed duckling on her hands. But within minutes she'd hugged the decoy to death as well, and I had to inform the tearful girl that maybe ducklings didn't make good pets after all.

While the crèche may have been a peaceful oasis, the rest of Crown Mines was starting to feel the government's increasing paranoia. People all over the city were getting harassed and arrested. Neil Aggett was picked up and kept in solitary confinement down at John Vorster Square, along with many others. Several activists went into hiding in the city or in neighbouring countries like Lesotho, Botswana and Swaziland. For many it would be years before they returned home, and a tragic few would die at the hands of the Special Forces in brutal cross-border raids. The iron fist of the regime was squeezing ever tighter.

An American academic named Philip suddenly appeared on the scene at that time. He had long hair, little round Trotsky glasses and all the lefty qualifications to fit into our social group. He told me he'd befriended a couple of white activists from Pretoria and wanted them to meet me. When he brought them around, I was immediately suspicious. Something about them raised an alarm, but I couldn't quite tell what it was. As we started chatting, I realised it was a setup. They claimed to be members of COSAS, the Congress of South African Students, which was a strictly black organisation, and invited me to join their group in "undercover" operations. I realised they were security police, and that Philip wasn't who he said he was. I cut all ties with these creepy imposters and Philip disappeared as mysteriously as he'd arrived. The country was saturated with these types during those days; you never knew who you could trust.

Then I woke to find my bedroom full of armed policemen one night. I thought I was dreaming. They moved silently around the house as if they didn't notice me, whispering as they emptied cupboards and rummaged through drawers.

"What are you looking for?" I asked one of them. He looked like quite a nice young man, even with the huge police pistol in his hand.

All niceness vanished in a millisecond.

"Shut up, you fuckin' communist."

There were about fourteen of them, and at some hidden signal, they holstered their guns and left. I sneaked a look as they climbed into the van parked in the trees at the bottom of the road. Back inside, Amanda slept on, purring quietly. I kissed her on the forehead and then walked into the kitchen and started laughing. The following day I told Sue.

"C'mon, Rog, you expect me to believe that? Why would they bother with you?" Why indeed?

My time as Le Chaim's barman was coming to an end. Dave Goldsmith's father had sold the building and the new owner was squeezing Dave out of the venue. During my time there, I'd got to know and befriend many of the country's great musicians. Le Chaim was incredibly popular and every band in town wanted a chance to perform at this quirky little venue. Among them was Sakhile, a bunch of Durban guys led by two incredible musicians, Sipho Gumede on bass and Khaya Mahlangu on sax. The band also featured Mabi Thobejane, a master percussionist who always appeared in full traditional dress. Mabi came across as a rural, ancestor-worshipping Africanist, so it was a huge surprise when he called me over one day and tapped his nose.

"Hey man, got any blow?"

I shouldn't have been surprised. After all, he arrived at gigs in Pierre Cardin and Bally shoes before changing into traditional gear. Mabi had started out drumming in the group Malombo with his uncle, the great Philip Tabane, a great musical innovator who played a lot at Le Chaim with his new outfit featuring two traditional drummers. The stage would be packed with drums of every shape and size while I served at the bar right beside the stage.

I'd had to come to terms with the fact that I was now just a barman at the venue where I'd been one of the brightest stars. The feeling of defeat ran deep, and little by little the blind confidence that had kept me going started dying as I faced the fact that I'd fallen off the ladder.

I still tried to do what I could to restore my marriage, but my breach of trust remained an insurmountable blockage to this goal. Sue didn't make life easy, and often disappeared for days on end, "staying with friends", leaving me alone with Amanda. I became increasingly depressed and desolate, and one cold afternoon, sitting alone at home, I knotted a length of red-and-white nylon rope to the rafters of the garage, stood on a plastic milk crate and secured the rope tightly around my neck. But I hadn't done my homework. The sudden pain as I kicked the crate away caused me to instantly regret this desperate act. I had two children, and the thought of the shame they'd have to face explaining the absence of their father had me kicking around furiously, trying to get out of this critical situation. I should have thought a bit more before I hitched myself to the rafters, but heartache can drive people to some crazy acts. My eyeballs felt about to burst as I managed to get one foot onto a wooden strut on the side of the corrugated iron structure. This enabled me to reach above my head and get a grip on the rafter to which the rope was tied. I have no idea how long it took, but when I finally managed to release myself, I sank to the dusty floor, exhausted and gagging, with tears streaming from my eyes. My tongue was thick and swollen and I couldn't swallow the thick spittle that had built up in my mouth. I lay there on the garage floor, the red-and-white nylon still tangled around my bruised and lacerated neck.

When I later looked in the bathroom mirror, I was shocked. My eyes were swollen and bloodshot like I had some dreaded disease. There was a massive welt around my neck, the blood almost breaking through the surface of the skin. I never told a soul about this shameful incident, and explained the wound on my neck by saying I'd run into a wire fence on the mine dump. My story was met with sympathetic but suspicious nods.

Years later my brother Patrick and I went to Durban's state mortuary to identify the body of my youngest brother, Michael. That sweet, smiley kid had become increasingly depressed and had attempted suicide more than once. This time he'd succeeded. As I looked at him on the shiny, stainless steel table, the sadness I felt was indescribable. Still tied around his neck was a red-and-white nylon rope. It took me days before I was able to weep and say goodbye.

Terry Acres, who'd done the sound for many of my gigs, had started Prosound, one of the first professional sound companies in the country. The sound business was booming in Jo'burg, partly because of an influx of international stars who were breaking the cultural boycott and playing not only at Sun City, but all over the country, including Frank Sinatra, Millie Jackson, Cliff Richard and Janis Ian. A promoter even dredged Bill Haley and the Comets out of some backwater for a South African tour. Terry had always been very generous to me when I needed sound gear for my gigs, but he and his partner, Simon Oates, were less than enthusiastic when I appeared at their offices to ask for a job.

"Yer a fookin' muso, ya coont. This work's not fer poofters, ya know."

Simon was a short, stocky Londoner who hadn't made it as a drummer. Many sound engineers were failed musicians, it seemed – Terry had been a bass player – and after convincing them that I could do the job, I joined their motley ranks. It seemed a good compromise; I was still in a field related to music, and at least I'd be learning a skill that could help in a music career I was determined to revive. After a couple of days, Simon flung me in at the deepest end.

"Righ', mate, see this mixing desk? It's a mono desk. By the end o' next week you'll 'ave turned it into a stereo desk."

I assured him I knew nothing about the inner workings of these things. I'd never shown an ounce of technical aptitude in my life.

"Piece o' piss, mate. Star' a' the beginning, follow the source." He turned on his cocky little heel and went up to his office.

I pored for days over the mass of diodes, cathodes, transistors and resistors, getting electric shocks even when the machine was off. My hands were soon covered in smooth, shiny burns from the soldering iron, but whenever I called Simon to tell him I couldn't go on, he'd say, "follow the source, mate," and hang up. Eventually the mono desk became a stereo desk, and I'd learnt an astonishing amount in a very short time. The deep end seemed Simon's way of approaching the learning process, and after about three months he sent me to the SABC as a "special consultant". I was horrified.

"Think ya know foockall, son? Wait till ya see wha' they know at the South African broadcorpsing castration."

The SABC was a big client of Prosound, and the butt of their jokes. At the SABC studios I realised that this derision wasn't unfounded. Dozens of "sound engineers" were milling about trying to get the system working for one of their dreadful live concerts. It seemed they had one engineer to put in a plug, another to take it out and a third to examine it – as if a long stare would fix it – and a fourth to push faders up and down even though nothing was working. It took me about three minutes to work out that the plug that should have been in the IN socket was in the OUT socket, and the plug that should have been in the OUT socket was plugged in where the earphones should have been. I quickly got the system up and running to profuse thanks from the "engineers". I drove back to Prosound feeling like a real sound engineer.

I got to do the sound for many big concerts featuring top acts of the time. Many of these performers had known me as a musician, but I managed to put my damaged pride and disappointment into a box in the back of my mind and get on with the daily challenge of making a living. Humiliating though it was to be a back-room boy where I'd once been in the spotlight, I was learning a new skill at a furious rate, which helped me regain some of my shattered self-confidence. I often worked long nights on shows, and there was always cocaine around to help with these tiring shifts. I developed an intense liking for that seductive powder, but its extreme costliness managed to keep my consumption under control, at least for the moment. But I was drinking far too much.

In a relatively short time I became extremely capable in the sound business. But my musical aspirations wouldn't leave me alone. I kept plotting and planning and speaking to musos about putting on a new show. By this time *The Road Is Much Longer* was history; the security police had confiscated all copies from the few shops that had stocked it. One September morning in 1982, I read in the *Rand Daily Mail* that possession and distribution of *The Road* had been banned. The penalty for possession was five years' imprisonment, a ten thousand rand fine, or both. Selling the album could have got the seller ten years in prison. The banning order stated that the songs were "dangerous for the safety of the state", and the song You Only Need Say Nothing was "equally dangerous in that the police are again shown in a very bad light. A climate of grievance and protest is being built up, and especially as the words are accompanied with the beat of African rhythm to enhance the impact of the words, the song can incite people towards insurgency and violence." The terms of the ban remain the most severe for any album in South African history.

Dave Dison, the young lawyer who'd looked the other way when Sue almost ran me over, encouraged me to appeal the ban. He gave his time and expertise for free, and coached me to conduct my defence. On the day of the appeal I put on my one and only scraggly tie and presented myself in Pretoria at the Publications Appeal Board. The chairman of the board, Professor Kobus van Rooyen, was surprisingly civil. He listened attentively as I talked about my songs and influences. But the state attorney gave me hell, harping on the "African rhythms" which could incite violence. His most bewildering accusation was that I had perniciously accompanied some songs with the saxophone, "an instrument known for inciting blacks to violence". The professor said he admired my commitment to my ideals, but the law was the law. There was nothing he could do. The album remains banned to this day, and Professor van Rooyen went on to become one of the country's most enlightened experts in the Broadcasting Complaints Commission, which does invaluable work to keep our country free of unwarranted censorship.

In the summer of 1983, Jonny Blundell was in Jo'burg on vacation from his studies at Berklee College of Music in Boston. On a whim, we put together a Zub Zub Marauders reunion concert at the popular Rosebank Hotel. When I arrived for the gig, the hotel foyer was packed with excited people milling around. I couldn't believe my eyes. At first I thought the doors weren't yet open, but it turned out the room was already packed. People started taking chairs from the foyer onto the pavement to watch through the high windows from the street. Soon there were three or four people standing on each chair, and the venue itself had not a spare inch of space. We played for three nights, each more packed that the last. It was a miracle that it slipped past the security police net, but it was barely advertised and I'd been off the scene for some time.

But after the third night when the lights went out on that steamy stage, I was back to obscurity and the daily grind of setting up sound systems for others. For me, the gaps between the highs and the lows were growing. It was almost as if my fleeting successes were passing dreams in an increasingly austere life. There were other successful shows, but they became less sustainable as time went on. My workload at Prosound grew heavier and more time-consuming, and eventually a back injury forced me to quit.

All around, meanwhile, evidence was mounting that the state intended to totally crush all resistance. A huge blow for us all at Crown Mines was the news that Neil Aggett had taken his own life while in detention at John Vorster Square. The police station was now notorious for its many deaths, and for the bizarre and cynical official excuses to justify these tragedies. Neil had been subjected to the most gruelling interrogation. He'd been forced to stay awake for long periods, and undergone both subtle and more overt forms of torture that the security police had turned into a fine art. A fellow detainee, Maurice Smithers, who was kept in a cell next to Neil's, described the horror of the little he heard and saw in the hours before Neil's death. It was clear that Neil could endure no more, and rather than buckle and tell his interrogators what they wanted, he took the only other option.

A massive funeral was held at the Anglican cathedral in the centre of Jo'burg. His coffin was then carried at a run, high on the shoulders of young comrades, all the way to West Park Cemetery many kilometres away. I found the event uncomfortable; it felt like Neil's life was being shoved into the background to showcase the agenda of young comrades. I felt I never really got to say goodbye to that incredibly committed and courageous man. But I had to accept that when one dies for the struggle, one's life becomes the property of the Party.

Neil's girlfriend, Liz Floyd, also a medical doctor, came to stay with Sue and me in Crown Mines. Friends felt she'd be better off in our community after the trauma she'd endured. But our house was hardly a haven of peace and harmony, and with Liz stretched to the limit with heartbreak, the arrangement only lasted a few weeks. Neil's death was a savage blow to us all, but its aftershocks lasted for years. The world around us was falling apart, and when I thought things couldn't get worse, Sue announced that she was moving out into another house in Crown Mines, and I wasn't welcome to accompany her.

Fortunately the rents for those little cottages were very low, and if I could get someone to share I'd be able to stay on. Happily Ian Herman, now playing with a couple of the top bands in town, moved in along with his girlfriend, Sue Dinner. I felt lucky that I still had a comfortable place to live close to my beloved daughter.

© Joe Weeber

26

Matabeleland, Winter 1983

MUGABE SAYS NO TO AN INDABA WITH NKOMO

The Prime Minister of Zimbabwe, Mr Robert Mugabe, yesterday ruled out a constitutional conference or indaba with ZAPU leader Mr Joshua Nkomo. He said such talks had been suggested by Mr Nkomo, who is in self-exile in London. Mr Mugabe told parliament during a special Prime Minister's question time, which was broadcast and televised live, that politically motivated dissidents were operating in Zimbabwe because Mr Nkomo was not Prime Minister.

The Star, 14 July 1983

DOCTOR TURNS FATALLY HURT CHILD AWAY

A seriously injured black boy who fell from a moving truck was refused admittance to Northdale Hospital and died as a result of his injuries in Durban's Wentworth Hospital the next day.

The Star, 14 July 1983

Roger Harris was a large, bearded Westcountry man from Devon whose sense of humour was as sharp as his temper. He was married to my cousin Miranda, and together they ran the South African office of United Press International TV News, one of the largest news agencies in the world. Roger started giving me freelance work and, in his temperamental way, training me as an assistant in the TV news business. One day in early July 1983, Roger told me to pack a bag and meet him at the airport. Together with ITN correspondent Peter Sharp, we were going to Zimbabwe to investigate a story put out by a Catholic priest in Bulawayo, Father Hebron Wilson, about a killing spree in Matabeleland by a North Korean trained unit. Zimbabwe's war of independence was fought by an alliance of Joshua Nkomo's ZIPRA army comprised mostly of Matabeles, and Robert Mugabe's ZANLA army, mostly Shonas. Soon after independence, these two main ethnic groups were at each other's throats. A major British newspaper was already on the story, but no-one from the TV media had yet ventured into this dangerous territory.

Matabeleland is a vast area covered by thorn trees with occasional rocky hills. Between the few tar roads was an infinite web of sand tracks linking villages, settlements and rural kraals. Father Wilson accompanied us as we thundered through the countryside, picking up information from people in the little settlements we came across. They'd alert us as to where the Fifth Brigade was operating, and we'd carefully avoid contact with them as we searched the countryside for signs of genocide. At one point we followed a plume of smoke to a hamlet of a dozen or so huts, all burnt out shells, still smouldering in the hot, silent afternoon. There were no signs of life. A dead dog lay outside, its blood still fresh and bright on the hot sand. On the village outskirts we came across a large mound of freshly turned earth, which we later discovered was a mass grave in which the inhabitants had been buried. An old man appeared out of the bush, sobbing dry tears, and told Father Wilson that the Fifth Brigade had come looking for ZIPRA soldiers. When they couldn't find any, they lined up the villagers and shot them all. We discovered many more instances of murder and mayhem over the next few days.

Unlike the video cameras of today, our equipment was huge and heavy. The camera and recorder were separate pieces connected by a thick cable; the trick was to constantly anticipate where the cameraman would go next. With Roger this was a nightmare. He was constantly on edge, ready to explode every time I slipped up. Despite his foul temper, or perhaps because of it, I learnt the ropes fast, which helped me later.

At one point, with the Fifth Brigade nearby and headed in our direction, the ancient Peugeot station wagon we'd hired stopped dead in the sand. I noticed we'd left a thin trail in our tracks, and when I looked under the car saw that the fuel line was completely severed. I dug frantically into the soft sand under the car to clear space to work, and managed to reconnect the ancient pipe with string, a few elastic bands and an old shopping bag. We got out of there with moments to spare.

As an avid supporter of Robert Mugabe and the ZANU government, I was having to face the truth that this liberation movement was becoming corrupt and evil. We sneaked out of the country through a rural border post into Botswana. In the bush outside the tiny town of Francistown, we visited a refugee camp packed with Matabeles who'd escaped. Peter Sharp interviewed several eyewitnesses to the brutality in Matabeleland. By the time we got back to Jo'burg, Peter Godwin's story had broken in the British press, but ours was the first visual evidence of what was rapidly becoming recognised as genocide. Robert Mugabe blithely rejected the allegations, but I can still smell the stench of rotting corpses in the eerie silence that hung over the land. It was the first major news story I'd been on, and I was learning to see the world around me more critically. I was also quite taken with the excitement that came with news gathering.

News wasn't my only source of income at the time; I was also getting freelance sound recording work for TV shoots. One time I heard that a young director, Duncan McLachlan, needed experienced crew to shoot a mountain-climbing movie in the Cape. The closest I'd ever got to a rock face was a weekend school outing with the mountain club. But I rushed to an outdoor shop in Braamfontein and bought a climber's handbook, which I quickly studied. Once I could safely distinguish a belay from an abseil, I went to see Duncan and presented my fictitious credentials. He then hauled out a huge map and started showing me the routes they'd be climbing.

A few days later I was standing on the top of Table Mountain with a tape recorder slung across my shoulders and a boom pole and microphone in hand, about to abseil down a massive, sheer cliff known as Africa Face. I don't know how I managed to keep up the pretence or avoid wetting my pants on this most terrifying day of my life. The film focused on a young tearaway, Chris Lomax, who climbs these rock faces without ropes. Also featured was a fifteen-year-old kid, Andy de Klerk, who scampered around these merciless rocks like a mountain goat on amphetamines. Despite his youth, Andy was a serious and intense boy, and his demeanour, when engaged in climbing, was nothing short of spiritual. As the years went by, Andy became South Africa's most legendary climber and a doyen of the international climbing fraternity. He's opened routes in far-flung corners of the world, and regularly writes eloquent articles about this extreme sport and the eccentric group who practice it.

Greg Lacey was a charming and kind-hearted climber who assisted me in the tricky process of getting into position to record every grunt and groan of the climbers as they went about their insane recreation. Greg told me with stoic melancholy how his girlfriend, Bev Opperman, had fallen to her death just weeks before on this very face where we were shooting. Quietly and meticulously he made sure I was safely secured as I went about my work. The shoot was incredibly dangerous, and during one sequence, on a climb known as Touch and Go, Duncan's safety harness came adrift and he plunged twenty metres to the rocks below. He hit a large rock that was sticking out at an angle, and slid down, coming to a stop on the edge of the cliff face. The angled rock had broken his fall, but he was badly injured. I was so full of adrenaline that I managed to carry him on my back down to the vehicles way below. After two weeks of shooting, with Greg's help and encouragement, I was an old hand at climbing and had conquered my fear of dangling thousands of metres above the ground. A few months later I drank a quiet whisky and toasted that fatalistic daredevil when I heard that Greg had died on a lonely mountain in the Alps above Chamonix. He'd already conquered most major climbing routes in the world, and after Bev's death had dedicated his life completely to mountaineering.

At a celebration meal to toast the successful completion of the shoot, bolstered by several bottles of Cape wine, I came clean with Duncan. I figured that with his leg in plaster from his fall, even if he was pissed off with me he couldn't do anything about it. I leaned across and spoke softly, hoping the others wouldn't hear.

"I lied to you about my climbing career because I really needed the job. I hope you'll forgive me."

Duncan's face was incredulous. "You fucking bastard. You bullshitted me? Hey guys, listen to this! This bugger's never been on a fucking mountain before... Well bugger me, you've got balls." He grabbed me round the neck, laughing and whooping, as the others broke into laughter.

But now they wanted to know what I really did for a living. I proceeded to tell another clanger of a lie.

"I've been writing music for films, mainly for my father in Durban, but things have been tight lately so I thought I'd diversify."

"Hmm," said Duncan. "You write music?"

Which is how I got to write and perform the music for Duncan's award-winning film, *Solo Ascent*, which was shown on television channels around the world, winning many international awards and which still pops up from time to time on late night TV.

Duncan went into a decline when his wife left him for another man. He moved to the USA and later Australia, where he was reasonably successful in the film industry. Not long ago I saw a familiar grey-haired man in a music shop in Cape Town, who looked at me and finally came over.

"Are you Roger Lucey?" I told him I was. "I'm Duncan McLachlan's brother." When I enquired after Duncan, he said things had been really tough for him lately, but were starting to come right. When I protested that I thought he was doing well in the film business, he lowered his voice. "I guess you haven't heard. Duncan's living as a woman now."

In spite of the work I was getting in the news and film industry, I still couldn't let go of my musical aspirations. My love affair with music was more painful and obsessive than any I'd ever had with a woman. With women, even through the messiest of breakups, I'd always reach a point when I knew I had to let go. Not so with music. By the end of 1983 I should have packed away my guitar and put my dreams to bed for good. But I'd been hanging around with a young musician and producer who'd started an independent label called Shifty Records. Lloyd Ross was the guitarist for the Radio Rats when they played at our wedding, and we'd stayed in touch. Lloyd was now working with people like James Phillips and many alternative Jo'burg bands, and I lent him a hand when I could with promotions, selling albums and technical assistance. The studio was housed in an old caravan, and when I decided to do a show at the Market Theatre, Lloyd agreed to record it.

The show was called After the Thunder, and I managed to assemble some of the finest musos in the country to play with me. My greatest joy was having Issy Fataar play lead guitar. Issy was Steve's youngest brother, who'd been too young to play with the Flames, but was by far the most talented of the family. He played a cheap, no-name guitar bought from a pawn shop, but in his hands it sounded like the finest instrument. Uncannily, whenever I was about to put on a big show and my face and name started appearing in the newspapers, Sue seemed more amenable to my overtures to restore our marriage. After the Thunder was no different. Once again, Mannie Manim gave me the best possible deal and all the support I could expect from that crusty old theatrical warrior. I am certainly the world's worst businessman, and when it came to music, my dreams always exceeded my budget. Before I knew it there were nine in the band, and while the music was sensational, there was no way we could make money. A few of Lloyd's recordings of the show have survived, and I'm still astounded at the power and energy we generated on that stage. There was also no sign of security police harassment at that time, but although we sent out press releases and photographs, not one newspaper in Jo'burg carried even the smallest mention of the show.

Predictably, when the lights went out at the end of that week at the Market Theatre, Sue walked out of my life once again, leaving me unable to pay the rent and unsure what to do next. So, as before, I packed my pride and headed home to my mother, this time with Amanda in tow. Sue was busy with her life and her work and had no qualms about me taking Amanda to Durban for what amounted to several months. My mother was delighted at the opportunity to spend time with her charming little granddaughter, but my father went ballistic. Although my mother now lived on her own property, it was right next door to her abusive estranged husband. He felt that a young man had no business looking after babies, and made his feelings clear from his bedroom window overlooking my mother's garden, where Amanda and I played outside.

"That child should be with its mother!" he'd shout.

"Fuck you," I'd hiss under my breath. "What would you know about child rearing?"

Blissfully unaware of the acrimony, Amanda would laugh and wave at him. After several weeks of the constant sniping, I lost my temper and stormed over to his house, grabbed him by the collar and pushed him into the wall. I was about to punch him when I saw the look on his face. It was one of surprise, disorientation and pain. I pushed him away and stormed back to my mother's house, frustration, confusion and anger welling up in my eyes. But there was no fence between the two houses and Amanda had free rein of the properties. She would wander into DJ's house and make herself at home while he worked on his films. I once found her on DJ's lap gleefully pushing buttons on his editing table while he laughed and spoke to her in baby talk. Somehow this four-year-old had managed to infiltrate the fortress surrounding my eccentric and very complex father.

One day Charl and Will von Witt, old Durban friends who now lived in Jo'burg, arrived at my mother's house with a proposal. For some time we'd toyed with forming a tongue-in-cheek country and western band, and they felt the time was right to put the plan into action. A few days later we piled into Charl's Volksie and headed back to Jo'burg. As we rumbled down the endlessly straight roads of the Orange Free State, Amanda sat on my lap in the back, stuffing her little face with chips and chocolates as Will dozed on the back seat. Suddenly without warning or effort, everything she'd eaten suddenly launched like a junk food sausage directly into Will's bag on the floor between my feet.

Charl pulled up on the side of the road and I quickly sat Amanda on a rock and started cleaning the multi-coloured vomit from Will's possessions. To add to the excitement, a large cobra emerged from under a rock and raised its head at us, but then thankfully slithered off into the veld. I wiped the slime off Will's passport while Charl and Will looked on with upturned noses. But when its inner pages revealed further sticky contents of my child's stomach, their own stomachs finally gave way. Will leaned from the car and hurled noisily into the grass, and Charl followed suit, eyes streaming from the effort. It was contagious, and after several attempts to calm my stormy guts, I was also barfing on the dry Free State earth. Amanda, still seated obediently on her rock, burst into giggles at the sight of these three men unceremoniously heaving away at the side of the road. Soon after dark we were back in Crown Mines, stomachs depleted and heads full of dreams.

I always left Durban with a heavy heart for my son Tay. His mother had married an abusive ex-cop who'd been kicked out of the police force for violent behaviour. Given that he'd been based in the same police station as Kat Ferreira, he must have been up to some pretty horrific stuff. Every time I went to fetch Tay to take him out, this pig of a man was always scowling over a drink, no matter how early in the morning. Having never married his mother, I had no legal rights over the boy, and could only worry and despair over his future.

I still always met up with Jabula, who still did the odd job for DJ, but also seemed headed for disaster. He was drinking heavily and his face was adorned with scars and lumps picked up in shebeen brawls. But it was always great to see him, and we'd often sit in the park smoking zol and talking shit. He was regularly in prison for petty crimes, but each incarceration left him hardened and more cynical about his prospects. With my own life such a mess, I could only look on helplessly as these two other lives, so close to mine, went on their journeys.

Despite the upheavals in my personal life and the daily trials of South African life, we led a relatively happy existence in that oasis called Crown Mines. It was a supportive and neighbourly village, and on warm evenings the streets were full of residents walking their dogs and chatting over slightly decrepit picket fences. Directly over the road from me lived David Webster, an anthropologist at Wits University, and his wife, Glenda. We often discussed music and its role as a political tool. We differed on many issues, as I did with most academic politicos, one being David's belief that there was no place for individualists in the struggle. I believed then, as I do today, that the individual voice can often afford to be more truthful than the collective one. Since the days when troubadours started their musical commentaries, the responsibility of the songsmith has been to reflect accurately, with heart and soul, the lives and times of their communities. Looking at the laager[1] mentality of South Africa's government eighteen years after the first democratic election, I believe it does itself a great injustice by squashing the individual.

---

1 a defensive circle of Afrikaner settlers' wagons during their Great Trek into the
country's interior

Many fine voices in the ANC have been crushed under the weight of the party's collective dogma.

I told David my new idea of putting together a country and western band that would sing lefty songs. I needed a nom de plume for this new persona, and when I told David the name I'd come up with, he laughed for days. Tighthead Fourie and the Loose Forwards would be the first and only lefty country band in South Africa. Charl and Will would sing harmonies and soon the band started taking shape. On Sunday evenings the residents would gather in the old scout hall and we'd deck out in ridiculous cowboy outfits and sing our country songs.

Jonny Blundell later joined as Ray Stadig[2], along with Brian Rath on drums as Gene Parkeering[3] and an ever-changing assortment of motley musicians, including Dave Marks as Lorenzo Marks. We got ourselves quite a following through the trying times we were all going through, and still managed our fair share of laughs. One of our best-known songs was No Easy Walk to Freedom. I'd written it in about 1977, and it called in plain language for Mandela's release. We also sang soppy love songs, and many a night I'd watch the butch and the cynical discreetly wiping tears from their eyes at the back of the hall. We even featured in a music show on Afrikaans TV. The host was genuinely taken in by the band's name, and the song we sang was a great little ballad of unfaithful love, broken hearts and alcohol abuse called Whisky Straight Up. Roy McGregor, a highly talented and eccentric director, shot a wonderful video of the band in and around Jamesons, a basement bar in the centre of town. This was said to be where the great South African writer Herman Charles Bosman and other literary lowlifes used to drink. In the 1980s Jamesons was taken over by Herbert Scheubmayr who once ran the Chelsea with Dave Marks in Hillbrow, and it quickly became Jo'burg's favourite alternative music venue, in many ways the centre of a youth culture that increasingly spoke out against the state. Despite the marginal success of Tighthead Fourie and the Loose Forwards, it was becoming clear that music was taking up a lot of my time for very little return.

I turned thirty in January 1984, and decided to put another band together. I managed to assemble a fine collection of musos that included my old mate Dan Chiorboli, who'd played with Neill Solomon and the Uptown Rhythm Dogs and whom I'd known since

2 to suggest "ry stadig", Afrikaans for drive slowly
3 to suggest "geen parkering", Afrikaans for no parking

my school days. He was a sassy, streetwise Italian kid who gave up a first class soccer career in favour of music. He was also partial to pulling a quick pipe with the ous in the bushes at the bottom of the park. The band got off to a good start, but as soon as word got out that we'd be playing, I started getting those nocturnal visits again. I once picked up the phone and a heavily accented voice on the other end said, "Roger Lucey, this time you die".

I didn't tell anyone about the visits; I still felt the humiliation of Sue's rebuttal when I'd last told her about the midnight raids. When I started making calls to venue managers to book gigs, I realised that once again we were up against the invisible enemy. I heard every excuse on the planet as to why we couldn't play at the popular venues in town. Eventually the Oxford Hotel, where the Zub Zub Marauders had played a very successful reunion concert, agreed to have us. But after one night the manager told me it wasn't going to work out and we should look for another gig. Once again I was in a corner, and it wasn't long before I was forced to abandon the group.

By 1989 David Webster had moved from Crown Mines into a house in the suburb of Troyeville with his partner Maggie Friedman. They'd been working on a paper detailing the state's increasingly repressive tactics – including assassination – to silence its opponents. He wrote that assassination was used "as one of the methods of controlling government opposition when all other methods such as detention or intimidation have failed. It is a very rare event indeed when such assassinations are ever solved".

On 1 May 1989, as he stepped from his car in front of his house, the occupant of a passing car fired on him at close range with a shotgun. David died soon afterwards. His killer, security policeman Ferdi Barnard, was later tried and convicted for the murder.

27

Aimless, 1985

BLACK LEADERS SCOFF AT MANDELA OFFER

The United Democratic Front said today that it had serious doubts about the practicality of the Government offer to release Nelson Mandela, and said that for him to accept the offer would entail breaking a deep commitment to the African National Congress and rejecting all he had fought for.

The Star, 1 February 1985

SWAPO BEGINS PUSH INTO NORTHERN NAMIBIA

Swapo's large-scale infiltration of Northern Namibia appears to have begun, security force spokesmen have said. In several skirmishes in the last month – mostly in Southern Angola near the Ngiva headquarters of the Joint Military Commission (JMC) – the SWA Territory Force claims to have killed 73 Swapo guerrillas.

The Star, 1 February 1985

THE FINAL DEADLINE

International media networks focused on the Rand Daily Mail yesterday as the newspaper – regarded as one of the best in the world – prepared its last editions after 83 years as South Africa's leading morning daily.

Rand Daily Mail, 30 April 1985

WITH ALL THE HEARTBREAK I'D BEEN through, you might think I'd avoid women like roadblocks. But, under the misguided notion that the best way to get over an old lover is to get on top of a new one, I plunged headlong into a series of infatuations that only brought me more grief. Annette was a bright and exotic journalist for a Jo'burg newspaper. She was also ravishingly good looking and I couldn't believe my luck when she made it clear that she wanted me in her bed.

For a while we were inseparable, but no sooner had we declared our deep and burning love for each other than I realised my heart wasn't on the market and I'd made a painful mistake. Tony Campbell, always a good friend and a shoulder to cry on at times like these, suggested I might have a commitment phobia. Years later, during a long spell of psychotherapy, I got to understand that most South African males are hopelessly unprepared for affairs of the heart. Ours was one of the most patriarchal societies in the world, and our preparation for true manhood had nothing to do with the reality of what it takes to be in a balanced relationship.

Unfortunately, I hadn't learnt this sobering lesson when I noticed Irna standing under the canopy of a huge banyan tree in Durban's Mitchell Park. A jazz quartet was playing on the bandstand and families were sprawled on blankets across the lawns. I'd returned to Durban for a few weeks to do a couple of gigs, and a friend suggested we spend that Sunday afternoon at Mitchell Park. Irna was tall and her unusual looks stood out among the crowd. She had the olive skin of an Afrikaans girl who's spent her time outdoors, enormous eyes that opened and closed languorously, and a feline gait that focused all attention on her exquisite legs and buttocks.

I was thunderstruck, and with the courage of temporary dementia,

197

walked up and introduced myself. She knew who I was from my musical reputation, and I managed to strike up a conversation. She was with a male friend I knew slightly through Steve Fataar, and while he gave me the evil eye, I learnt that she was a teacher who'd made a point of going to work in a poor coloured township school. She had all the credentials for me to fall ridiculously in love with her, which took all of about twelve minutes. Irna's father was an Elder in the Dutch Reformed Church, and it had taken enormous courage and principle for her to turn her back on the flock and make a new life in Durban.

When I finally got to meet her parents at their Pretoria home, it was a dismal encounter. Her father was aggressive and hostile, and we weren't even offered a cup of coffee. This wasn't simply a family matter, but was symptomatic of the deep divisions that existed in every nook and cranny of our ruptured society. As we drove back to Jo'burg, Irna was the picture of melancholic beauty as she quietly accepted the consequences of the life decisions she'd made. Soon after meeting her, I had to get back to Jo'burg for work. I'd moved into a communal house in the gang-ridden suburb of Mayfair, and was still getting lots of freelance work as a soundman for a variety of TV and news crews.

Although I was living in Jo'burg and regularly travelling around the country for work, Irna and I got together at every chance. Dennis Rubel was an activist doctor who lived in our communal house with his wife Sally Candy, also a doctor. Dennis had an old Moto Guzzi motorcycle, which he'd occasionally lend me. I'd head off to Durban, bones shaking and my bum as stiff as a board, but knowing that just across those plains and mountains, Irna was waiting. Apart from our frantically athletic bouts of lovemaking, we were getting closer and closer as friends. I was starting to feel that the dark days were behind me and that a real and sustainable healing was taking place.

But as always, as the good times settled in, something would turn the world upside down. I received a formal letter from Sue in which she told me she was taking Amanda and going to live in Windhoek, Namibia. The modicum of peace and civility we'd managed to achieve went straight out the window, and we started a new round of ghastly battles. Sue's friend, Gwen Lister, was starting a new, progressive newspaper called *The Namibian*, and had invited Sue to help her set it up. Despite my shortcomings, I considered myself a dedicated father, and I spent much of my time looking after my daughter. But Sue was unyielding, and in due course she left for Windhoek. Amanda's sudden departure left a huge hole in my life, but was only a taste of things to come. They were away for about a year, with Amanda coming to me for holidays, before Sue finally returned to Jo'burg and Gwen went on to create one of the bravest little newspapers on the continent.

By the beginning of 1985 I was doing a lot of news work, although it was becoming increasingly difficult for journalists to function. The country was on fire and I was running around with a microphone watching it burn. The foreign press was now a target for the police, and every day in the field was filled with danger. Where I'd once sat on stages and in nightclubs singing about how close we were to freedom, I was now in the battlefront watching our freedom drift further away towards an uncertain future.

Like so many times before, I was slowly being enveloped in a cocoon of blackness as all my systems started shutting down. It was my defence against the overwhelming crush of the outside world. It was a strange feeling, as the line between waking and sleeping became unclear and unstable. The world took on an almost dreamlike quality in which the pictures were crystal clear, but with no feeling or emotion attached. The first victim of this shutdown was Irna. She was everything I wanted and admired in a woman. She was beautiful and brave, talented and funny, and yet I shut her out without explanation. I still read the extraordinary letters she wrote me, lyrical tomes that, if they weren't confidential, belonged in an anthology of poetry. Several times I tried to write to her to explain, but I barely knew what had happened myself. It took years to slowly unravel all the mysteries that tortured me, but by then it was too late to make amends.

One thing that helped during these desperately alienating times was cocaine. Well, it helped while the rush surged through my bloodstream, blocking out the relentless pressure of life. The trouble was that it was very expensive. So when an old friend from Durban told me he'd located a bulk source of high-grade coke, it seemed that one problem was solved. Everyone in the news business then was living on cocaine, so there was a constant demand for the Bolivian marching powder. All I had to do was buy a half-kilo bag, package it into one-gram sachets and sell them at a huge profit. Macullum, a friend I'd known from Durban who now also worked for various news organisations, was keen to be in on the deal. We had to put up a fair amount of money to buy the first batch, and his healthy list of potential customers was helpful.

I flew down to Durban, collected the powder and headed straight back to Jo'burg. It struck me as ironic that my friend was now a major supplier. While at school, his father had always warned him off me, saying I had the look of evil about me. On the plane home I must have gone to the loo at least six times in the one-hour flight, to toot a hastily chopped line up my nose. During the last visit I noticed that a white crust had formed around my nostrils which I quickly wiped away. I was flying like a rocket, and suddenly realised that my behaviour must seem mighty suspicious. I tried to calm my shaking hands as a sudden rush of paranoia overcame me. It was a great relief to finally get off that plane.

Macullum was waiting to pick me up and we hurried back to Crown Mines, keen to get the business going. Driving through Mayfair on the way home, a police car with flashing lights and sirens raced past us, forcing us to the side of the road. The bag with half a kilo of cocaine was lying on the back seat of the car, and I started counting my years in prison as the cop walked over to us. It turned out to be a traffic policeman who'd noticed that a brake light wasn't working, but I was a nervous wreck. He waved us on after I apologised and promised to attend to the problem immediately, and we went home to weigh out the nose candy and supply the anxious customers.

As the stock got depleted, Macullum became desperate to keep himself a private stash. He started cutting it with a laxative called mannitol, which has the colour and texture of cocaine. While customers realised that the goods were getting less pure, their complaints got lost in the frenzy of chopping, snorting and sniffing. Macullum had changed, and was now prepared to cheat his friends in his quest to keep himself supplied. I no longer recognised this old friend who now sneaked around with his little scale in a quiet conspiracy like a wicked alchemist, moving piles of white powder around a large glass mirror on his desk. I made a tactical withdrawal from the business and let him carry on alone. I was also starting to feel a toxic madness creeping into my head that could only be calmed by vast quantities of alcohol.

This crazy period happened while Sue and Amanda were in Namibia. How quickly I fell apart when she wasn't around; the simple fact of having a child to care for, I realised, had a sobering effect. While all this madness caused me untold physical and emotional damage, it was nothing compared to what would follow.

28

Love and War, 1985

BOYCOTTS LEAVE SCHOOLS IN 26 TOWNS DESERTED
Tens of thousands of pupils across the country are continuing their mass stayaway from classes this week, leaving schools virtually deserted.

The Star, 17 July 1985

TWO POLICMEN'S HOMES PETROL BOMBED AS SOWETO UNREST CONTINUES – FIVE MORE UNREST DEATHS REPORTED

The Star, 18 July 1985

WIDESPREAD VIOLENCE CONTINUES
A man was shot dead in Soweto, 122 people were arrested on the East Rand and townships near Maritzburg erupted in violence as stone throwing, petrol bombing and arson continued countrywide yesterday.

The Star, 19 July 1985

TWO WHITES INJURED IN SOWETO STONINGS
The unrest took a new turn yesterday when it spread to larger black residential areas and smaller rural townships.

The Star, 20 July 1985

STATE OF EMERGENCY

A State of Emergency is to be enforced from midnight in 36 magisterial districts in South Africa, the President, Mr PW Botha announced today. He told a press conference that conditions of violence and lawlessness around the country had increased recently and had become more severe and cruel, especially in black townships.

Weekend Argus, 20 July 1985

441 HELD, 8 DEAD BY DAY 3 OF EMERGENCY

A total of 441 people have been detained without charge, about 60 were arrested on criminal charges and at least eight people have died violently since South Africa entered a state of emergency at midnight on Saturday.

The Star, 23 July 1985

THE HIGHVELD GRASS CRUNCHES LIKE cornflakes underfoot. The sun is already high, but in the spots of shade under the sparse trees, in ditches and behind gravestones, the morning frost remains. Andile Fosi is tall and quiet and, I suspect, disapproving of the clamour and lack of decorum around the graves, as comrades compete in their sloganeering and news crews trip over gravestones for a better shot. I don't consider myself one of those types; I wear a red jumpsuit I once performed in and a ridiculous pair of sunglasses, the left half red, the right bright blue, hiding my bloodshot, heavy lidded eyes. The pipe I smoked less than an hour ago softens the grimness of this very South African tableau. Four coffins lie beside freshly dug graves at the top of a long sloping cemetery in the Duduza township. I follow Andile around with my microphone as he picks up the shots needed by the editor back in the office to package the piece for ITN's evening news: the weeping mothers, enraged friends, sombre ministers in their heavy black vestments. The dead are young MK[1] operatives whose arms cache was intercepted and booby-trapped by the security police. They died as they pulled the pins from grenades which then blew up in their faces. The war has turned very ugly, and the mood on this wintery afternoon is frightening. The rising dust lines my nostrils as comrades toyi-toyi[2] on the bare earth around the graveside. I start sneezing and feel idiotic as I follow Andile with a microphone in one hand and a hankie in the other.

I point to a commotion by the trees at the bottom of the slope, but Andile is busy with a close-up of a grieving mother. Below us the crowd is getting bigger, and again I point it out to Andile. He looks

---

1 Umkhonto we Sizwe, Zulu for Spear of the Nation, the military wing of the African National Congress
2 A dance expressing protest and defiance

downhill and trots off reluctantly, with me sneezing behind him. At the bottom of the hill my sneezing fit has subsided, so I wipe my eyes and pocket the hankie. The crowd has formed a circle and is shouting and waving fists in the air. Andile pushes through the crowd to where Jeff Chiltern from Visnews is already shooting towards the ground in the centre of the circle.

A woman sits on the dusty earth, legs folded to one side the way traditional women sit around the cooking fire. She's propping herself on her arms, her face swollen with patches of blood around her mouth, ears and nose. Her eyes are swollen almost shut, but what I can see of them shows the shock and terror of one facing death.

As Andile starts the camera rolling, a young man breaks from the crowd and kicks her savagely in the head. Her arms give way and her upper body sinks to the ground. The crowd cheers. Another youth breaks the line and kicks her in the face. She rises slowly to her feet and once again the crowd cheers. Yet another youth takes a box of matches and lights the hem of her skirt. The synthetic fabric bursts into flame, leaving a molten, tar-like substance that welds itself to her skin. She flounders inside the circle, wisps of smoke rising from the remains of her clothes. A boy no older than thirteen, in dirty shorts and gumboots, enters the circle and starts beating her with a length of hosepipe. The crowd is ecstatic at one so young engaged in the affairs of the revolution. An older youth moves into the circle, takes slow and deliberate aim, and then kicks her on the side of the head. She goes down and doesn't come up. The boy resumes his whipping as the jubilation reaches fever pitch.

Suddenly the circle parts as three young men enter carrying a large, uneven chunk of concrete about a metre in diameter. Positioning themselves above her prone but heaving body, they roar in unison and drop the crude weapon on her head and chest. The boy beats whatever flesh pokes out under the concrete block. The three youths grasp the block again, grunting with effort, and raise it to head height before dropping it triumphantly on the now limp body. Her legs are splayed and her underwear torn, exposing her pubic hair. The boy takes a burning stick and fishes around between her legs, poking it into her vagina.

Andile suddenly breaks from the crowd and falls to his knees at a nearby ditch, retching and spitting. We're going back to the office, he tells me, as the attack on the butchered body continues: a petrol soaked tyre is being placed on her upper body and set alight.

Carefully he drives the hired Mercedes through the throng. Suddenly the boy rushes up to the car and shoves his piece of hosepipe through the window into my face. "I'm going to kill you!" he screams, and then bursts into laughter. As we drive off I look back and see him enveloped by the crowd as they dance around this young hero. Andile and I say nothing as we drive back to Jo'burg with our precious tape.

Her name is Maki Skosana, and her death is the first "necklacing" to be filmed and photographed in South Africa. Along with a handful of news crews and photographers, we document the event without saying a word or trying to stop the murder.

In years to come, as the Truth and Reconciliation Commission slowly and painfully unravels this country's mysteries and shames, it emerges that she had a relationship with a cop named Joe Mamasela. What she didn't know was that Mamasela worked for an undercover commando of security policemen based at Vlakplaas, a rural farm where these notorious murderers carried out their cruel acts. Mamasela had booby-trapped the hand grenades that killed the boys, and Maki paid the price. Certain youths had become suspicious of Mamasela, and when Maki arrived at the funeral, she was pointed out as a collaborator, or impimpi.

Back at the office, ITN correspondent Peter Sharp waits anxiously for our return; word is out that there was trouble at the funeral.

"Did you get any bang-bang? How many dead?" They always ask the same thing.

Peter looks at the first few seconds of pictures and then reels out of the edit suite into the corridor. "Fuck's sake, that's gross! Jesus, Andy, you got to be more careful when you shoot. We can't show these fucking pictures on TV."

But they do. Over and over they show these pictures, and fifteen years later I still get that acrid smell in my nostrils and the tremble that racked my body for days afterwards.

I still believed passionately that the state needed to be overthrown, but on that day everything that had seemed so clear became muddied. When Allan Boesak told the international media that South Africa's youth were the most politically aware and progressive in the world, I wondered if that included the likes of the boy with the hosepipe. Would Boesak have lauded the youths that cheered and jeered as Maki Skosana was beaten, stoned and burnt to death? I saw many kids carry out acts of terror, revenge and stupidity in the name of the struggle, and many young revolutionaries censured for trying to bring discipline to the lawless young psychopaths in their ranks.

The *City Press* carried a colour picture of the Maki Skosana incident, with me among the crowd in my crazy sunglasses and red jumpsuit. My face has a look of dislocated shock. I will never know whether my stoned state softened or intensified my experience that day, but whatever the case, I couldn't touch zol for many years and my guitar remained untouched in its case until it was cracked and unplayable.

A few months after Maki Skosana's necklacing, I was offered a fulltime job at WTN, Worldwide Television News. I'd turned down their offer a year earlier, certain that success as a musician was imminent. This time, with the realisation that no such thing was going to happen, I gratefully took the job. My friend and housemate at the time, Jonathan Partridge, had taken the job I turned down, and now I was to be his soundman. The company's executive vice president, Robert E Burke, was out from England to check out the new staff members and introduce the new South African bureau chief, Freddo Gueddes. Freddo was a blindly ambitious little man who'd made a name for himself in the conflict zones of Nicaragua and Salvador. He'd started out in South Africa, and his images of Steve Biko's beaten body sneaked in the state mortuary in 1977 shocked the world. For all his bombast and arrogance, Freddo understood the pressures in the field and was a reasonable bureau chief.

But these were busy times and we hardly spent any time at the bureau. In July, PW Botha had appeared on national television, licking his lips and wagging his finger as he declared a State of Emergency. Despite the restrictions the State of Emergency imposed, international media swarmed all over the country and new stories were breaking daily in newspapers and TV around the world, most of which didn't even make South Africa's evening bulletins. Jono and I would trawl the townships, following the palls of smoke from barricades of burning tyres or vehicles that had been hijacked, looted and burned. There was always something going on, and input editors in London and Geneva were spoilt for choice. Our pictures were offered to clients via telephone conferences held throughout the day. The more sensational the pictures, the more likely they'd sell.

"Students stoning a police convoy, hmm, and cops retaliating with teargas and rubber bullets? Nine injured, you say?" The input editor might have been buying fresh fish. "Problem is, Visnews got a hell of a bun fight in Port Elizabeth this morning… two dead, and beautiful shots of cops beating comrades… Tell you what, get back out to Soweto, maybe things have heated up by now. With a bit of luck we can offer some hot stuff for the next conference. Maybe even a few stiffs."

It was a perverse competition, all these macho boys and a few girls cruising the townships bristling with cameras, lenses, flak jackets, and the defining swagger of the electronic cowboys. Loose alliances were formed, and groups would pull up beside each other in the dusty streets to swap information. The crews had immunity from the venom of the comrades – the international press, after all, were on *their* side showing *their* cause to the world. How were the comrades to know that many working for British and American broadcasters were ex-Rhodesians who saw South Africa going down the same shithole as their beloved country? To this day they still cover events in South Africa with glib told-you-so smiles as they point to the north as a sign of things to come.

We flew around the country in business class and chartered jets, covering funerals, marches, speeches and the rise of the Afrikaner resistance movement, the Weerstandsbeweging. Wednesday's march would provide bodies for Saturday's funeral, and Saturday's funeral would provide more bodies for the following week. It was an endless cycle.

Jono and I once arrived at a mass meeting in the township of Mamelodi outside Pretoria to find no-one there, just hundreds of shoes littering the dusty red field. As we got out to investigate what appeared to be a few people lying on the ground, a cop car screamed up beside us. Two cops grabbed us and hurled us violently into the back of their car. One had his pistol drawn and the other brandished a shotgun, which he pressed to the back of my head, screaming at me to get down. We were both squeezed into the narrow space between front and back seats, and when Jono tried to move, the cop shoved the gun down on him, forcing his head to the floor. The cops drove us around for maybe an hour, screaming and swearing with tyres shrieking around corners as they tested their brakes to the limit. Then they yanked us out of the car and pointed their guns at us, threatening to shoot as we got into our car and drove away.

They were part of a police battalion that had just killed twelve people, and were out of their minds on adrenaline. A routine protest meeting had rapidly expanded, and by the time fifty thousand people were raising fists and voices against their increasing repression, the police opened fire into the crowd. The news crews were everywhere except in Mamelodi that day. Just another of those days with little to show at the office and not much to tell. The next day we'd be in Cradock, then Durban, then Botshabelo and Inanda. Once in a while the army would cross the border and kill suspected ANC operatives in Swaziland or Lesotho; so we'd get a charter, follow the trail of blood, and rush home in time for the late feed to London.

In Cape Town the cops started putting purple dye in their water cannons to try to identify the enemy. Jono and I were on the pavement on a main road in the city centre, filming the purple rain as a student protest turned violent. The students took shelter in St George's Cathedral, Archbishop Tutu's parish, leaving us as the next best target for the cops. Suddenly a huge policeman was beside me with his sjambok[3] raised over his head. Jono ducked behind me as I tried to lift the recorder to protect myself, but it was too heavy. The first blow landed squarely on the small of my back, the next three ripped into my upper back. After a few more, the notorious cop, Dolf Odendaal, got distracted and we dashed off down the street. I shat on Jono for letting me take all the punishment but he didn't see my point.

Somehow we needed to get back to our car, but the cops were everywhere. Like urban warriors we ducked from building to building, using parked cars as cover. Suddenly, from nowhere, the brute form of Odendaal reappeared, sjambok twitching. Jono quickly backed into the entranceway of a bank, leaving me once again to the full fury of Dolf's sjambok, this time raking my legs and thighs. It turned out that a cameraman from another agency had filmed my first assault, and the pictures were beamed around the world that night as an example of how the regime was now clamping down on the international press.

A few weeks later, we went to interview Archbishop Tutu. He looked at me and burst into his insane cackle.

"Hey man, yoo, yoo, yoo! I was in Philadelphia and I saw them on the TV and they were beating you. I said to my friend, 'Hey man, I know this guy.' They were *beating* you."

With that, he burst again into his gleeful giggle, clapping his hands and slapping his knees through his purple cassock. I saw a lot of the

---

3 a traditional whip, originally made from rhinoceros hide

Arch over the next few years, and though I'd long since walked away from the flock, I was always moved and humbled in that great man's presence.

A short while before I started with WTN, I was down at Jamesons one night with Stan James, when his girlfriend arrived with a friend of hers. The friend's name was Ruth, and one look at her dissolved all my resolutions to remain a bachelor. Her hair was naturally blonde and furiously curly like a great mane of golden corkscrews. I was still smarting from the sudden end of my relationship with Irna, but Ruth was so startling to look at that I became instantly intoxicated. It was extraordinary how common sense could so quickly and absolutely abandon me just when I needed it most. I can't remember how long the courtship lasted but I was resolute and focused on my mission, and before long Ruth and I were floundering in the pool of deep affection. Life was very busy. Amanda and Sue were back from Namibia and I had a fulltime job for the first time in my life. It's amazing the energy of a rejuvenated heart. But even with this new and heart-warming presence in my life, I still drank heavily. Alcohol was a quick and effective way to draw the curtain on the violent events I was witnessing daily. Yet it was frightening how it could blot out great chunks of memory. One Saturday morning, after a particularly big night at Jamesons, I woke to find Ruth tidying the house.

"What you up to?" I called as I reached for a cigarette on the bedside table.

"Shit, I'm still shaking from last night," she replied.

"What are you talking about?" I asked.

According to Ruth, she'd woken in the early hours to find a bunch of cops in the bedroom, and climbing in the window. I allegedly leapt out of bed naked, shouting and abusing them. Ruth said they swept quietly through the house, pulling clothes and other stuff out of cupboards and then left silently by the front door, after which I collapsed back into a deep sleep. I didn't have a trace of memory about the incident.

My erratic behaviour didn't seem to deter Ruth, and we soon acknowledged that we were in danger of falling in love. But soon after I introduced her to my mother I noticed a problem. I knew all about her parents – she spoke about them freely – but when I asked about meeting them, she backed off. Eventually she revealed that her parents would be horrified that she was seeing a gentile. To that point her Jewishness had played no part in our relationship. Now it stared us down and wouldn't go away. The divisions in our society ran deep. Ruth was politically active and also worked for an organisation called POWA, People Opposed to Woman Abuse. She was feisty and independent, but when the chips were down, she ended up bowing to the pressure of her social group. Had times been less hostile, I might have fought harder to keep her, but back then, there seemed a certain inevitability that she'd end up with a nice doctor or lawyer within the faith. After a particularly bad night of tequila and angst, Ruth and I walked away from each other. Once again, it was an ending strewn with loose ends and raw nerves, another closed drawer in the closet of regret.

Meantime, home, kids, work, morning traffic, PTA meetings and letters from the tax man all combined into a daily burden I found increasingly difficult to handle alone. Which is probably why I saw in Rachel the perfect partner for these tough times. Racing around the country with Jono, on one Cape Town trip I bumped into Simon, a strapping man I'd met at a gig years earlier. He was one of a new breed of young South African farmers who believed the only way forward was to respect the rights of farm labourers, who were still treated with appalling cruelty, although their sweat had helped build this country. We met for dinner later in the week, and along with his charming wife, Isobel, he brought his younger sister, Rachel, a drama student at the University of Cape Town. We got along easily, and before I left for Jo'burg we went out for another meal. Over the next few months we spoke frequently on the phone as she prepared to move to Jo'burg to follow her acting career.

Thick black smoke rising beyond the green hills looks like it might be from a factory near Umbogintwini. As the plane banks towards Durban, I see that it's coming from the side of a valley opposite the factories. The Sony Betacam sits like a baby on my lap; it's a new system that records pictures and sound on one machine, and I'm the first at WTN to use it. Jono is away shooting with Spokes and I was alone in the office when the news broke about shit going down between Pondos and Zulus in a squatter camp near Umbogintwini. Freddo showed me how the Betacam worked and hurried me to the airport. My first time as a cameraman, and I'm alone, the Betacam clammy in my hands.

The police are hanging around their armoured troop carriers. I step out of the hired car and walk across to them. I ask if I can go into the maze of broken and burning shanties stretching uphill in front of us.

They shrug. "Do what you fucking what. But don't come back crying if you get fucked up."

I walk into the swirling smoke, silence hanging over the wreckage of charred metal sheets and timbers strewn in my path.

It's steep and hilly, and soon I'm descending a broken pathway into darkness almost like night. Up the other side I come across a pack of dogs, snarling at each other as they feed on some remains. Ignoring me, the jumpy, feral hounds jostle around their meal. I notice a pair of splayed human legs beneath them. I stop. A burnt out tyre lies on the head and chest of a corpse, the dogs ripping at the charred flesh. Steadying myself, I begin to shoot the scene from different angles.

I walk on. The place seems deserted. Then suddenly a bare-chested man appears out of the smoke, wild eyed with a spear in his hand and a red scarf around his head. I blanche as he looks at me. But he walks right on, back into the smoke. I go on and on, walking around the desolate scene. Filming as I go, I come across more bodies, more wreckage. Eventually, after about an hour, I find my way back to my car, where the cops still linger, laughing among themselves as I drive away. On the way to my hotel I buy a bottle of whisky. Soon it's half empty but I hardly feel drunk. The phone rings; Freddo tells me that the feed came in fine and the pictures are great. I've just made my way from being a soundman to a cameraman.

At the beginning of December 1985, Rachel arrived in Jo'burg and moved into my spare room in Crown Mines. At the same time my brother, Patrick, also arrived in Jo'burg to start a new life. He'd been working as a music teacher at a girls high school in Paarl near Cape Town. He was tired of teaching but not quite sure what to do, so I offered him part-time work as my soundman. On the morning of 17 December, I was sent to cover an unfolding story in the rural region of Moutse, east of Pretoria. The government was trying to forcibly incorporate Moutse into the nearby homeland of KwaNdebele, but the Moutse residents weren't cooperating. Patrick and I arrived in the village where the local chief lived, and found our way to his house to interview him.

During the interview we heard shouting and chanting nearby, and we all ran outside to see what was happening. At the bottom of the dusty street was an armoured police vehicle. We couldn't make out what was happening, so Patrick and I grabbed our gear and headed towards the fracas. As we approached, we saw a group of youngsters shouting and waving sticks and other crude weapons at the police. We started filming just as the police opened fire on the crowd. Chaos broke out on this previously deserted rural road.

Suddenly, a phalanx of police vehicles became visible, racing across an arid field towards the now scattering crowd. Patrick and I held our ground, camera rolling as the commotion unfolded. One vehicle, a bakkie, headed in our direction and slid to a stop beside us with a cloud of dust. Two cops leapt out, grabbed Patrick and me and threw us into the back of the bakkie. For the next half hour they drove that bakkie like the devil through ditches and clouds of teargas, ramming on brakes and doing everything possible to batter us and our gear against the sides of the vehicle. Finally they took us to the nearby police station, confiscated our gear and locked us in a cell.

As usual, I knew we'd be out in a few hours; this was nothing new. I assured Patrick we'd be home for supper. But supper came in our prison cell that evening in the form of dry bread and tepid tea. I consoled my brother again: we'd definitely be out by morning. The following morning, a huge uniformed cop wordlessly ushered us into the back of the bakkie again, and drove us to another police station about half an hour away. We still hadn't been allowed a phone call. I was becoming concerned about my responsibilities back home, including that of driving Amanda to playschool. I tried calling through the barred door, but the only time we saw anyone was when a black constable silently pushed a tin plate of food through the hatch.

After three nights in this cell, we were finally ushered into the charge office where a young attorney from Dave Dison's law practice was waiting. After a very brief whispered consultation in the corner of the charge office, we were marched across the compound into a small crowded courthouse, where our attorney exchanged a few words with the state prosecutor. We all stood as the magistrate entered the court. Only then did I discover that we were in the small town of Dennilton. It seemed we were to be charged with some minor contravention.

The prosecutor started speaking. "Mr Roger Lucey and Mr Patrick Lucey, you have been charged under the Terrorism Act, no 83 of 1967..."

I couldn't believe my ears. This was ridiculous. The terror laws allowed detainees to be held without charge for ninety days. Conviction carried the death penalty.

Our attorney had a long discussion with the prosecutor. Eventually we were given bail and released. Outside the compound, a press photographer and TV crew were waiting for us. The story had hit the papers, and WTN in London was already hiring one of the top advocates in Jo'burg to defend us.

During the time we were in custody, Rachel had run around taking care of the kids and harassing Freddo regularly to make sure WTN was doing everything possible to get us out of the slammer. We later learnt that during the first forty-eight hours of our incarceration, the police denied any knowledge of our whereabouts. The testimony of the chief in Moutse persuaded them to admit that we'd been arrested, but it was still another day and a half before they would tell the lawyers that we were in the cells in Dennilton.

Over the next six months we had to appear several times before the magistrate in Dennilton, and finally he dropped the charges against us.

By this time Rachel and I had gone from sharing the house to sharing the bedroom. We settled into a combative but regular routine, and managed to bring a sense of order to what had previously been my chaotic life. Rachel was bossy and almost Victorian in her ways, but like an old-fashioned school mistress she made sure the house ran to her rules. For me it was a relief to have help. By now Sophie, still living in the servant's quarters, had another child, a boy called Lerato fathered by her new beau, a driver from the mining company, and the house was often like a nursery school. My friends didn't care much for Rachel and stopped coming round. This created a greater sense of calm and order which I welcomed. Rachel knew little about my previous life as a musician, and didn't seem to care. I once told her how my album had been banned and how I was harassed by the police. She responded with a tirade against my feelings of injustice when so many blacks in the country were suffering so immeasurably. Sympathy wasn't her strong point.

One day an old friend from Durban who worked for Child Welfare phoned to tell me she'd received a query about my son Tay, now eight years old. Things looked bad, she said, and the authorities suspected physical abuse. They'd found cigarette burns on his arms, which his mother and grandmother claimed he'd accidentally caused himself. I drove to Durban a few days later and went straight to Sheila's apartment, where her husband was scowling on the sofa, beer in hand. I told her I was taking Tay to Jo'burg with me. With hardly a word she packed his clothes and twenty minutes later I was on the road home with Tay. Rachel took it in her stride, and once again I was grateful for the ordered, if somewhat severe, calm that had descended on my life.

Things at home may have calmed down, but the rest of the country was sinking into anarchy, and I had a front row seat.

At the beginning of 1987 we got notices that Crown Mines was going to be demolished, and we should make alternative living arrangements. Objections and papers were filed with the National Monuments Commission to try to prevent them knocking down this historic village, but in April the axe fell and everyone had to move out. At Rachel's advice, I bought a rundown old house in the suburb of Observatory, and sadly we left Crown Mines along with Sophie, Joshua and Lerato. The Crown Mines community had overflowed with warmth and friendship, and formed a sanctuary of mutual support through some very trying times. Despite all that had happened, both personal and political, I remember Crown Mines as one of the finest periods of my life. It was also a time when Joshua and Lerato, two little boys with no blood ties to me, became an intrinsic and loving part of my life. It was illegal to adopt children across the colour line, but over the years they became as close as any adopted child could have. For the previous few years, the children had been attending Sacred Heart College, the only school in the city at that time that defied the state and admitted black pupils. It was always a huge operation getting the kids to and from school, but now the school was within walking distance of home, and the pressures of daily life became more manageable. But there was no let-up in pace at WTN as I raced around in planes, chartered jets and helicopters covering the daily diet of killings, funerals, riots, mass meetings, and still more killings and funerals.

No sooner had we settled into our lovely old house than I got a call from Sue. She was now involved with a *New York Times* journalist, Alan Cowell, and she and Amanda were moving with him to Greece. The government had expelled him from the country, offended by something Alan had written, so he'd been redeployed to Athens. His punishment ended up hurting me more than him.

I hired a lawyer and took the matter to the Supreme Court. After all, I'd been a committed and dedicated father, and despite the problems I'd been through, I was well on the road to recovery. Sue's lawyer, a well-known human rights attorney at the time, was ruthless. It was hard to believe that a man of principle, as he claimed to be, could so horribly falsify who and what I was. I was no angel, certainly, but I was made out to be a demonic and savage person who would inevitably abuse my daughter if she stayed with me. When I asked Sue why they'd resorted to such tactics, she simply blamed the lawyer. When I lost the court appeal with costs, the same "human rights" lawyer sent a letter of demand threatening to attach my assets if his fees weren't paid in one month. My only "asset" was my mortgaged house – I'd saved enough to pay a ten per cent deposit, and was now in danger of losing it. I borrowed from my mother, increased my hours at WTN and shaved my living down to basic necessities. It was an awful time. I was heartbroken at losing Amanda, shattered by what I witnessed daily in my work, and still harboured a deep, lingering bitterness about the sudden, inexplicable collapse of my musical and creative dreams.

Over the next couple of years I covered events in every corner of South Africa that boiled over into conflict, confrontation and death. If things quietened down at home, Angola, Mozambique or Zimbabwe were always good for a war story. Every couple of months I went to the Angolan battlefront, and the sights and sounds of that war still linger deep in my psyche. On my return from these sojourns I would often see my family doctor, feeling ill and out of sorts. At the time he could never find anything wrong, and would blame it on depression or a "non-specific virus" caught in the warzone. Only years later were these symptoms identified as post-traumatic stress disorder.

Ian Herman was my soundman for a while, and he made a great companion as we raced from one story to another. Resistance to the apartheid regime had spread to every corner of the country, and we often found ourselves in rural places we'd never heard of. At a funeral outside the town of Thohoyandou in Venda, a large group of highly agitated young men surrounded us as we got out of our car. They weren't used to news crews in their territory, and because I was white, they thought I was a plain-clothes policeman there to film the funeral. They began pushing me around as a circle formed around me, poking their fingers in my face. Ian, being coloured, was sidelined at the back of the crowd with all the attention on me. A black news cameraman working for an American broadcaster climbed onto the hood of my car and started filming the altercation. This raised the temperature among the crowd, and a car tyre was fetched while others tried to open the petrol cap of my car to siphon petrol into a bottle.

I knew my time was up; I'd seen necklacings by now, and a strange calm overcame me. Suddenly Peter Magubane, a famous photographer colleague, pushed his way to the centre of the melee. He pushed the youths away from me, shouting at them in the Venda language, then nimbly leapt onto the hood of my car and ordered the other cameraman off. He then raised his hands in the air and called for silence. Miraculously, the crowd obeyed, and he addressed them in a firm and reproachful manner.

I didn't know what he was saying. But the crowd quickly calmed down and dispersed, many young men slapping me on the back with friendly smiles and laughter. He had told the crowd that I was there doing the same job as he was. If they wanted to kill me, they had to kill him as well.

As I fished in my car for my equipment to film the funeral, a squad of police vehicles came racing around the corner, firing teargas and rubber bullets into the crowd. They arrested Ian and me, locking us in the back of a bakkie for several hours before releasing us.

On the way back to Jo'burg, we stopped at the home of a Catholic priest who was politically active in the area. After telling him what had happened, he went off to the kitchen and returned with three tea cups, each filled to the brim with Scotch. "Here lads," he said, handing us each a teacup. "This'll make you feel better." And it did. Whenever I see Peter, we still joke about that incident. But it would have been no joke if Peter hadn't put his life on the line to save me from a crowd that wanted to watch me burn.

Ian soon left to continue his music career, and Carlo Guidozzi, a brawny Italian South African, came to work with me. He was tough and funny, which made a huge difference to staying sane in that kind of work. And although the work was hard, I was financially stable for the first time. The long hours paid off, pulling me back from the financial precipice that almost sank me when I lost my case in the Supreme Court. Amanda came to South Africa twice a year, and I looked forward to those visits like an elixir. Tay, Joshua and Lerato were happily in private schools, and the spectre of debt was slowly diminishing. Rachel and I continued our uneasy relationship, but we'd come through against heavy odds, and, hopeful that things would improve, we got married on 17 May 1989.

My mother came to Jo'burg to look after the kids, and we took off for England where Rachel's parents had their permanent home in the village of Ewelme in Oxfordshire. We were married in their local church by one of Rachel's mother's old friends, the Rev Barney Pityana, a former friend and comrade of Steve Biko. Years later, I went to interview Barney, who was then Vice Chancellor of the University of South Africa. He'd heard that Rachel and I were divorced. "Obviously," he said, nodding ruefully, "I didn't pray hard enough for you." But no amount of prayer could have saved our marriage.

29

Cape Town, Summer 1990

FREE AT LAST

Nelson Mandela stepped into freedom yesterday and immediately called for the intensification of the struggle, including armed resistance and the international isolation of "the apartheid regime".

Cape Times, 12 February 1990

AWB: "HANG MANDELA!"

"Hang Mandela!" a crowd of Afrikaner Weerstandsbeweging supporters chanted on Saturday as they marched through central Pretoria to deliver 30 pieces of silver – in two rand coins – to State President FW de Klerk.

Cape Times, 12 February 1990

Pictures of pain in a frame without purpose,
The name of the game in a cynical service.
Pictures of death and destruction is good business;
Understanding the story doesn't need to be part of the process.
                                    Pictures of Pain, Roger Lucey, 1990

Rachel's mother owned a beautiful farm in the mountains outside Cape Town, and a cottage overlooking the sea just miles from where the Indian and Atlantic oceans meet at the tip of the continent. In the summer of 1988/9 we spent a wonderful three weeks swimming in the ocean, riding horses and walking in the mountains. Amanda now lived with Sue and Alan in Cairo, and getting her to South Africa for holidays was increasingly difficult. There was no diplomatic contact between the two countries, and she had to travel enormous distances to get to South Africa. Nonetheless she was with me, and life was as good as it had ever been. Towards the end of 1989, word got around that Mandela would soon be released from prison. He'd been moved from Robben Island to Cape Town's Pollsmoor Prison in 1982, and then to Victor Verster Prison in 1988. Instead of a prison cell, he was now housed in a prison warder's house in a pretty field away from the prison complex, a sign that the government was starting to treat its prime prisoner with a newfound respect.

Since 1985, various meetings had taken place between the government and Mandela, and by the end of 1989, rumours of his release dominated newsrooms around the world. WTN was considering a permanent bureau in Cape Town to cover what would surely be the story of the decade. They had a freelancer, or stringer, in Cape Town, but no fulltime operator for the company. Their young stringer, Craig Matthew[1], was an incredibly courageous cameraman in such high demand from other organisations that he couldn't always fulfil his obligations to WTN. So this seemed the perfect job for me. I'd done well for the company over the previous five years, and just a few days after I volunteered for the position, I got the go ahead to pack for Cape Town.

---

1 Craig's iconic footage still appears in historical documentaries today

We're hovering in the sweltering heat of the Cape summer, the town of Paarl below to our right and the village of Franschhoek to the left. The door of the Bell JetRanger helicopter has been removed, but it's not just the wind making my hair stand on end. The engine's overheating, and the pilot shouts that we must either land or start circling. Circling's out of the question: we're at the front of half a dozen helicopters all after the same view; circling will take us to the back of the queue.

"Put it down right here," I shout.

"I can't," he hollers back. "It's a prison; we'll be shot."

"Not today, we won't. Put it down."

I can see the crew in the next chopper cursing as we descend into a field of freshly mown rye. We stay down until the temperature stabilises, then rise again, just as Nelson Mandela walks out of his prison bungalow and into that memorable day. I'm strapped in, but my feet are on the runners and my bum on the chopper floor. Through my lens I see him hugging and shaking hands with a long line of comrades who've come to walk with him to freedom: Cyril Ramaphosa, Ahmed Kathrada, Jay Naidoo, and his wife, Winnie. As he drives away I have a clear shot of him through the side window of the car, his grandchild on his knee. I'm overcome with exhilaration; it's one of the few times I don't feel that familiar tackiness at poking my lens into someone's life. This moment is so much bigger than that.

The months that followed Mandela's release were everything the news editors had looked forward to: massive political rallies to introduce the newly liberated revolutionaries to the masses, backlashes from the extreme white right, attacks from the shadowy Third Force and an epidemic of worms crawling out of the woodwork as talk of a Truth Commission was bandied about. It was a busy time, but there was Rachel's family farm or the beach cottage to escape to and relieve some pressure. As the ANC and the Nationalist government started the CODESA talks (Convention for a Democratic South Africa), the story moved from Cape Town to Jo'burg. But that didn't ease things for me.

The Jo'burg crews were run off their feet as a new development came to dominate daily events: the so-called Third Force was randomly attacking train commuters coming to the city from the townships. They'd enter the compartments wearing balaclavas and armed with guns, knives, spears and pangas[2], and lash out viciously at everyone on the train. The suspicion was that they were allied to Mangosuthu Buthelezi's Inkatha Freedom Party, which was talking of self-governance for the KwaZulu-Natal province. For years, Inkatha had been at war with United Democratic Front supporters, and with the UDF's mother organisation, the ANC, now out in the open, the fight had reached new levels of brutality.

As things calmed down in Cape Town, I was sent to help former colleagues in Jo'burg. On the first morning back in my old town, I went out with Carlo to the nearby Jeppe train station. Before long a commuter train from the eastern townships sighed to a halt in the station. The windows of almost every compartment were smeared with bloodied hand marks, forming grotesque patterns on the glass. As the doors opened, screaming, blood-soaked figures staggered off the train, directionless and terrified. We recorded the scene and then ventured onto the train. Bodies lay on the seats and the floor, many without limbs, individuals almost indistinguishable from each other in a mass of bags, flesh and blood.

I don't remember much else about that day, but that night I had supper at Stan James's house. After the meal Stan pulled out a small envelope of white powder. It was a new substance called ice, he said, as he chopped up some lines on a mirror. Before we knew it, it was four in the morning, the whisky bottle was empty and we were flying. Most evenings that week were spent tooting ice and drinking whisky, and most mornings hanging around commuter stations where the bodies kept rolling in.

By the time I got back to Cape Town, I was out of my mind. My memories of that week are like a shattered mirror: jagged shards but no cohesive picture. I rode my bicycle furiously around the neighbourhood, trying to exorcise the grotesque, dislocated images that overwhelmed every part of my consciousness. I remember sitting on a bench at the edge of Rondebosch Common, trying to work out whether I was really there or just imagining myself there.

Within a week I was telling my whole story to a young psychologist, Steve Brokensha. He was also a musician, and I felt safe enough in his company to speak freely about the events that had led to this crisis point. For almost two years I saw Steve every week, a time during which many tangled pieces of my past were put in their rightful places

---

2 traditional African machetes

and many plans for my future were mapped out. Unlike so many psychologists, psychiatrists and councillors I'd come across, Steve had a great sense of humour, and our sessions together produced as much laughter as tears. He understood my deep frustration at losing my musical voice, and helped me to understand the dreams, signs and signals that began emerging as I embarked on this healing journey. I was able to reveal to him my darkest secrets, most terrifying fears and what then seemed utterly futile hopes. When I described my dream of building a house in the mountains, he not only encouraged me but gave me reading matter on the value traditional societies placed on the act of home building. Through Steve I discovered a new view of the world, a vision in which my future began to look not only bearable but challenging and exciting.

I now recognised the damage my job at WTN had inflicted on me, and knew I had to get out of the news business. But I was still responsible for kids at private schools, and couldn't make impulsive decisions. I also realised that I needed to start playing music again after not touching an instrument in almost five years. My old Martin guitar, bought on my first trip to London, had survived all the hard times, but was cracked and broken from misuse and neglect. I took it to my old friend, Marc Maingard, one of South Africa's finest luthiers. He looked at it long and hard, and then let out a slow whistle.

"Hey, Rawj!" Marc had lived in the communal house at Rapson Road, and still used my old nickname. "This thing is totally poked. The only hope is my legendary skill – and a miracle."

Marc had a justifiably high opinion of himself. After many months in his workshop, my guitar was rejuvenated, and I started the long, finger-aching process of playing again. But I was still busy with WTN assignments, and started covering events even further afield, like the failed revolution in Madagascar and the military coup in the Comoros Islands. But every spare moment was spent playing and writing new songs.

In October 1990, I drove up to Durban and started recording my latest songs in Dave Marks's new studio. Kenny Henson played guitar and Dan Chiorboli played every type of drum and percussion instrument imaginable. It was one of the last sessions that master fiddler Dave "Plod" Tarr played before he died, and I also got three great Zulu singers, Vika Mthiwane, Queen Mbothwe and Winnie Zondi. Dave released the album, *Running for Cover*, at the beginning of 1991, but the bad smell that accompanied my name still stuck, and no-one would touch it. In Cape Town we arranged a concert to launch it at the Little Theatre on the University of Cape Town's Hiddingh Campus.

An article in the Cape Times announced the release of the album and its launch concert. Within days, I received notification of a registered letter waiting for me at the post office. A registered letter requires a signature on receipt, but as soon as I opened the envelope, I regretted signing for it. It was from the South African Defence Force, calling me up for a three week camp. It was a bizarre situation; I was thirty-seven years old and had completed my commitment to the army a decade and a half earlier. Mandela was out of prison, and despite the on-going unrest, the country was slowly pushing towards a negotiated settlement. I decided to ignore the letter.

Kenny, Dan and David all came down to Cape Town for the concert, which ran for a week at the Little Theatre. Attendance was half-hearted, but I was pleased I'd broken my musical drought and was a muso once again. I was invited to perform that April at the Splashy Fen Festival on a farm in the foothills of the Drakensberg. I also started doing solo gigs around Cape Town. Later that year we did a week at the Dawson's Hotel in Jo'burg, which took over when Jamesons closed. I was back in the musical saddle, and it felt good.

I'd almost forgotten my nasty invitation from the army. But soon after Splashy Fen, I arrived home one day to find the military police parked in my driveway. I casually reversed and drove nonchalantly down the road, parked out of sight around the corner and waited until I saw them drive off. Then I immediately contacted a young lawyer who'd been a conscientious objector himself and represented cases against the military. He wrote a slew of letters to my regiment, but received nothing in return. Call-up letters continued to arrive in my post box and I continued to ignore them. One day the military police delivered a letter by hand to my house, but luckily I was out on a job. I was to be court martialled, it said, and was expected at the military base the following Monday.

This was the only case of its kind the lawyer had come across. I was beyond the age of camps, and in any event I didn't qualify for them. Over the next few years the military police occasionally came to my house, but it seemed more of a game of harassment than a real effort to get me back in uniform. Only when conscription officially ended in August 1993 did I finally stop hearing from them.

By this time South Africa had slipped off the front pages

internationally, and the various political parties hammered out the terms of what would eventually be our first democratic election. But things didn't cool off for me. There were other conflicts going on in the world, and I was still on the payroll at WTN.

AT WORK: Acclaimed photographer Dennis Lucey who died in Durban a few days ago.

Adventurer Dennis Lucey dies

Daily News Reporter

DURBAN adventurer, flyer and film-maker Dennis John Lucey, 70, died in a city hospital a few days ago.

Mr Lucey...

photographer before moving onto making film advertisements.

Mr Lucey's work won wide acclaim

Hotspots, 1993

ADVENTURER DENNIS LUCEY DIES

Durban adventurer, flyer, and film-maker Dennis John Lucey, 70, died in a city hospital a few days ago. Mr Lucey, who caused a sensation in the 1950s when he and a friend flew a light aircraft from Durban to Europe and then repeated the trip a number of times, suddenly fell ill and was taken to hospital. Doctors discovered that he was suffering from cancer and his condition deteriorated rapidly.

Daily News, 6 January 1993

CROATS ATTACK MUSLIM TOWN

Bosnian Croat forces launched a tank and artillery attack on Muslim-held Gornji Vakuf yesterday, while Muslim units reoccupied the town of Fojnica in an upsurge of fighting in central Bosnia.

Cape Times, 16 November 1993

THIRD FORCE UNDER SPOTLIGHT

Human rights and research organisations are investigating whether a third force actually exists, as well as other covert operations.

Cape Times, 6 November 1993

THE HAIRDRESSER ON RONDEBOSCH Main Road has its blinds down against the afternoon glare. Soft, fat fingers rub the conditioner through my scalp in slow, circular movements. For a moment I feel drowsy, but I wake up quickly as she turns on the shower hose, rinsing the fragrant conditioner from my thinning hair. I sit up as she rubs the warm towel across my head and over my ears and forehead. My face in the mirror is hard and lined; I wonder how people see a similarity to my father; he remained handsome to the last, his aquiline features even more pronounced as the cancer ate through his body.

My mom would appreciate me looking neat for his funeral; I haven't bothered much recently, my hair loose and scraggly like those men in the bar down the road. I drink at home, not in the bar, but quietly and consistently. After the funeral I must fly to Nairobi; it's my turn in Somalia, but I'm looking forward to getting away; life with Rachel has become unbearable.

I'm thankful for the trips I made to see my father during the past year, as he rapidly became a skeleton. We never talked about our battles, but managed to find some sort of peace. He'd smile wanly when I kissed his forehead and call me "my boy".

He breathed his last in Addington Hospital, alone at three a.m.; the last breath of a Celtic warrior. In the mirror my face looks sad, and way older than my thirty-nine years.

The more it became evident that I needed to get out of the news business, the deeper I seemed to be getting into it. Joshua and Lerato were now at school in Jo'burg – closer to their mother – and only Tay remained with me and Rachel. Although he was becoming increasingly disruptive at school, it was more manageable for me to undertake the trips WTN required of me. I hired a young psychology student I'd met when I first arrived in Cape Town to mentor Tay. Paul Haupt had grown up in the neighbourhood and was enrolled in the University of Cape Town's clinical psychology programme. Paul often stayed at the house while I was away and took care of Tay. Rachel had started a clothing business, importing exotic African garments from Senegal, and was often away. Apart from the regular news duties like Somalia, Namibia and any other conflict that flared up in the region, I also worked as a producer/cameraman for European and Asian correspondents who came to South Africa on news or documentary assignments.

The day Chris Hani was shot I was in Maseru, doing a soft story about migrant labour with a Finnish correspondent. Chris Hani was a rising star among the recently returned ANC exiles, and to many, the likely successor to Nelson Mandela. By the time his killers – two right wing extremists – were caught a few hours later, Hannu Vaisanen and I were racing across the country towards Jo'burg. Hannu was the Africa correspondent for the Finnish Broadcaster YLE, and I'd covered many stories with him around South Africa and Namibia. The CODESA talks were reaching a climax, and violence in the country had decreased dramatically. A negotiated settlement seemed within sight, and a tentative new spirit of hope was awakening. Hani's assassination shattered it in a single burst of gunfire.

The response was immediate and frightening. Crowds took to the streets calling for a return to armed conflict; the police and army responded by increasing their numbers in the townships. At a rally at the Kings Park football stadium in Durban, Mandela addressed the massive crowd, urging them to throw their weapons into the sea. They booed him vigorously. But, in what is often seen as a South African idiosyncrasy, the mood turned, reeling back once again from the edge of the precipice.

Hannu and I spent two weeks covering the story as it unfolded, and he made a powerful documentary about the emerging democracy in a country he came to love. In the evenings, over copious frozen Finnish vodkas, he told me how happy being in Southern Africa made him, and how he wished he could find a way to live in its warm if unstable climate. But Hannu was eventually transferred to the Foreign Desk in Helsinki, ending his days as a roving reporter. There he sank into an ever deepening depression in a life he felt consigned to, rather than one he'd chosen. A short while later, as snow swirled in the half-light on the outskirts of Helsinki, he stepped deftly and deliberately into the path of an oncoming goods train.

At times during the CODESA talks the news story died completely, and almost nothing from South Africa made international news. The story grabbing the headlines was the increasingly intense war in the states of the former Yugoslavia, and soon the foreign editor told me to get on a plane to London. I was to take an armoured Land Rover from central London by ferry to France, then through Italy and onto another ferry to the city of Split in Croatia.

This should be a simple assignment. Sally Becker, self-styled angel of Mostar and loose cannon of the aid business, is off to East Mostar to evacuate a Jewish family and a Muslim man whose wife and kids she's already taken out. Along with local sound man Elvis Barukcic, I am to follow her and record the event for an ABC documentary programme. We will meet her at Split airport on Sunday evening and follow her, her bodyguard and her interpreter to the town of Citluk, a Croatian stronghold in central Bosnia about two hours away.

For three days the interpreter scurries in and out of the Citluk Hotel, trying to arrange permission and a ceasefire so the evacuation can take place. The Citluk Hotel feels like Brakpan's Royal Hotel on a Saturday afternoon. Half-pissed HVO[1] soldiers check out strangers, making anyone not in uniform feel like a dog turd on a bowling green. A guy who wouldn't be out of place in a pub in Brakpan is suspicious of Elvis. He hasn't heard the name Elvis before and wants to know if he's Muslim. Elvis does some fast talking and things cool off. The conversation ends with the big guy drawing his finger across his broad throat, saying in his heavy accent, "all Muslims". This is fragile and dangerous stuff; the encounter could have gone either way. We see a soldier greeting another with the Nazi salute. I'm starting to get the measure of this place, and can't help drawing parallels with South Africa.

The dining hall is blue with cigarette smoke and tense with the self-consciousness of soldiers fresh from battle; it's the only place to hang out as we wait for the endless stream of messages from the militia. War attracts weirdos, and the Citluk Hotel is where they're staying. There's the bald Scot who joined the HVO after being turned down by the South African Defence Force "because of the language barrier"; the wiry Londoner who got bored with the Putney fire department after eight years, so what the hell; the Croatian American,

---

1 Hrvatsko vijeće obrane or "Croatian defence council" militia

born and bred in Newark, New Jersey, who's back home with all the nationalism of a native and all the showbiz of one who's spent his life in the shadow of New York; and there's the Pole who lurks on the hotel steps all day, saying nothing, just waiting to go into battle. It's a relief when word finally arrives that we're clear to move.

Finally we're on the road, and after many checkpoints and endlessly hauling out the half-dozen press cards required here, we're driving across the old airstrip, the no man's land between East and West Mostar. We have two hours to get in and out. Sally Becker and two independent aid workers are in a borrowed Irish relief agency ambulance, and we're following in a brand new armoured Land Rover, the showpiece of my company. The ceasefire is to last until four pm sharp, when we'll meet the HVO patrol at the edge of the airstrip.

When we arrive at the hospital, something's gone wrong. In place of the red carpet welcome we'd been told to expect, the assembled hospital staff eyeball us in silence, and a hard-faced man with a black leather jacket and ancient machine gun orders me to switch off my camera. Elvis suggests I oblige. Something Sally Becker said during her previous trip appeared on Croatian TV and made the Croats look like the good guys. The head of the hospital accuses her of betraying the Muslims. There are accusations and counter accusations, voices rise and tempers flare; too many people are putting in their penny's worth and the whole thing is being conducted through an interpreter. It's a mess, and time's moving on. Come four o'clock, things have eased; explanations are given and once more TV journalism gets the blame. There's plenty wrong with the TV news business, but this time it's a damn convenient scapegoat.

We're back to square one. Permission to evacuate the family and the father needs to be obtained from the military commander, but he's out in the field and can't be found. I've been allowed to turn my camera back on and start shooting around the hospital. It's an old house, with windows and doors sandbagged; from the street it looks wrecked and deserted. You enter from the back and descend into the basement, which houses the operating theatre and the doctors' eating hall. Everyone smokes incessantly. There's no running water and the smell of shit and smoke overpowers the smell of death. The ceasefire has meant a lull in activity here, but the place is still packed with beds and stretchers, the kids two to a bed. Doctors walk around in blood-stained theatre gear and rubber sandals. They're short of everything and it shows. Elvis has set up our satellite phone in the hospital grounds, and I call the office in Split to say we're spending the night. When I hang up, a doctor from Sarajevo starts talking to me. He's been saving a bottle of wine since he arrived in Mostar, and he'll give it to me if he can call his wife who he hasn't seen for eighteen months; his daughter's now three. I tell him not to worry about the wine. He rings but there's no reply.

That evening we eat in shifts in the doctor's dining hall. The day's work is showing on their faces and they eat mechanically, yet another bowl of "humanitarian aid" rice and beans. There's little conversation; the TV in the corner gives the Croatian version of the day's events, and the extreme isolation of these people begins to dawn on me.

Lying in the back of our Land Rover later – my head propped up on my bulletproof vest while rifle fire rattles across the river – I drift in and out of sleep, wondering if Cape Town could ever reach this desperate state.

Early the next morning I call Citluk. I'm told that a ceasefire has been arranged for between eight and ten a.m., and we must get out, whatever happens. Sally Becker's still waiting for a reply from military command, and come ten o'clock, nothing's happened. Elvis wants to get the hell out. He's picked up grapevine talk that the commander doesn't give a shit for her evacuation, so I call Split and explain the position. It's pushing midday by now, and as I talk there's a huge explosion. I'm the only one out in the open, I notice, as another shell lands just up the road. I finish talking and grab the camera from the car.

As I make my way down the road towards the centre, a soldier who's been hanging around the hospital runs after me, waving his arms in the air. At first I think he's telling me to stop filming, but with a manic smile he beckons me to follow. I realise I've picked up a tour guide for the pending battle. By now shells are falling thick and fast, and my guide takes me to the fifth floor of an apartment building in the centre of town. In the room furthest from the source of the attack a family is huddled, a young girl quietly weeping. The view from up here is shocking. The entire hillside is exploding in pockets of dust and smoke. An ambulance screams down the street below. I turn the camera on and point it out the window; the rest simply happens.

My guide beckons again and we race downstairs onto the street. He's identified some houses that have been hit, and we wind our way up the narrow streets near the worst-hit part of town. Whenever a

231

shell lands close by, he looks at me and lets out a crazy laugh, like a cowboy on a Saturday night. I laugh with him, and we slap hands like basketball players. What is this? A quick celebration of staying alive? We pass through a doorway into a destroyed courtyard. It's a mess of soil, fragments of shrub and terracotta suggesting a once-neat patio; the garden furniture is now a tangle of wire that snares my legs as I walk. Inside, an old man sits weeping on the remains of a chair, ignoring us. At his feet, blood is still flowing from his dead wife's head. As the soldier takes a tablecloth and covers her, the old man's wail reaches fever pitch, strangles itself, and subsides.

We take refuge for a while inside a sandbagged tailor's shop, where the tailor and his apprentice are drinking Turkish coffee and smoking. They fall into easy conversation with the soldier. I refuse their offer of coffee; I'm wired as it is, and being unable to speak the language forces me into the role of silent observer; my senses are heightened to almost hallucinogenic proportions. A woman somewhere between forty and sixty – it's hard to tell around here – wanders in to bum a cigarette. She doesn't speak but cries without tears; the tailor shuts her up with a cigarette and a stern warning. She sits on a pile of camouflage trousers and smokes the whole thing, staring at the floor. I bump into her many times in the next few days and realise that this is all she does: wander around crying her tearless cry and bumming cigarettes. On one occasion she sits in a shattered doorway in the most exposed part of the street, staring at the floor and smoking, while locals urge her to take cover. Miraculously she finishes her cigarette safely before wandering off.

The soldier takes me into the old part of town, past the public park now packed with graves, where he points out those of his cousin and brother. We continue up the narrow lanes; despite the gaping holes and pock marks from rockets and machine guns, the charm and beauty of these old buildings is still evident. At the end of a long, dark passage he opens the door to his parents' house. I meet his father and mother. His aunt brings his grandmother downstairs on her arm, and she shakes my hand, her toothless face breaking a beautiful warm smile. They sit me down and give me lunch, and I'm stunned by the generosity and fortitude of these humble people under such horrendous conditions.

Back at the hospital I find the Land Rover's taken a near hit from a mortar: it sits glumly on flat tyres, its bullet proof panels looking like Swiss cheese. Good thing I wasn't in it. This will be a source of consternation for management back in London. The basement looks like a scene from the trenches in World War I. There are people everywhere, the place is thick with smoke, and among it all the doctors are doing their best to keep things under control. The steep staircase is jammed with blood-stained orderlies rushing the wounded down, and carrying the dead slowly up again. A young fighter is brought in – half his leg blown off – and taken into the operating theatre. Minutes later a massive blast shakes the building, and doctors and nurses covered in dust and sand reel blindly out of the theatre. It's taken a direct hit but the sandbags have done their work. Within a few minutes the patient is brought out into the corridor where the doctors continue cutting the blasted flesh from his severed leg.

There's a limit to how much of this I can take, so I head outside. The Land Rover has suffered another hit; diesel is pouring from a dozen holes in the tank. The satellite phone has been hit by shrapnel. I try to call Split, but the line's dead.

I'm given a bed in the doctors' quarters for the night, where six double bunks are squashed into a narrow room, and the windows sandbagged shut. The light stays on all night as doctors, nurses and orderlies come and go in shifts. It's hot and stuffy and there's no privacy. Sleep doesn't come easily, and in my pissed-off state, I wish I could bring the Big South African War Talkers on a tour of this place, to let them see where war gets you. Terreblanche and Constand Viljoen and Yengeni and Winnie, Benny Alexander and Buthelezi and every other bastard politician who talks the talk and doesn't give a shit where it all ends up. I've got to sleep; this place is getting to me.

During the night the hospital takes another twelve direct hits. Come morning, nothing's changed. The shells are still falling and the basement is chaotic. The saddest is when kids are brought in, dead on arrival, with mothers and fathers hoping hopelessly, desperately, for some small sign of life, while the traffic of the dead and dying is so busy that no-one has time to offer compassion.

By now I've stopped filming; I no longer have the black-and-white eyepiece to distance me from the reality of it, which, I so often think, allows people in my business the callous unconcern that characterises so many news hacks.

The frequency of death is shocking, especially among the fighting men, I realise, as a group bolts down the stairs with a badly wounded comrade shouting for attention. A doctor kneels next to him on the floor and tries to get a drip up while a nurse pushes a plastic tube down his throat. But it's too late. The realisation settles slowly among his comrades; one weeps silently and another bites his trembling lip. As they remove their battle gear in the heat of the basement, I realise that these fighting men are just boys: not one is older than eighteen. But they too must make way for the constant stream of casualties. They put on their helmets, check their weapons and leave at a run for the front. They'll have to grieve their fallen comrade on the battlefield.

There's a kid about ten years old who hangs around the hospital, bumming cigarettes and offering to find loose women for us foreigners. His head is shaved and his cheeky smile capped by a row of rotten teeth. A nurse strokes his spiky head and tells me that both his parents have been killed in the last eighteen months. He puffs away and checks me out, his naughty smile giving nothing away. He's being looked after by an aunt, but she has her fair share of kids and troubles, so he cruises, more or less taking care of himself. He shows no outward signs of his personal tragedy; just another kid, cruising around the war zone. On the third evening as I walk around, I see him in an open lot next to a burning apartment block. He gazes at the flames and the residents trying to save their possessions, and I notice that his smile is gone; in its place is sorrow tempered with resignation, his eyes deep, mouth hanging. It's a picture as vivid to me now as it was then. I struggle with the ridiculous desire to take him from this place, to make it better.

I've always heard that love does extremely well in wartime, and when I return to the hospital, I've got front row seats to a little passion play. Since we arrived, Elvis and a beautiful young nurse have made no effort to hide their attraction to each other. They spend minutes looking at each other intimately, unabashed, as if there's licence to make up for lack of privacy. They speak to each other in whispers, mouths inches apart, seemingly unaware of the crush of orderlies carrying stretchers, shocked soldiers and weary doctors, and no-one seems to notice their frantic courtship. All the rules are different around here, and while the people are charming and warm, there's an urgency that does away with unnecessary social graces. When Elvis gets hit by ricocheting shrapnel, she takes control, ordering the other nurses into action, pulling the burning twists of metal from his body and covering him with kisses. Elvis later tells me that he knows it's an impossible situation, but now they sit in the corner of the dining hall, kissing gently and smiling sadly at each other.

It's become clear that Sally Becker won't be evacuating anyone this time, and Elvis and I decide – since the story is dying – that in the interests of our wellbeing we should get out of here. The UN Spanish battalion have agreed to take us out whenever the shelling subsides, and a burly man with a moustache has let us sleep in his fortified room over the road from the Spaniards. So far they have three wounded troops and nine blasted tyres out of four armoured personal carriers, and their relief shift is four days overdue. They're keen to get out. The burly man makes us a pot of Turkish coffee, and when he takes off his shirt I discover that his burliness is an illusion created by his battle fatigues and his big moustache. He's suddenly small and spindly, his arms thin and white and his ribs visible through his undershirt.

He shows a snapshot of himself with a bunch of other soldiers in a tavern, and tells how they vowed that night to resist the ethnic separation being forced on them. These were the residents of Mostar, Muslims and Croats who'd been living together peacefully for years. But days after the photograph was taken, a tide of madness swept through Mostar, and Muslim and Croat faced each other across the river that divides East from West. Elvis sleeps soundly even when the shells land on our doorstep. He's from Sarajevo and this is nothing new to him. But I'm from Cape Town, and sleep dances just out of reach around the edge of my consciousness. It must be the Turkish coffee.

I'm on the street before sunrise and the sight is staggering. A bus has been blasted across the street, rubble is everywhere, tail fins of mortars jutting out of the tarmac. There are about ten crowded in an area of fifteen square metres. The shelling has subsided, and people are on the street, collecting water in an assortment of containers, while others sweep away the debris outside their shops and houses. At the water tanker is a gynaecologist I met at the hospital, and he introduces me to his wife who speaks good English. She's a striking woman, about sixty, with a shock of grey hair and a look that belies the hardship she obviously endures. She tells me she and her husband were about to visit South Africa when the war came. They lived in a rambling villa overlooking the river; now they share a basement dormitory with many, sleeping on mattresses on the floor. Yet there's enormous dignity as she asks about the state of theatre in South Africa, and how many orchestras we have. The Spanish are about to leave, so I shake her hand and ask her to call me if she ever gets to South Africa.

Elvis and I squeeze into the armoured vehicle, the crew on bucket seats while we and our bulky equipment fill every other inch of available space. As the vehicle starts limping down the road on its flat tyres, we crouch on our knees to stop our heads banging against the metal ceiling. We peer through the driver's window for a view of what's outside. All we see are kids with outstretched hands, then suddenly the road's deserted. We're crossing no man's land.

At last, the driver breaks the silence with a great whoop to celebrate our safe passage. The army doctor hits the play button on his ghetto blaster and Credence Clearwater Revival blasts through the space. He produces a bottle of piss yellow liquid from his first aid kit. "Bosnia Cognac," he grins. Two good pulls on an empty stomach and things soften around the edges. I poke my head out to inhale some clean air and absorb the eerie serenity of this tortured, bombed out place. We stop to meet the maintenance crew who've come to change the tyres before we can carry on. The Spaniards walk around, talking excitedly, making jokes to the maintenance guys about the last couple of days. Once again the language barrier isolates me, my mind spinning over the events of the past few days. I walk over to the armoured carrier and polish off the bottle.

Foreign assignments took their toll on my mental health, but one consolation was the good money I earned doing this dirty work. My mother had always advised me to invest in property, and now with more financial security, I decided to move up in the property market. The house on Wolmunster Road was huge and pink. The front door had a magnificent stained glass panel the size of a bed, and the hallway was covered in ornate Victorian tiles. Despite tenuous links to a grand past, the house was falling apart, so I managed to buy it well below its real value. Rachel was spending most of her time in Senegal and Jo'burg now, but soon after I moved into the big house, an old friend from the early days of the Market Theatre, Nicholas Ellenbogen, asked if he could camp out for a few weeks. He'd just relocated his theatre company, Theatre for Africa, to Cape Town, and was looking for a new home for the company and himself. An actor friend of Nicholas, Andrew Brent, took refuge with him after a traumatic relationship in England ended, and when Nicholas found a house and moved out, Andrew stayed on as my housemate.

On 21 January 1994, I celebrated my fortieth birthday with a party and a concert at the big house on Wolmunster Road. I built a small stage in the corner of the garden and covered the rest with a large marquee. This was a symbolic event, meant to mark my return to music and the end of my news career. It was a wonderful evening with many friends turning up to grace my stage, although it took another year before I could finally turn my back on WTN.

Meanwhile, Andrew and I started talking about a theatrical collaboration. We booked ourselves onto the fringe of Grahamstown's National Arts Festival in July of that year, and in between shooting the run-up to South Africa's first democratic election – scheduled for 27 April – I started writing my first play, *The High Cost of Living*. Grahamstown schools and colleges are all on their winter break during the annual festival, and the whole town gets converted into makeshift theatres, restaurants, bars and all types of accommodation.

Before the first rehearsal, Rachel confronted me. I was not to ask her for help producing the play just because she'd gone to drama school. This was entirely my endeavour and she was having nothing to do with it. In truth, I hadn't even thought of asking her for help. She was frequently away, and her drama career had been virtually non-existent. Since her arrival in Jo'burg she'd produced a two-woman revue that was panned by the critics, and that had been it.

To play opposite me in *The High Cost of Living*, Andrew and I hired David Muller, a smiley barrel of a man and an evergreen on the Cape Town theatre scene. Having missed out on theatre school in London years earlier, I still hankered to take to the stage, and this was my chance. David was a treat to work with, quietly encouraging and sensitive to the fact that I was a total novice. Andrew directed, and since we lived in the same house, he coaxed me into my role at all hours of the day. Although I was still running the WTN office from home, apart from the occasional outbreak of violence, the appetite for news stories from South Africa had diminished considerably. We rehearsed in the large dining room, and every so often I'd have to break away and rush off to some or other political disturbance. Although I still did my job dutifully, my heart was now in another place.

Work on *The High Cost of Living* was put on hold as our first democratic election approached. Foreign correspondents starting drifting in and I had to get seriously into news mode. Planning meetings took place, schedules were set out and daily satellite feeds were booked. The mood was one of quiet apprehension. Correspondents, producers and news crews were preparing for one of Africa's great bloodbaths: there was enough evidence to suggest that this would be the catalyst to unleash combatants from all sides upon one another. That April morning we all went out with that familiar dry mouth and hollow stomach, anticipating trouble. But as the morning wore on, anxiety turned to smiles, as thousands upon thousands of people emerged from their homes to form long, winding queues at the polling stations. Word filtered in that it was the same all over the country: quiet, peaceful lines of humanity waiting their turn to make their mark. By the following morning, half the satellite feeds had been cancelled; audiences can take only so much of a peaceful scene. As the votes were counted, the bloodbath still hadn't materialised, and by the end of the third day, many correspondents and crews were packed off to Rwanda. Now *there* was a bloodbath.

Three weeks later at home in front of the TV, I watched as Nelson Mandela was inaugurated as the country's new president. It was a moment that changed the whole world. It was also a moment in which I felt a massive wave of personal healing sweep over me. I whooped and wept and danced myself dizzy in the big, empty house on Wolmunster Road.

In addition to our play, Andrew and I decided to make a documentary of what would be the first National Arts Festival since the advent of democracy. We arrived in Grahamstown loaded with props and camera gear, and set to work immediately.

The High Cost of Living was produced under the patronage of Nick Ellenbogen's Theatre for Africa, which immediately lent it some weight. The story was partly autobiographical, in which we played two old friends who were once in a band together. In the story, David arrives on my doorstep after many years and suggests that we reunite the band. It's a story of the pain and joy of being an artist, and fortunately the critics gave it good reviews.

When we weren't on stage with the play, Andrew and I were merrily shooting the documentary, meeting artists, actors, writers and directors from every corner of South Africa. Two nights before the festival ended, Rachel called to say she was coming to Grahamstown. She arrived in time for the penultimate performance, and despite the freezing weather, we had a sizable and appreciative audience. Afterwards, in the small apartment we'd rented, Rachel attacked with the fury of a woman scorned. It seemed I'd misread the signs; she had very much wanted to direct my play. Totally bewildered by her reasoning, I tried to let the tirade pass without too much damage.

But when Andrew and I dropped her at Port Elizabeth airport for her flight to Jo'burg, and then drove off towards Cape Town, I knew my marriage was over.

31

Walking Away, 1995

RUSSIA TIGHTENS GRIP ON GROZNY

Chechen President Dzhokhar Dudayev was reported by Russia's government press centre yesterday to have left Grozny on Friday – though it said his forces still controlled parts of the city. Thick black clouds of smoke covered Grozny as Russian artillery, mortar and rocket fire poured into the centre of the city where 400 000 people once lived.

Cape Times, 9 January 1995

GOLDSTONE'S SECRET REPORT REVEALED... AT LAST

Today we publish the secret report of Judge Richard Goldstone. The explosive document links top-level police officers – including former police commissioner General Johan van der Merwe – to "murder, fraud, blackmail and political disinformation". Goldstone handed his report to then-president FW de Klerk weeks before the April 1994 election, calling for urgent steps against the "depraved" SAP leadership. De Klerk sat on the report.

Mail & Guardian, 7 to 13 July 1995

NATIONAL ARTS FESTIVAL

From Cape Town is Roger Lucey's realistic portrayal of life behind the scenes in a newsroom, aptly called Newsroom. *Directed by Nicholas Ellenbogen, with Andrew Brent playing the archetypal boozing bastard of an international correspondent and a support cast of engaging characters, the play takes a touching look at how "getting the story" might make a public career but can break a personal life.* Newsroom, *set on the eve of the 1994 South African elections, is sensitive without being schmaltzy.*

Cape Times, 10 July 1995

MUSIC TO SECURITY BRANCH FEARS

In a second extract from his book, former security police "dirty tricks" expert Paul Erasmus tells how he put the brakes on singer Roger Lucey's career.

Mail & Guardian, 7 to 13 July 1995

AT THE END OF 1994, TAY WENT back to Durban to live with his mother and stepfather. He'd become increasingly unhappy at school and had been to three different schools in three years. His behaviour had gone beyond simple teenage upheaval. I was regularly called to the headmaster's office to discuss a problem, and Tay would always resolve to make things better. Several times I had confronted him about money that had gone missing, which I'd find hidden among his clothes. He always denied the infringement, first suggesting that he could have been framed by Joshua and Amanda. We had let it pass, but now there was no excuse. During a consultation at Cape Town's Child and Family Unit, Tay revealed that he constantly worried about his mother's wellbeing, and desperately wanted to be close to her. The psychiatrist persuaded me to let Tay go; at the age of seventeen, he was old enough to make his own decisions. He hadn't been an easy child, so with sadness but also relief, I helped him pack his bags and board a plane for Durban.

Now only Andrew and I were left in the vast house on Wolmunster Road. To fill up at least some of the empty space, we decided to pack an entire room with cases of wine bought at a discount from a winemaker friend. And with the same enthusiasm as we'd filled the room, we applied ourselves to depleting the stocks.

A few days after Christmas 1995, I was called by the foreign editor at WTN to London. The city of Grozny in the Russian province of Chechnya was under siege by Russian troops. Reluctantly I drove to the airport. I was trying to get out of this crazy world of news gathering, and here I was heading into a desperate conflict in a place I'd barely heard of. The only consolation was that I'd return via London, where I could spend time with Amanda, who was now at boarding school in the lovely city of Bath.

The dark moods and brittle alienation that had plagued me for years had now been given an official name: depression. I resisted the antidepressants I was told could help, and instead spent hours tramping Table Mountain. Wolmunster Road is a stone's throw from the Table Mountain Nature Reserve, and I found that vigorous walking in all weather helped keep the darkness in check. But nothing could prepare me for what I was to find in Chechnya.

The words and phrases scribbled in my small black notebook jolt my memory. The past month has all been so turbulent that I need to go back and retrace my steps; to put it all in order.

I remember my desolation on the flight from London to Moscow, the bitter taste in my mouth and heart after the cold, formal parting with Rachel. Getting off the Aeroflot plane, I head for a grey, snow-covered building at the edge of the runway, so far away from Cape Town.

The hard-faced woman at customs finally waves me through. I push past a steamy throng of taxi drivers with furry hats and smelly Russian cigarettes, all hustling for my foreign currency. My driver speaks no English, so I sit in silence watching this wild new world unfold. It's minus fourteen outside and everywhere is snow and ice. We overtake a bus. It's from the fifties, lopsided and rusty like a Nairobi bus without the colour, with bits hanging off it, a thick mat of snow on the roof and steamy windows: inside the anonymous faces under big furry hats look huddled and silent. Our radio's on loud, a local FM station playing the early Beatles: *picture yourself in a boat on a river...*

A huge concrete apartment block looms out of the mist; Stalinist architecture, ugly as sin. Down one side is the Marlboro cowboy, ten stories tall in neon.

I enter and check in, then head out again, not quite sure where I'm going. I find myself in Red Square with snow falling, gently icing St Basil's as waves of history rock me. This was the centre of what for some was the core of all evil, and for others the source of all liberation. I recall the old saying: If you're not a communist at twenty you have no heart; if you're still a communist at thirty you have no brain. I'm forty one; fuck knows what I am.

But right now I'm on my way to Chechnya with other things on my mind. Come morning, a different driver picks me up from my hotel, and he doesn't speak any English either. That's fine by me. It's well before dawn and I'm happy to look out at Moscow as it passes by. We pass the White House, the seat of power that was taken out by tanks only a few months ago. It's the only white building in this great grey landscape; it's been repaired and its spotlights are back on. Over the river, the spectacular Hotel Ukraine is one of Stalin's "seven brides", designed to stun the world and show the power and glory of the Soviet spirit. Further on is a power station, steaming away into the surreal morning, and next door the university – so here you have it all: workers, students and politicians all mixed together in the same neighbourhood. The Great Leveller, the proletarian revolution. Too bad about all the shit pouring out of the power station.

I board a chartered jet with a gaggle of other TV hacks for a place called Mineralnye Vody in southern Russia, an outpost of snow, ice and miserable authorities trying to squeeze a couple of roubles out of you. From there it's onto an old school bus for the twelve-hour trip to Khasavyurt, where all the networks and agencies are based. By this time these "dogs of war" as the hacks call themselves are growing inebriated, and war stories start flowing. None of them is listening to the other; they all just butt in to tell their own story that's yet more courageous and more cynical than the one before. I long to escape this depressing display of macho voyeurism, but it's too uncomfortable to sleep, and every hour or so there's another Russian checkpoint looking for another payment of Marlboros and vodka. We arrive well after midnight. There's just time for a few vodkas, and I get told I'm "it" for Grozny tomorrow.

It's still dark as we leave in our armoured Land Rover whose windows don't open, and the first thing everyone does is light up. I've given up smoking and I find it offensive now, but by the end of the day I won't care.

Soon after sunrise we reach a suburb of Grozny where we stretch our legs and don bulletproof vests and helmets. These may protect us from sniper fire, but won't help against the Grad missiles raining down on the city centre. The windows of the dull grey apartment blocks have all been blown out, yet women are still hanging their washing over the balconies and shouting at the kids running around in the snow. Pavement market stalls are selling a variety of basic provisions, oblivious to the boom of heavy artillery and thick black smoke just over the bridge.

A photographer with rotten teeth and smelly breath tries to bum a lift with us into the centre; his driver is refusing to go in. "Fuck him," says Avdaly our driver, who doesn't need anyone more to worry about. Avdaly's pale blue eyes – unusual in a Chechen – are bright with adrenaline as he guns the motor. In no time we're across the bridge and racing towards the centre. He's got a job to do and he means to get it over with, fast.

First stop is the well, the city's sole source of water, where old people and kids are queuing with an assortment of containers on sleds, carts and even an old pram. The guy handling the hose chivvies them on, his hands pink from the freezing water. As I film these scenes, an old woman starts talking to me in Russian, and soon she's sobbing loudly and wiping her eyes on a tattered sleeve. The others look on blankly until a man in the queue barks sharply at her. She moves off into the snowy street, pulling her sled, still sobbing. The word is out that the Russians are concentrating their attack on the Presidential Palace today, so it's safe to come out and replenish supplies. But the respite doesn't last. When two fighter bombers roar low over the city, the streets quickly empty, apart from a couple of white-clad soldiers trudging to the front, and a teenage boy yelling with great bravado after the planes.

Avdaly shouts at us; he doesn't want to stay too long in one place. We drive a short way on and park behind a bombed-out apartment block, only four city blocks from the Presidential Palace. The earth rocks with each deafening explosion. Still, there's something vaguely unreal about this whole scene, as if it's on TV, sanitised. I wander around, a bit dazed. Kids run out of a basement and throw fireworks into the air; a soldier shouts at them from the balcony of a destroyed building, and they run back underground, laughing. A soldier with dark-ringed eyes and swags of ammo belts crunches through the snow towards the front, smiling tiredly at me as he passes.

I step on a dead dog half buried in the snow. It feels creepy and sets my heart racing. Then I notice something in the snow across the street and set off to check it out.

"Get back!" Avdaly screams as bullets crack over my head. "Russian sniper," he says laughing, eyes flashing. "That's what happened to that poor bastard." He points across the road.

My heart's really pumping now. I zoom in on the body across the street. It looks like a young man in his early twenties. There's no sign of any wound, just a thin trickle of dark, congealed blood snaking out of his ear. This is one body the soldiers can't retrieve; they've already lost one man trying. We pass the body several times over the next couple of weeks, and each time it appears just a little less real.

A boy no older than sixteen comes running from between the buildings, an ancient shotgun over his shoulder, and bangs on the heavy metal door of a basement. A soldier lets the kid in. Avdaly waves me in and we wind down a dark, foul-smelling stairway.

The basement is full of fighters drinking tea around a small fire of planks and rolled-up cardboard. One is playing a guitar and singing sad anthems about Chechnya. We accept a glass of tea, while the muted boom, crash and crackle pounds the city in the background. Then we head off for a look at the Presidential Palace.

As we get closer it gets visibly more dangerous, the level of destruction increasing. Bodies are scattered over the roads and pavements, lying in awkward positions. Some look almost alive; others are shattered, barely held together by bits of uniform or webbing. Avdaly is silent, mourning written over his face. Finally we're in a building a couple of hundred yards from the palace, peeping through holes in the walls and ducking from one room to another. The experience is extremely unnerving. There's no sign of life out there, except for the deafening mélange of shrieking mortars and clattering AK47s, punctuated by the regular deep swoosh and thunder of Grad missiles. A Chechen fighter tells us to be quick; you never know where the next shell will land.

Grozny's main street is a scene of pure carnage. Blackened carcasses of Russian tanks and armoured personnel carriers stand here and there, the legacy of earlier street battles that stunned the powerful Russian military machine and set this war on its hopeless trajectory. In the middle of the main street a tank still smoulders from a Chechen rocket fired at point blank range into its turret. The bodies of the Russian soldiers that tried to escape remain bizarrely statuesque in frantic positions on and around the smoking wreck. Everywhere in the snow lie dead soldiers and civilians. Sprawled and twisted, they must wait for a lull in the fighting or warmer weather – whichever comes first – before it becomes necessary to bury them. This doesn't apply to the dead Chechen fighters; soldiers brave the brutal barrage to collect the remains of their comrades, and wait for nightfall and hopefully relative calm to bury their dead.

Up and down the street, mortar shells keep landing, several each minute, but they seem far away and almost innocuous. Suddenly one lands nearby, raising dust and fear. It's time for us to back out of this hideous theatre of death.

Around the corner from our parked Land Rover a couple of kids and a wounded soldier sit around a furiously burning gas line that's been shot up. In a bizarre way it's like being in a farmyard: chickens are clucking, a cat sleeps on a pile of burnt-out mattresses and kids with AK47s smile for the camera. A middle-aged man comes out of an apartment block with what looks like a big balalaika wrapped in a blanket. Behind him, a fighter with an RPG over his shoulder carries an ancient amplifier. Avdaly tells me he's a famous Chechen musician who's finally decided to get the hell out before his beloved instruments get blown up. He says something about the "Ruskies" and everyone laughs. Then he does a little dance – arms in the air, legs kicking brisk and high – before getting into his clapped out little car and racing up the road, swerving between bomb craters.

We follow, and soon we're out of Grozny, driving through the oilfields with their nodding donkeys and derricks, pumps and pipes. This is what the fight is all about; the main pipeline from the Caspian Sea runs through Chechnya, and the Russians fear Chechen independence will shut them out of the picture. What I'm hearing is that the average fighting man doesn't give a damn about the oil. His fight goes way back to the time of the czars and before, when they were denigrated, harassed and turned into the monsters of Russian nursery rhymes: throat-slitters with great cauldrons for boiling Russian babies in. Stalin banished them to Siberia, moving in Russian settlers in their place, many of whom are still here. The look in the eye of one of our drivers, as a Russian soldier at a roadblock slapped his head and shoved him with a rifle, smouldered with centuries of unfinished business.

As the light fades, we drive through the nearby villages of Gudermes and Shali. People crowd around little sidewalk stalls loaded with hunks of red meat, piles of bread, pale plucked chickens with forlornly lolling heads, as well as Pepsis, Marlboros, Hershey bars and other American junk food. The effect is otherworldly. There's a colourful mosaic of Lenin in the village square, with a cannon hole right through his forehead. Nearby on the village green, half of a huge concrete hammer and sickle sticks out of the mud and snow.

The day's over and my head's spinning as we return to Khasavyurt.

The area has no hotels, so the hacks are staying in a vacated preschool and any spare rooms they can find in the town. At the preschool we sit on kiddie chairs nine inches high and sleep on camp beds or nursery beds pushed together. There's no hot water and the toilet is the kind of place you don't hang around in any longer than necessary.

The noisy, smoky atmosphere is dominated by Vanya, a huge Georgian from Tbilisi who fills our cups with vodka and makes endless toasts in the Georgian tradition: to beautiful women, to the children of war, to our parents – we stand up for them, but sit to toast our employers – then we toast Nelson Mandela and our own dead colleagues... and in no time the day's terrifying events have slipped into a quiet, dark place behind a wall of laughter, vodka and boisterous camaraderie.

Once again we leave early. Today two young English satellite operators accompany us; they want to see the battlefront for themselves. They sit in the back while I ride up front with today's driver, Alhun, a stern, thickset Chechen with a mouthful of gold teeth, a hawk-like nose and eyes that bore right through you. Like so many of these people, I soon discover that he has a heart of gold. When we reach the bridge that leads into Grozny, yesterday's buzzing market street is deserted. Sensing that all is not well, Alhun pulls into an alley between the buildings. The Russians have tried to destroy the bridge overnight; it's riddled with craters, and one lane is blocked by the smoking skeleton of a truck. From the shadows of buildings locals peep nervously around corners, while a steady stream of refugees crosses the frozen river under the bridge. Alhun is reluctant to go in, but finally agrees. As we don our protective vests, a man walks up and hands me a tangerine – fresh and bright orange against the monotonous white surroundings. I look into the man's rheumy eyes and we share a smile.

Alhun races us across the bridge and we hold our breath as he slows to manoeuvre around the burning truck. He takes a back route into the city and stops before we reach the centre. He won't go any further. The English boys in the back haven't said a word. There's no animosity as I take my camera and head off on foot to see what's going on.

The craziness of what I'm doing suddenly fills me with doubt. Here I am, completely unfamiliar with the area, walking alone to the front, into this sorrow and madness, and for what? Am I just an adrenaline junkie, trying to fill the holes in my own sorry life? I hurry across the open streets, making an effort to be extra careful. My efforts feel foolish; the scene is much like yesterday, only steadily disintegrating.

I meet a fighter on his way out of the city, his grimace weary and sad. He motions me to stay with him and we dash from one bombed building to the next, stopping occasionally to let me film the awful scenes around me. The buildings are devastated; huge craters in marbles floors and the remains of ornate ceilings that I imagine were once banks or state offices, it's now impossible to tell. I no longer catch my breath each time I come across another body; they've become part of the scenery. Between the skeletons of two buildings a woman lies face down in the snow, still clutching her shopping baskets. Her head is turned to face me, a neutral look on her waxy face. She seems perfectly normal, except that the clothes and skin on her back are gone. Her internal organs are all still there, almost bloodless, neatly cauterized by the white hot fragment of whatever missile created this horror. My heart lurches as I suddenly think of my daughter at school in England, expecting me for a weekend on my way home. I'm relieved when we finally get back to the Land Rover. Alhun shakes my hand and hugs me when I arrive. As we drive off I stick my head out the door to wave goodbye to the fighter who's been guiding me – but he's gone.

I peel the tangerine and we share its sweetness in silence.

Captured Russians soldiers are being kept in a prison in Shali near the Chechen headquarters. Here a group of mothers are about to visit their sons. The press are allowed into the prison first, where we interview these frightened kids, not one more than nineteen years old. Hands blue with cold, one stares at the ground and speaks in fits and starts, his brow deeply furrowed for one so young. They were told they wouldn't be going into Grozny; they'd be in a support role. But on their first day they were sent into the city. The battle lasted thirteen minutes and took sixty of their comrades. He begs us to tell the truth: they had no choice, their officers are drunk, please tell the truth. They're demoralised; they never wanted this fight from the beginning. It's a profoundly unsettling moment. Eventually the mothers are allowed in and the sound of sobbing fills the place. The boys are disorientated and embarrassed as our lenses stalk these intensely private moments.

An exchange of prisoners is being brokered. After a few false starts and accusations of bad faith from both sides, it finally happens on a bridge between Chechnya and Dagestan. The snow is starting to melt and the roads are turning muddy. Cars get stuck and chaos builds as everyone yells instructions simultaneously, each with a different solution to the problem. The prisoners' trucks pull up on either side of the bridge. The Chechen prisoners disembark – ragged boys and middle-aged men, civilians picked by the Russians and now being used to cut deals. Despite the obvious disparity, the exchange goes ahead. A young Russian soldier hugs a comrade, trying to hide his tear-stained face. They've said they'll refuse to return to Grozny, facing instead a threatening and uncertain future within this crumbling and corrupt military edifice.

For me, it's been a good day – hope and happiness instead of death and despair – and we arrive at our base in a buoyant mood. For Vanya it's been a bad day. He makes a sorry sight on his tiny chair, belly sagging between his thighs, doe eyes pools of sadness that won't let go. I sit down next to him and put my hand on his shoulder.

"Vodka?" he says, looking up. And he fills two cracked teacups to the brim.

The days are starting to blur into one another. It's been more than a week and I battle with this thing called "objectivity". I'm feeling at home with the Chechens and the Georgians, themselves the victims of Russia's ill-considered internal policies. By now I know my way around; I drive myself into the beleaguered areas, accompanied most days by Maya, a young woman who's a news producer in Tbilisi. We usually pick up Askir, a Chechen officer from Shali, who guides us into the battlefront. At the little grey town of Argun, Russian tanks and heavy artillery are positioned across the river, trying to drive out the Chechens. On the edge of the town, Askir makes arrangements to get us to the front. Two ancient women walk past bent beneath heavy sacks, the last of the refugees. We pick up a couple of soldiers and head into town. Soon we're in a suburban street that's taken a hammering from artillery.

Sharieb, a tall, imposing soldier whose face Maya finds beautiful, leads us through the ruins of a home and across a small paddock. His courage in battle is unprecedented, and fellow combatants call him the Legend of Argun. Fighters stand behind bits of concrete wall or piles of bricks and stones, firing at the Russians across the river. Through a hole in the wall I can see a tank, side cannons blazing, tracer fire almost in slow motion as it cracks overhead. Sharieb crouches beside a huge gun mounted on a tripod, and loads the magazine. The air is thick with tank and cannon fire. He cocks the gun, leans his knee on the tripod for support, and empties the magazine in a series of murderous explosions. All the while, as I kneel beside him, I see the tracers racing overhead. He pauses to load a new magazine and blasts away again.

Maya's waiting for me in a dugout shelter, grinning, eyes bright with the rush of adrenaline. Soldiers dash in, laughing wildly, and quickly reload. I'm bellowing with laughter too. What the hell for? Sharing the untameable spirit of these naïve yet wonderful warriors, or simply rejoicing at staying alive? Whatever it is, it must be good for the health.

Driving back at the end of the day to drop Askir at Chechen headquarters in Shali, I notice that Maya's strong Georgian looks aren't lost on him; his face softens when he speaks to her. He's become her special guide these last few days, and I enjoy the warmth of these two young hearts reaching out to each other; gentle words amid a terrible war. When we reach headquarters our vehicle is quickly surrounded by soldiers wanting to know what's happening on the front. We stand and chat for a while, and as we take our leave to head back to our base in Khasavyurt, Maya reaches up to kiss Askir's cheek. He stiffens and pulls back; a Chechen man mustn't show signs of tenderness. Smiles and guffaws break out in the assembled ranks as Maya gets back into the vehicle. Askir's face is stern as his ears redden. I turn and give him an exaggerated wink; his frown breaks into a grin, the man becomes a boy.

The next day Askir takes Maya and me into the Chechen areas that are putting up the strongest resistance. The barbarism of war becomes more and more evident, the sheer mediaeval brutality and total destruction. As we stand listening on the outskirts of Grozny, trying to gauge our best route in, a woman walks by pulling a sled with a small suitcase on it. She asks in English where I'm from. I notice that she's well-dressed, her face neatly made up. She weeps, her eyes puffy but dry as she tells me that her husband's lying dead in their wrecked apartment, and she waited all night for her own death. Then she continues down the road, joining a long line of her fellow residents dragging sleds or carrying bags and suitcases, trudging towards the desolate countryside.

Suddenly the fleeing townsfolk start running toward the ditch and sparse forest on the side of the road. It looks like total chaos, the older people falling over in the snow and everyone screaming and shouting directions. Only then do I notice a line of helicopters appearing through the thin cloud on the far side of Grozny. Large puffs of snow appear over the hillside, and I realise that the choppers are firing rockets at the escaping civilians from multi-barrelled pods on each side of these anonymous killing machines.

As I stand filming, a Chechen soldier in his late fifties runs up to me, shouting and waving a large pistol in the air. He sticks his face into mine and I'm forced to lower my camera. By now he's screaming at me, pointing the gun to my head. I don't know what's going on but I hold his gaze and try to stay calm, my heart leaping in my chest. Askir runs up and shouts at him, and suddenly the scene is diffused. He puts his gun into its holster and smiles at me, while the choppers continue circling and firing rockets.

A group of soldiers dashes towards a small banged-up car parked nearby, carrying a youth of about twenty, shouting and gesticulating as they run. I approach with my camera rolling. The young man seems asleep, head on his chest, until I notice his ashen face and his legless body. One foot is trailing behind, still in its boot, attached by a strand of sinew to the stump of his shattered leg. Askir comes and pulls me away to our vehicle, while Maya guns the engine and races off down the pockmarked road.

On the outskirts of Argun, we join a group of fighters in their rudimentary barracks, thick with cigarette smoke and the smell of boiling soup. They insist we eat with them. The thin grey liquid with hunks of floating meat is delicious on this cold, heartless day. Someone hands Askir a beret, and he gazes at it sorrowfully; the remains of a fallen friend. As he sits, I notice his similarity to a portrait on the wall of a distant Chechen hero, turbaned and defiant; he's part of a long, sad history of struggle.

We go on to a nearby hospital. The thick, oppressive smell bores into me; even breathing seems dangerous. These are conditions from another time: blinded men moaning gently under blood-soaked bandages, while friends and relatives sit around making food for the wounded and dying on small open flame cookers. The odours of gangrene and boiling meat meld into a sickening stench that wrenches my stomach. I'm overcome by a sense of panic, and it's an enormous relief to get out of there.

Back at the base we're told that Grozny is no longer the big story: floods in Holland and a car bomb in Algeria have pushed it out of the headlines. We need to move out. Looking at the material we've collected during the day, I realise that pictures *do* tell lies. They can't convey the horror, nor the staggering resilience of the human spirit. What is TV news but another form of entertainment, while we, the collectors of these images, dish out just enough to boost the ratings so audiences can say, "Wow, just like the movies"? But this is not a war of neat holes in the head or handsome soldiers tended by syrupy Florence Nightingales. This is legs torn off, gaping holes in flesh, whole shattered body parts disappearing without trace. It's jets appearing from nowhere, evil in their anonymity, arbitrary in their violence. The face of Boris Yeltsin appears on the screen, justifying it all, content in his ideology, and I want to grab him and force him to look into the face of the woman on the ground with her back blown off, or the legless kid in the back of the shot up car. I'm aware of my naïve and irrational ravings, but I'm half insane from the events of the day and I'm fucked up on vodka. It's the only way on a night like tonight. But soon I'll fall asleep.

As we fly out of Makhachkala airport in a decaying Aeroflot plane with surly cabin staff and filthy toilets, the past weeks feel almost dreamlike. I think of Vanya roaring with laughter or silent in sorrow; of Maya, daughter of the Caucasus; of Askir and Sharieb living from one desperate battle to the next. I'm relieved and buoyant to be getting out of here, but I'll probably never return, and the lives and spirit of these people have touched me too deeply.

I took Amanda out of school for a few days and we drove to London in my hired car. We ate in restaurants, went to a show in the West End and spent hours at the largest amusement arcade in Europe. By the time I took her back to Bath, I could feel the fire and ice of Grozny slowly dissipating. But I knew I couldn't carry on being a silent witness to other people's wars. It was hard enough facing my own.

Within weeks of my return home, Rachel and I were divorced. The Wolmunster Road house was put up for sale and I started looking for a new, more modest place to live. Like many times before, I swore I was done with relationships, and set out on a mission to live the simple, single life.

Mo was just a friend, a beautiful and caring person I'd known for two decades since we first met in Crown Mines, but "just a friend" nonetheless. She was also recently divorced, and as she worked around the corner from Wolmunster Road, we often met for tea and a chat. Despite the difficulty of raising two small children, she'd recently qualified as a psychiatrist and set up in private practice. She had a jungle of the thickest, curliest black hair and the softest almond eyes that could switch from gentle, dark pools to fiery black lasers when angered. Somehow Rachel got wind that we were "seeing" each other, and I woke one morning to a faxed note accusing me of infidelity. Aware that Rachel's own love life had moved on, I was surprised by her double standards, but I didn't respond. Except that, once accused of infidelity, it felt appropriate to invite Mo upstairs to view the beautiful carpet I'd brought back from Dagestan. My resolve to stay single vanished in a flurry of discarded clothing, and by the time I came to my senses, Mo and I were deeply entangled.

The house on Wolmunster Road was sold at a handsome profit, and with the extra income from being in the war zones, I bought a modest house in the same neighbourhood, and still had money left. During therapy sessions with Steve Brokensha, we'd discussed the issue of manhood and the attainment of that state in the Western world. I'd read Robert Bly's thought-provoking treatise *Iron John*, Robert Johnson's ideas on emotionally wounded men in *The Fisher King*, as well as a book Steve gave me about young indigenous men building their own houses at the advent of manhood. Ever since, I'd spent my quiet news days driving around the countryside looking for a place to build my dream cabin.

Soon after Chechnya I resumed my search, and heard of some plots in a private nature reserve at the foot of a mountain range overlooking the Breede River Valley, just an hour and a half from Cape Town. I went out to meet the developer, an unkempt man with a huge, walrus moustache. In his ancient Land Rover we drove along a rocky track into a valley that ended in a huge amphitheatre against the side of the mountain. It was a hot, dry day and when he killed the motor, the only sound was the occasional shrill whistle of the yellow and black Cape Bishop and the whisper of invisible water. We stood among the fynbos – the indigenous vegetation unique to the Western Cape – and looked out over a wide river valley towards the distant mountains. I pushed my way through the tough but pretty vegetation towards the burble of water, and found a strong flowing stream amid a tunnel of bush and vines. The water was clear and cool as I splashed and dunked my head into a deep recess between the smooth rocks.

I'd found what I was looking for. I signed the deed sale and drove back to Cape Town with a head full of plans and dreams.

The next time I went to look at my ten acres in the mountains I took Mo along, excited to share my fantasy. We drove up the rocky path, the exhaust scraping and knocking as I nursed my old red Mercedes up the treacherous track. The journey had been pleasant until then, but in my blind enthusiasm I hadn't realised how awful the mountain track was. With each bump and knock Mo shrieked with fear, and by the time we arrived at my barren, rocky piece of nature, her eyes has turned to lasers.

"What the fuck is this?" She only swore under extreme duress.

"It's where I'm going to build my cottage."

"Your *cottage*? What in fuck's name do you know about building a cottage?" Her voice was hard and hostile.

I was totally deflated. All the excitement, the expectation that she'd see my dream as I did, vanished in the stifling heat. Till now we'd shared nothing but joy and love, and her fury took me by surprise. I reddened with shame, and responded a bit lamely that I was reading a book on how to build a house.

"You're going to build a house by reading a book?"

"*An Introduction to Good House Construction*," I mumbled. "I borrowed it from Paul."

Paul Haupt had done a year at the Cape Technical College before taking up psychology, and one of his subjects was civil engineering. The book was part of his syllabus; all twenty-eight pages of it.

Mo got into the car and slammed the door, and we slowly bumped and banged our way down the rocky track in silence.

Just before Andrew and I moved into my new house, I started writing my second play, *Newsroom*. Andrew was to play the lead role of a British reporter in South Africa, and Nick Ellenbogen would direct. By this time international interest in the South African story was at an all-time low and I had loads of free time to pursue my own interests. So it came as a jolt when, at the beginning of April, WTN's assistant bureau chief in Jo'burg, Vincent Francis, called on me to cover the troubles in Burundi. But I was all packed up and about to move from Wolmunster Road into a rental until I could take up my new house. I told Vincent I could only go the following week. Vincent was a "desk jockey", a slight man who lacked the rough-and-tumble temperament for hard news gathering. Nonetheless, he enjoyed escaping the office occasionally and set off for Burundi with a freelance cameraman until I was free. Three days later Vincent and the cameraman were ambushed on the outskirts of Bujumbura. Of the four in their car, only the cameraman escaped with injuries; the others were killed outright.

I attended Vincent's funeral in Jo'burg and then handed in my resignation. It was a huge relief to have finally taken this decisive step, and I felt ecstatic as I served out my notice and started packing up the office. It was just a week later that my sister, Louise, called to say that my brother Michael had hanged himself. For my mother, it was a turning point that she never quite recovered from. Michael had a special place in her heart and until her death many years later, the anniversary of that tragic day brought inconsolable grief.

While in Durban for Michael's funeral, I tried to contact Jabula. At the funeral I asked Japhet, who'd worked for my father, to enquire about him in KwaMashu. I phoned Japhet a few weeks later with a sense of foreboding. "Eish, Rog, he must be dead, sorry," was all he said. I went back to Cape Town and finished packing up all the gear that was to be returned to WTN. I was now free to turn all my attention to the new life that I was re-inventing for myself.

Once again I made the pilgrimage to the National Arts Festival, but this time I was even busier than the year before. As well as writing *Newsroom*, I was also in the cast of Nick Ellenbogen's new play *Hippo*. Nick's Theatre for Africa company was founded on the principles of Physical Theatre, and most of his works dealt with environmental issues. Working with Nick was hard work but great fun, and I learnt an enormous amount. I also did a solo music revue that year called *Turning Points*, which Andrew directed. It was an autobiographical series about my life and songs, and judging by the poor attendance, not of any real interest to anyone. It was after one of these performances that I met James Phillips in the Cathcart Arms, and got to read about a part of my life that had been hidden for almost thirteen years.

There in the *Mail & Guardian* Erasmus described raiding my house, tapping my phone and intercepting my mail. He admitted to threatening club owners and venue managers that associating with me would implicate them in the terrorist activities I was about to be arrested for, and even threatening Dave Marks with arrest if he had anything more to do with me. It was Erasmus and his colleagues who'd confiscated every copy of *The Road Is Much Longer* from the record stores. And everything was done covertly. He had orders that none of it must be traceable to the security police. They didn't want to turn a common rock 'n' roller into a martyr.

In the bar that night, James's voice seemed to weave in and out of my consciousness as these revelations and the tequila sank in. I'd always known that something like this had been happening, but now as I looked at the words on the page, I found it impossible to take in. Yet it made such sense, and put into perspective what had been horribly skewed for so long. After a while, the tequila did its work and James and I drifted into a cloud of bullshit and reverie for the rest of the evening.

When the bar started closing and the barman began coaxing drunks out of their seats and into the cold night, I gave James my customary hug and said goodbye.

"Hang on, take this," he said, fishing in his bag and handing me the *Mail & Guardian*. And he wobbled off into the night, on his way back to the farmhouse where he was staying a few miles out of town.

Along the dirt road he lost control and his car rolled several times before ending up in the dry veld. I went to see James in hospital the following evening; his face was cut and bruised, his fractured skull wrapped in a slightly comical bandage. But in spite of his injuries, he was as full of mischief as the previous evening. When the nurse told me that visiting hours were over, I gently kissed his bruised cheek, and as I left he shouted that we should put a band together. A few days later he checked out of the hospital against the doctor's wishes, and returned to Jo'burg. He died soon afterwards.

I spent the next year playing small gigs and working in a variety of Theatre for Africa productions. I'd gone from earning a lot to earning very little, but at last I felt my life was making sense. Mo and I had recovered from a brief, unsuccessful attempt at cohabitation and were in a happy and loving relationship, albeit living in separate houses. And, as the hidden story of my past slowly came to be part of my present, so I gingerly began rebuilding my broken self-confidence and esteem.

In December 1996 I drove up to my piece of land and spent the day hacking and chopping at the tough fynbos on a sandy rise beside a small stream. By the end of the day, I'd hammered four white poles into the newly cleared ground, marking out an oblong six metres by ten. My hands were blistered and red, unaccustomed to this type of backbreaking labour. My sunburnt arms stung as I sat in the stream to wash off the dirt and sweat. Even after the sun had set behind the mountains that rose steeply behind me, the heat of the day still shimmered in waves above the fluorescent green of the fynbos. I sat in my shorts on a patch of sand near the front corner of my oblong – where my front door would be – and swigged a cold beer, then three fingers of tequila from the ice box.

As I sat, a profound sense of satisfaction began to settle over me. More than satisfaction, it was something larger, something deeper.

As if I could see myself from above, it dawned on me where I was. This wasn't just the future doorway of my own little cottage in the mountains, but the threshold of something far more significant.

In my talks with Steve Brokensha, the idea of building a house had become the cornerstone of a bigger plan to rebuild my life and reclaim the parts of my soul that had been savaged by decades of upheaval. I had no idea how it would all work out, and even less how I'd actually go about building a house. Yet for a couple of years I'd been roaming scrapyards, collecting doors and windows – an old bathtub here and a kitchen sink there – and my garage was now full of what looked like the debris of a demolished house. But these were the building blocks of my new life.

I'd clung to the thought that if I could just get started, the momentum might carry me forward. And now, as I sat on this rough patch of sand and looked around, imagining where the old teak window and the cast iron bath would go, I knew I'd started a new journey, one that would take up the dream I'd talked about to Steve and make it real. I gazed out through my non-existent doorway over the magnificent Breede River Valley and on into a life of new hope, and a profound sense of wellbeing swept over me.

Suddenly I started to laugh. There wasn't another human soul for miles around, and I stood up and laughed some more. I thrust out my arms into the hot evening stillness and whooped, then shrieked and whooped some more. Soon I was dancing around on that dusty patch of sand, laughing and stomping until my bare feet were filthy and sore.

I had survived.

Epilogue

I'm AMBLING DOWN THE BANKS OF the river Main in Frankfurt on a beautiful autumn day. A ferry pulls up to a landing just ahead, and a dozen or so men and women in tailored suits and power skirts alight briskly and disperse towards the tall city buildings beyond the trees on our left. My heavy set companion hobbles along beside me, shirt buttons straining over a generous beer belly. Beneath a shock of thick grey hair, his face streams with sweat.

"Fok[1] it, boet. My feet are killing me."

Pain is showing on Paul's face, a face that bears scars whose stories I might one day come to hear, and a nose that's taken a few punches over the years.

"Would it help to take off the boots?" I ask, feeling helpless and slightly guilty for suggesting this walk. I hope he doesn't think I meant any harm.

"Naw. Bloody blisters are on my soles." And so they are, open and inflamed.

We've still got eight hours to kill before our flight leaves. We reach a mediaeval square between the city centre and the river, and settle at a pavement café to take it easy. We waste no time getting ourselves a pair of cold beers. As the afternoon wears on, the headiness of the alcohol draws us into the past, and we reminisce, laughing out loud about the intersection of our lives. Two slightly portly, middle-aged men sharing a sunny afternoon in Europe before returning to South Africa, our strangely compelling, infuriating, but achingly beautiful land. There's nothing very odd about sharing a companionable afternoon together, except that Paul Erasmus is an ex-member of South Africa's notorious security police, and I'm one of his victims.

---

1 Afrikaans for fuck

260

In 2001, I got a call from a sociologist at Rhodes University in Grahamstown.

"Paul's agreed to tell his side of the story," he told me. "How would you feel about telling yours?"

Michael Drewett had been researching the Roger Lucey/Paul Erasmus story, and had secured a grant from an international organisation to shoot a documentary on it. I'd met Michael once before, when he interviewed me as part of the doctoral thesis he was writing on music censorship and resistance in South Africa. His funding for the documentary was from Freemuse, a Copenhagen-based organisation that deals with issues around music censorship, and works to highlight the problem around the world.

Paul's revelations in the *Mail & Guardian* had come as a relief, but the saga was still churning round and round in my head, and felt like a huge chunk of unfinished business. So, after a short think, I concluded that it could be a good way to put the whole saga to bed once and for all.

And – I'd get to meet Paul.

The venue for our meeting, chosen by Michael and film director Doug Mitchell, was the Devonshire. It was a bar in Braamfontein frequented by cops and other undesirables during the dark years, around the corner from Mangles where I'd first made my musical name, and very close to Wits, a place powerfully connected with my early years as a young muso.

As I drove into Braamfontein for the meeting, memories came flooding back: memories of friends and colleagues who'd died at the hands of the police; memories of my own rise and sudden fall from grace. My hands were clammy as I greeted Michael and Doug outside the Devonshire. Paul was already in the pub with the camera crew, they told me, and I was to wait in the service passage and only come in when they called.

"Okay," came a muffled voice through the thick swing doors. "You can come now."

Two cameras were set up at the end of the long, narrow room. Paul was sitting at the bar, leaning on one elbow. I don't know what came over me, but as I saw him I erupted into laughter – not derisive or cynical laughter but more nervous, mildly manic. Maybe it was just the relief.

"Howzit, Roger? I've organised you a beer. I've already started on a whisky." And he too began to chuckle. "I was *so* nervous, man!"

I took a deep slug of beer and we got chatting.

Later that afternoon we all went down to the Market Theatre together, where I'd had some of my most memorable concerts. Alone on an empty stage, I played one of my old songs for the solitary member of the audience, Paul Erasmus. It was all a setup for the film, and I wasn't fully prepared. I stumbled through the first verse of a song I hadn't played for twenty years, and then had to stop. I called out that I needed time to refresh my memory. I just couldn't remember the second verse.

"And the cars just shoot by you and the sun's in your eyes..."

Paul's gravel voice came from the darkness.

"And you stand and you sweat and you swear at the flies."

The world premiere of this documentary, titled *Stopping the Music*, was screened at the Second World Conference on Music and Censorship in Copenhagen in October 2002. I received an email from Marie Korpe of Freemuse inviting me to attend, along with Dave Marks, Michael Drewett and Paul Erasmus.

After a slightly boozy and uneventful flight, we were met in Copenhagen by a smartly dressed man holding a small South African flag. He was from the South African embassy, but I recognised him from the bad old days. Machiel van Niekerk had worked for a conservative Afrikaans daily in Johannesburg. Without the remotest sense of irony, he introduced himself as First Secretary to the Ambassador.

With him was a slightly bohemian looking man called John Hansen, a South African who'd gone into exile in the early 1970s and was one of the movers and shakers of the early anti-apartheid movement in Denmark. John took us on a tour of the delightful Christiana area of Copenhagen, and he and I couldn't stop yakking about mutual friends from the old days, life in present day SA, and music and art. When I told him a few choice South African jokes, he almost wet himself laughing. We spent some great times with Machiel and John and even got to have lunch with the South African Ambassador, a charming old man who'd spent most of his life in exile in London.

The screening of our documentary was to be the first event of the conference. We arrived at the Royal Danish Film Institute and I took my seat – right beside Paul. After a few opening words from Ole Reitov, a director of Freemuse, the lights went down.

The film tracked both Paul's life and my own, going back to our youths and tracing the paths that had led us to opposite sides of the political divide. I felt myself being dragged back through all those years of turmoil that I so wanted to forget, although a part of me still couldn't quite let it go. Yet I couldn't help but acknowledge the many hard and ugly truths that Paul had faced up to about himself as he talked candidly and honestly about his life. Watching the film was like riding a supercharged rollercoaster; the memory of it still sends shivers through me.

Then came the conference, a gathering of wonderful people from every nook and cranny of the planet. There I heard the stories of many musicians in their quest for truth and justice, and for the first time in my life I truly grasped the power of music and song. I heard great musicians like Amal Murkus singing for Palestinian justice, and Marcel Khalife from Lebanon, alone with his oud[2], whose songs silenced the hall. What a rare pleasure to share so much with so many; crossing so many barriers, connecting so many divergent points in such a brief period of time. Those nights of hard talking, hard laughing and hard drinking helped me to better understand and put to bed the bad times we'd come there to talk about.

And that was how Paul Erasmus and I ended up in Frankfurt with a day to kill before our flight back to Jo'burg. Many people like to criticise the process of reconciliation taking place in South Africa at the moment. I've certainly been censured for my attitude towards Paul. At a recent party, an old friend, barely able to hide his venom, said, "So you and Paul Erasmus are big chommies[3] now?" I didn't rise to the bait, merely told him that I do what feels right for me.

Paul and I went on to attend many more events, talking about our own reconciliation to audiences from conflict-ravaged countries around the world. After a while, we agreed we'd spoken enough on the subject, and it was time to leave the past behind. Yet we kept on getting invited to talk about our experience "one last time". One night, after a long and emotional conversation with Ole Reitov of Freemuse, we had to acknowledge that our story had become bigger than both of us, and that we had a certain responsibility to speak about it when asked. Paul and I have spent long nights in far-off places and all over South Africa addressing both school kids and adult audiences. I always accompany these appearances with a few songs, and as I get

2 Arab lute
3 Afrikaans for mates

older, I'm glad to still get these chances to perform.

In Paul, I've come to know a man haunted by the savagery of his past who's gone to great lengths to put things right. He continues to suffer from the events of his past, and I believe he'll always carry a heavy burden. I guess we all have to get on with our lives as best we can, but we in South Africa have been through a savage and cruel time, and I have the greatest sympathy for those who must carry that pain to their graves.

I still feel the loss of friends and colleagues who died, not only at the hands of that terrible state, but also as the unwitting victims of its cruel laws. I never did find Jabula, and I now accept that he must be dead. With sadness I've watched many fellow travellers die still carrying the bitterness and poison of the past.

I believe forgiveness can cure those ills. And I believed Paul when he said he was sorry for what he'd done to me and to so many others. For that I'm thankful. It's allowed me to leave the past in its rightful place and to move into a new part of my life where I've found peace, creativity and love.

Through forgiving Paul, I discovered that I could also forgive myself. For years I had lived under a crushing yoke of anger – anger at myself, anger at the world, anger at what could have been and wasn't. Now it was finally starting to lift. And as it did, very quietly, almost imperceptibly, the walls of my prison began to dissolve and float away.

Postscript

© Gale McAll

In 2004, Amanda returned to South Africa to live with me while reading for a master's degree in Justice and Transformation at the University of Cape Town. The title of her thesis was "A Psychological Analysis of Political Violence: A Narrative Case Study of an Apartheid Policeman". The thesis was recently published by a German academic publisher, LAP Lambert. Her primary source of information was an extensive interview she conducted with Paul Erasmus. She recently completed a year-long tour of duty for the United Nations as a Rule of Law Officer in rural South Sudan, and continues to work in that field.

Acknow-
ledgements

THIS STORY MIGHT NEVER HAVE TURNED out the way it did if not for some fortuitous turns along the road, and the love and caring I continue to be blessed with from so many friends.

Lee le Roux and Chris Charles have steered, pushed and pulled me through some of the darkest times, and it's now a privilege to share the bright times with them.

In 2005 I ran into Paul Weinberg, who told me about the MA he'd just finished at Duke University in North Carolina. When I expressed my envy he suggested I do the same. My problem was that I hadn't finished my schooling. "No problem," said Paul, and before I could get cold feet he'd introduced me to Donna Zapf, director of the Master of Arts in Liberal Studies programme at Duke. Donna had me apply for a "recognition of prior learning" exemption, and in 2008 I entered the programme. Susan Mann, my friend and compadre, always pushed me to "find my own voice", and this was the beginning of a process of doing just that. Donna was amazing as she coaxed and guided me through this sometimes frightening but utterly stimulating new world.

When I arrived at Duke, I took a room in the home of an archivist for the university library, Karen Glynn. Paul Weinberg introduced us and assured her that I was an experienced handyman, so I got a free room on the arrangement that I'd do work on Karen's house. Karen was a great sounding board during the early days of my studies and a source of encouragement over our shared evening meals. Today she still stands beside me – now as my wife – despite having read this story.

My supervisor Margaret Sartor worked tirelessly through this manuscript, helping me unlock many parts of my memory that had clammed up. Paul also introduced me to Bridget Impey at Jacana, and I couldn't imagine a more encouraging publisher, who welcomed me so warmly into Jacana's fold. I also love telling as many of my friends who will listen that my editor is Gwen Hewett. Gwen has given me the licence and the encouragement to say things I initially thought were too close to the bone to mention, and sharpened the manuscript into a work I'm extremely proud of.

My daughter Amanda has always been a source of great joy to me. Without her in my life, I have no idea where I would have ended up. I am also blessed with many friends and family members who fill my life with love and happiness. Thank you one and all.